Treaty Politics and the Rise of Executive Agreements

Treaty Politics and the Rise of Executive Agreements

International Commitments in a System of Shared Powers

Glen S. Krutz and Jeffrey S. Peake

The University of Michigan Press | *Ann Arbor*

First paperback edition 2011
Copyright © by the University of Michigan 2009
All rights reserved
Published in the United States of America by
The University of Michigan Press
Manufactured in the United States of America
⊛ Printed on acid-free paper

2014   2013   2012   2011   5   4   3   2

A CIP catalog record for this book is available from the British Library.

Library of Congress Cataloging-in-Publication Data

Krutz, Glen S.
    Treaty politics and the rise of executive agreements :
    international commitments in a system of shared powers / Glen S.
    Krutz and Jeffrey S. Peake.
        p.   cm.
    Includes bibliographical references and index.
    ISBN-13: 978-0-472-11687-4 (cloth : alk. paper)
    ISBN-10: 0-472-11687-8 (cloth : alk. paper)
        1. Treaty-making power—United States.   2. United States—Foreign
    relations—Executive agreements.   3. United States—Foreign
    relations—Treaties.   I. Peake, Jeffrey S., 1970–   II. Title.
    KF5055.K78   2009
    342.73'0412—dc22   2008047853

ISBN 978-0-472-03462-8 (pbk. : alk. paper)
ISBN 978-0-472-02211-3 (e-book)

for Julie and Lori

Contents

Acknowledgments

The idea for this book came in spring 1999, when we were finishing graduate school in the Department of Political Science at Texas A&M University. Glen Krutz approached Jeff Peake with an idea to collaborate on a project about the politics of treaties, combining our mutual interests in the Congress (Krutz) and the presidency (Peake). Little comprehensive research existed on the topic, and we sought to fill this gap in the empirical literature on presidential-congressional relations. We soon discovered that, despite the paucity of empirical work, a strong conventional wisdom had emerged: modern presidents routinely evaded the Congress (and the requirements set forth in the Constitution) by using executive agreements instead of treaties. As a result, the domestic politics of treaties were not all that interesting, because presidents normally obtained what they wanted without consulting with or requiring the assent of the Congress.

This conclusion did not fit well with our understanding of the way American politics works. Certainly, as we document, the relationship is more interesting, and the politics are more complicated. Our training at Texas A&M prompted us to question the received wisdom on treaties and to explore the question from an empirical perspective. Aggieland proved to be an ideal environment in which to ponder questions about presidential-congressional relations and policy making. There we had the opportunity to study American politics with Jon Bond, George Edwards, and Patricia Hurley and public policy with Jim Anderson, Frank Baumgartner, Bryan Jones, and Dan Wood. Learning from such a fine group of senior scholars spawned a career's worth of ideas from both of us. From A&M, we each moved in 1999 to institutions where this project would take off—

Glen to Arizona State University and later to the University of Oklahoma and the Carl Albert Congressional Research and Studies Center, Jeff to Bowling Green State University.

As we reported our research in the various conference papers that would form the core chapters of this book, several individuals provided helpful comments. We received constructive feedback at the 2003 History of Congress meeting in San Diego from Jeff Jenkins, Mathew McCubbins, Barbara Sinclair, and James Snyder. In 2007, as the book came together, a collection of University of Oklahoma faculty and graduate students gave very insightful feedback at a ninety-minute brown-bag session. Comments from Gary Copeland, Greg Russell, Jim Sheffield, and Justin Wert were much appreciated. Others providing helpful comments along the way include Rick Beth, Dion Farganis, Richard Fleisher, Victoria Farrar-Myers, Lyn Ragsdale, and Adam Warber. Several research assistants helped with data collection, including Michael Humphries, Karen Kuns, Jason Truett, and Walt Jatkowski.

Two key funders of this research were the Dirksen Congressional Center and the Carl Albert Center, both of which made possible our being together to conduct research in the same place at the same time for several days. A Dirksen Center Congressional Research Award funded our fieldwork visit to Washington in 2004, during which we were able to interview officials in the State Department and Senate about the rise of executive agreements. We are indebted to staffers of the Senate Foreign Relations Committee, the Office of the Assistant Legal Adviser for Treaty Affairs and the Senate Liaison Office in the State Department, and the Congressional Research Service, for graciously addressing our questions. Their commentary forms an important component of our research. The Visiting Scholars Program of the Carl Albert Center generously funded Jeff's visit to Oklahoma in 2005, during which we utilized the Carl Albert Center Congressional Archives, which were especially helpful with the case studies that make up part of this book. Other institutions that supported research assistance or travel assistance for this project include the political science departments at Bowling Green State University, the University of Oklahoma, and Arizona State University.

We are especially appreciative of the hard work of our editor at the University of Michigan Press, Melody Herr, and editorial assistant Scott Griffith. Their guidance as we revised the manuscript was most helpful. Chapter 2 is a much-revised version of an article that originally appeared in *Presidential Studies Quarterly* (Krutz and Peake 2006).

On the family front, Glen thanks his children, Matt (14), Ryan (11), and Rachel (9), for their love and support. He also thanks Jim and Peggy Gann for their encouragement and positive outlook, and he thanks his parents, Larry and Diane Krutz, for their love and for having showed him, through their example, how to balance work and family. Jeff thanks his two boys, Jacob (6) and Nathan (4), for their encouragement and love. He also thanks his parents, John Peake and Beverly Vermillion, for their consistent encouragement over the years; Gary and Phyllis Kimmel; and Ron Vermillion. Most important, we thank our respective wives, Julie Krutz and Lori Peake, for their patience and loving support. It is to them that we dedicate this book.

Introduction: Power Grab or Institutional Bargain?

In early 1964, a mere fifteen months after the resolution of the Cuban Missile Crisis, President Lyndon Johnson sought to build a bridge to the Eastern Bloc by negotiating the first formal, bilateral treaty between the United States and the Soviet Union since the beginning of the Cold War. In Moscow on June 1, 1964, President Johnson and Secretary Khrushchev signed the pact, which would lead to the establishment of consulates in both countries. Johnson submitted this agreement as a treaty to the U.S. Senate for advice and consent, as required by Article II of the U.S. Constitution. Nearly three years later, after committee consideration and reconsideration, intensive lobbying campaigns on both sides, and eight days of final floor debate, the Senate finally approved the treaty by just three votes more than the required two-thirds supermajority.

Four decades later, on July 18, 2005, President George W. Bush and Indian prime minister Manmohan Singh announced a bilateral agreement that would allow for full civil nuclear cooperation between the two nations, whereby the United States would provide nuclear fuel and know-how to India. This agreement was followed up by a second, allowing international inspectors access, for the first time, to India's nuclear facilities. The agreements significantly improved relations between the world's two largest democracies but were controversial because India had not signed the Nuclear Non-Proliferation Treaty. While the president was free to complete the agreement as a treaty or executive agreement, he chose the latter. His decision, seemingly contrary to constitutional requirements, caused barely a ripple in the American press or in the U.S. Senate.

Different from what the framers of the U.S. Constitution intended, executive agreements are completed unilaterally by presidents. They do not require two-thirds support from the Senate as do treaties, yet they are considered interchangeable with treaties in the legal sense, both domestically and internationally (see *United States v. Pink*, 315 U.S. 203 [1942]).[1] Article II, Section 2, of the U.S. Constitution states that the president "shall have power, by and with the advice and consent of the Senate, to make treaties, provided two-thirds of the Senators present concur." No other form of international agreement is mentioned in the Constitution, other than confederations and alliances, which states are prohibited from entering (Article I, Section 10).

Despite the Constitution's silence in regard to international agreements other than treaties (what practitioners in the State Department call "executive agreements"), "no objective distinction exists," in the words of James Lindsay (1994: 82), between what is a treaty and what is an executive agreement, other than that treaties require Senate consent. Arthur Schlesinger (1973: 104) recounts one humorous exchange on the topic: "When Senator Gillette of Iowa asked the State Department in 1954 to make everything perfectly clear [on the distinction between treaties and executive agreements], the Department . . . replied 'that a treaty was something they had to send to the Senate to get approval by two-thirds vote. An executive agreement was something they did not have to send to the Senate.'"[2]

The approach used by President Bush in the agreements with India exemplifies the dominant trend in the way modern presidents decide to formalize relations with other nations. Use of the classic Article II process, as followed by President Johnson on the U.S.-Soviet Consular Treaty, has become relatively rare. The modern era has seen presidents utilize executive agreements rather than submitting treaties to the U.S. Senate for advice and consent. Of the 15,894 international agreements completed by the United States between 1946 and 1999, only 912, or just 5.7 percent, were formal Article II treaties. From 1930 to 1945, the percentage of treaties was much greater, as 176 of 641 (27.5 percent) of international agreements were treaties. The year 1937 marks the last year that the number of treaties surpassed the number of executive agreements (Fisher 2001: 39, table II-2). The trend has continued into the twenty-first century. Through the first six years of the George W. Bush presidency (2001–6), the United States completed 1,172 international agreements. Only 73 (6.2 percent) were treaties transmitted to the Senate for advice and consent.[3]

Political observers in Washington and academia point to the rise of executive agreements as one of the most fundamental changes in the foreign policy process of the twentieth century. Some even argue that executive agreements have pushed Article II treaties into the dustbin of history. Hyperbole aside, executive agreements have been used time and again to complete consequential international agreements, including such significant agreements as the North American Free Trade Agreement (NAFTA) and the General Agreement on Tariffs and Trade; agreements on U.S. membership in the World Monetary Fund and World Bank; the Paris Peace Accords, ending U.S. involvement in the Vietnam War; the Quadripartite Agreement of 1971, which provided a diplomatic framework for dealing with West Berlin; U.S.-Israeli agreements in 1976 and 1979 that have made Israel the largest recipient of direct U.S. foreign aid; and the Kosovo Military Technical Agreement, which ended hostilities between the United States and Serbia in 1999. William Howell (2003: 19) notes that while the vast majority of executive agreements "concern very specific (and often technical) matters, the sheer number issued during the modern era has increased at such an astronomical rate that collectively they now constitute a vital means" by which presidents make foreign policy.

Thomas Franck and Edward Weisband (1979: 135) note, "Of the various foreign relations initiatives open to a country, the most crucial are the making of war and the undertaking of solemn commitments." Making international agreements lies at the core of foreign policy, as such agreements affect a vast range of American foreign policies, including foreign trade, fishing rights, transportation, monetary policy, foreign aid, nuclear energy, international crime, immigration, terrorism, communication, space travel, environmental policy, human rights, arms proliferation, arms transfers, deployed military personnel, and military interventions. A drastic change in the way foreign commitments are approved, especially one that alters constitutional design and the separation of powers, should be considered major and fundamental.

Despite the topic's importance, we know little about the rise of executive agreements beyond the basic trend previously identified. Political scientists have yet to deliver a comprehensive theoretical and empirical treatment of the topic and the implications for the domestic politics of international agreements. Political scientists routinely list executive agreements among the modern president's unilateral powers, yet when doing so, scholars do not address their usage directly in their analyses (Canes-Wrone, Howell, and Lewis 2007; Howell 2003; Moe and Howell 1999; cf. Shull 2006, chap. 6). The paucity of systematic political science research on the domestic politics of international agreements lies in stark contrast with the attention given by scholars to the domestic politics of war and military force (see, e.g., Hess 2001; Howell and Pevehouse 2007). To be sure, a few legal and historic treatises on the rise of executive agreements exist (e.g., Ackerman and Golove 1995). Moreover, some recent systematic studies on the politics of the Senate treaty process have begun to emerge in academic journals (e.g., Auerswald and Maltzman 2003; DeLaet and Scott 2006). Yet much of what we know about treaty politics stems from book-length treatments of single cases (e.g., Caldwell 1991a; Moffett 1985).

As we will document shortly, strong conventional views of the domestic politics of international agreements and the institutional change that is the rise of executive agreements have nevertheless developed, despite these limitations. One of our purposes in writing this book is to offer a fresh theoretical account, based on multiple methods of evidence, for why presidents use executive agreements rather than treaties. A second purpose of the book is to describe and systematically explain the U.S. domestic politics of international agreements, including the politics that occur when presidents decide to take their treaties to the Senate.

Explaining the Change: Existing Perspectives

The dominant explanation for the rise in the presidential use of executive agreements over Article II treaties holds that presidents utilize executive agreements strategically to evade the Senate's formal treaty role (Crenson and Ginsberg 2007; Lindsay 1994; Margolis 1986; Nathan and Oliver 1994). This account of the change has been referred to as the "evasion hypothesis" (Martin 2000). Presidents are constrained considerably when using the treaty power, for treaties require supermajority advice and consent in the Senate. Moreover, the Senate often amends treaties in the process. A president thinking strategically might ask, why not therefore complete international agreements without that noisome step by evading the Senate altogether? Such a perspective proceeds from the fact that presidents, according to the U.S. Supreme Court (*Pink*, 351 U.S. 203), may legally use treaties and executive agreements interchangeably when completing their international commitments. Gary King and Lyn Ragsdale (1988: 112) explain, "According to this view, executive agreements enable presidents to enhance their autonomy in international affairs and thereby to promote their ability to act as independent policy makers."

Matthew Crenson and Benjamin Ginsberg (2007: 194–95), in their recent book entitled *Presidential Power: Unchecked and Unbalanced*, write, "The presidency affords broad opportunities to govern without interference. Executive orders, national security findings and directives, executive agreements, proclamations . . . enable presidents to legislate unilaterally without consulting any legislators . . . In foreign policy, unilateral presidential actions in the form of executive agreements have virtually replaced treaties as the nation's chief foreign policy instruments." Similarly, Nathan and Oliver (1994: 99) contend that presidents employ "the executive agreement to circumvent Senate involvement in international agreements altogether." Underscoring this conventional wisdom is the notion that presidents evade the Senate treaty process due to political considerations. For example, Crenson and Ginsberg (2007: 320) write that decisions to use executive agreements rather than treaties to complete America's international commitments are "largely at the president's discretion and based mainly on political considerations." Lawrence Margolis (1986: 46–47), after examining trends in the use of executive agreements and treaties, finds that presidents' use of executive agreements corresponds with domestic political calculations. He concludes, "Hence, the treaty process, the Constitution's main safeguard against presidential excesses in foreign policy, is no longer much of a constraint." While examples abound of presidents completing major agreements as executive agreements rather than as treaties, research on presidential behavior in this realm has not really tackled the issue that Crenson and Ginsberg, among others, believe to be fairly settled—that modern presidents, with domestic political considerations in mind, routinely circumvent the Senate on their "chief" international agreements. To argue that treaties have been "virtually replaced" belies cases of modern presidents taking their consequential treaties to the Senate, even when they cannot bank on swift Senate consent.

This conventional wisdom of evasion with executive agreements dovetails nicely with recently resurgent unilateral theories of presidential power (P. J. Cooper 2002; Howell 2003; Mayer 2001; Shull 2006) and related discussions about the imperial presidency (Rudalevige 2005). According to the unilateral perspective of presidential power, the U.S. Constitution was designed to provide a general framework. The founders designed separate branches with checks and balances, but they had no way to anticipate what challenges might subsequently be presented to the new nation. Later, as society evolved, issue agendas ebbed and flowed, and crises occurred, the stage was set for additional constitutional context to be filled out.

Unilateral scholars expect that presidents will step into such contexts or power vacuums created by the environmental changes and develop unilateral authority above and beyond the shared power designed in our system. In this way of thinking, the unilateral presidency was and is inevitable. Howell (2003: 16) draws theoretical guidance from John Locke's notion of "prerogative powers": "According to Locke, certain public officials ought to enjoy the 'power to act according to discretion, for the publick good, without the prescription of the law and sometimes even against it' . . . These powers are necessary, Locke argued, because the designers of any constitution cannot foresee all future contingencies and therefore must permit certain discretionary allowances . . . In order to meet new expectations, and serve the public when laws cannot, the president may act unilaterally, even when neither the legislature nor the Constitution has mandated appropriate powers" (Howell quotes Locke [1689] 1988, 237).

Although emphasizing the time period since Watergate, Andrew Rudalevige's notion of the new imperial presidency also assumes an executive accumulation of power and similarly takes theoretical guidance from Locke. It is the nature of presidents to "push the limits of their power," argues Rudalevige (2005: ix), who adds that "it is inherent in the office's position in the constitutional framework." Power within a system of shared powers is relative—as presidents push the boundaries of power, it is up to Congress to maintain those boundaries (Rudalevige 2005: 14). When Congress fails to protect its position of power from executive encroachment, an imperial presidency is the natural outcome. The expansion of executive power was especially evident during and immediately following the Franklin Roosevelt presidency and is indicative of the modern presidency. One important component of the modern presidency is the ability of presidents to make use of "formal and informal powers on their own initiative" (Rudalevige 2005: 40). Modern presidents' reliance on unilateral authority is part and parcel to the development of the imperial presidency.

The unfettered use of executive agreements is an important plank of this view of presidential power (Rudalevige 2005: 48–49). Rudalevige (2005: 49) documents President Franklin Roosevelt's use of the method: "He [FDR] also concluded a series of executive agreements, thus evading the Senate ratification needed for treaties. One created provisional governments in Latin America that kept French possessions in the region away from the Vichy government. Another formed a Permanent Joint Board of Defense linking the American and Canadian military staffs. A third, more dramatically, transferred fifty destroyers to Britain in return for eight Caribbean naval bases." The last transaction violated existing statutes that banned the transfer of warships to belligerent nations.[4] Crenson and Ginsberg (2007: 321) invoke FDR as well, writing that when he first took office, he "had no intention of allowing a small number of sena-tors to block his foreign policy decisions and initiated the now standard practice of conducting foreign policy via executive agreement rather than Article II treaty."

Howell (2003) describes the resultant tool chest of such unilateral powers that presidents have assembled over time: executive orders, procla-mations, and national security directives. While Howell does not focus at all on executive agreements in his empirical analysis, his tool kit includes executive agreements, which allow presidents "to unilaterally commit the United States to deals involving such issues as international trade, ocean fishing rights, open air space, environmental standards, and immigration patterns" (2003: 19). Executive agreements are typically viewed as holding both characteristics associated with unilateral powers: presidents have "the ability to move first and act alone" (Howell 2003: 15). Additionally, executive agreements were central to three major Supreme Court cases during the FDR administration that bolstered presidential prerogatives to act unilaterally, particularly in regard to external affairs (Howell 2003: 20–21).[5] Executive agreements, therefore, are a significant part of the pres-ident's unilateral powers. Their increased usage underlies unilateral theo-ries of the modern presidency and, indirectly, claims of executive power aggrandizement; but, heretofore, the rise in executive agreements has been given little systematic empirical treatment by presidential scholars.[6]

That executive agreements are part of the president's tool kit of unilat-eral powers is widely understood. However, this understanding overlooks the significant proportion of executive agreements that flow directly from statute or previously ratified treaties or require congressional action in or-der to take legal affect. Loch Johnson (1984) estimates that 87 percent of executive agreements completed from 1946 to 1972 were of this variety. In some instances, what scholars have lumped together with other unilateral powers (proclamations, national security directives, etc.) may not be en-tirely unilateral. In other words, presidents must at times act in conjunc-tion with the Congress to complete an international agreement. We con-tend that the modern use of executive agreements deserves additional empirical scrutiny before scholars offer such broad, sweeping conclusions about how presidents use this important foreign policy power.

Additionally, it is unclear how modern presidents have utilized their authority to complete international agreements and whether or not Con-gress provides significant institutional constraints that structure presi-dents' use of this power. If significant constraints exist, their use may not be as important a blow to the effective workings of a system of shared power as has been argued. Conventional perspectives on treaty politics indicate presidents will evade the Senate, through their use of executive agreements, to complete agreements that would otherwise be blocked in the Senate. Hence, executive agreements provide a strategic alternative to the Article II treaty when the president faces off against an opposition majority party. It is possible, as unilateral theorists have demonstrated, that presidents may take seriously congressional constraints on their unilateral powers and utilize them most when Congress is least likely to object. For example, Howell (2003; 2005) demonstrates, both formally and empirically, that presidents more commonly employ significant executive orders when their own party controls both chambers of Congress. Similar patterns emerge when the theory of unilateral powers is applied to presidential uses of force. Constraints on presidents' unilateral actions depend, in part, on the discretion Congress affords presidents and the significance of the policies affected (Howell and Pevehouse 2007: 47). In a similar vein, in our theory that we present shortly, we take seriously the constraints placed on a president in a system of shared power.

The political tenor of the presidential use of executive agreements is only part of the picture, however. If presidents are using executive agreements to avoid tough treaty battles in the Senate, the treaty consent process may have become pro forma. Indeed, many observers suggest that it has indeed become a rubber-stamping affair. In summarizing the entire time series of treaties submitted by presidents to the Senate from 1789 to 2002, David M. O'Brien (2003: 73) stated, "While the Senate has ratified over 1,500 treaties, it rejected twenty-one proposed treaties. Of those, fifteen were rejected between 1789 and 1920, when the Senate refused to ratify the Treaty of Versailles, which ended World War I. By comparison, after 1920 just six treaties have failed to receive Senate ratification." Only three treaties were rejected after 1945. Along these lines, Lindsay (1994: 30–31) suggests that presidents may buttress their success rate on treaties by entering into executive agreements instead. Their use, he concludes, has eroded the significance of the treaty power. Crenson and Ginsburg (2007: 355) similarly conclude, "Presidents have all but abandoned the constitutional process by which the Senate ratifies treaties." Moreover, textbooks on American government (e.g., Lowi, Ginsberg, and Shepsle 2004; Tannahill 2004), the Congress (e.g., Davidson and Oleszek 2004), the presidency (e.g., Edwards and Wayne 2006), and American foreign policy (e.g., Hastedt 2000) spread far and wide this conventional wisdom of evasion on executive agreements coupled with a treaty process that is typically pro forma. Professors describe to college and university students each semester, with clarity and concern, the provocative tale of evasion and the accompanying demise of the treaty consent process and thus of constitutional checks on presidential power.[7]

All in all, the juxtaposed perspective of the rise of executive agreements as presidential evasion and the resulting pro forma Senate treaty consent process provides, it would seem, for a cornerstone of presidential dominance in foreign policy and an important plank of the imperial presidency. With the rise of executive agreements, modern presidents appear to have grabbed the treaty power, intended by the framers to be shared with the Senate, and made it their own, thus diminishing an important check on executive power and thwarting the constitutional principle of shared power. Indeed, scholars conclude (and have not been challenged otherwise) that presidents now use executive agreements and treaties interchangeably as the result of the Senate's surrender of its treaty prerogatives.

Certainly, such provocative conclusions deserve empirical scrutiny. Why would the Senate, known for its collectively large ego and a history for guarding Senate prerogatives, stand idly by as modern presidents routinely stand the Constitution on its head? Given the apparent go-ahead of the Senate's surrender of its treaty prerogative, why do modern presidents submit any of their consequential treaties for Senate consent? If presidents are unconstrained, what is served by taking a treaty to the Senate and suffering the indignity of a high-profile rejection, as occurred to President Clinton with the Comprehensive Nuclear Test Ban Treaty in 1999? In this study, we seek the answers to two empirical questions. First, why has the United States witnessed the rise in use of the executive agreement mechanism by modern presidents? Second, when modern presidents decide to take their international agreements to the Senate as Article II treaties, what does the process entail, and what sort of politics are they likely to find? These two empirical questions are inextricably linked, as how we answer the second question certainly informs our answer to the first. As is typical of social scientists, we look to the vast empirical record for answers, employing both qualitative and quantitative methods. We asked practitioners for their views and delved into congressional archives. We start, of course, with an underlying theory.

Our Theoretical Framework

Our theoretical framework stands in stark contrast to the conventional wisdom that the rise in executive agreements represents a power grab by an imperial presidency bent on supplanting constitutional practices through unilateral action. At its core, our framework proceeds from the notion that while treaties and executive agreements are, for the most part, legally interchangeable, they are not politically interchangeable. In other words, their use has important political ramifications that presidents are likely to consider. We believe that the juxtaposed logic of executive agreements and treaties found in the conventional understanding of their political use runs counter to a broader theoretical understanding of political incentives, interbranch relations, and institutional evolution. In this book, we recast the critical constitutional relationship between the president and Congress on international agreements. We see the two institutions as interdependent parts of an adaptive system that must together forge and implement internationally binding agreements with a vast array of nations and international organizations, all while maintaining the constitutional and political prerogatives of shared power (Neustadt 1960; M. Peterson 1990).

We see the rise of executive agreements as a rational response by the president and Congress to the challenges faced by the United States during the daunting complexity brought on by the emergence of its international leadership in the twentieth century. To be sure, under a system of shared powers, the framers created what many scholars have referred to as "an invitation to struggle" between the presidency and Congress in foreign affairs, which tends to force the institutions toward consensus in order to effectively make policy (Corwin 1984; Crabb and Holt 1984; Davidson 1988). In their struggle to confront an uncertain and dangerous world, where domestic political consensus is seen as a premium (Melanson 2000), the two political branches, with a supporting role played by the Supreme Court, constituted an institutional bargain grounded in requirements for efficiency that are demanded by modern realities. As is the case with institutional relationships in the U.S. system of shared powers, conflict often arises and is mitigated by the degree to which Congress and presidents are willing to work together. Hence, presidential power in this realm ebbs and flows much like it does in other areas of presidential-congressional relations.

The Framework Elaborated

Presidents do not make decisions on the format of international agreements while working in a vacuum; their relationship with Congress is multifaceted. Were a president to exercise unilateral authority in the diplomatic realm by using executive agreements on every single important international agreement, it would have significant and negative repercussions for the president in many other areas of activity in which presidents are reliant on the Congress—including budgeting, confirmations to the executive branch and judiciary, and policy making. Therefore, congressional constraints are to be considered real and significant in a theory that considers mechanisms of shared power.

Moreover, if presidents proceeded in a truly unilateral fashion, with no regard for the Senate or House, the vast majority of such agreements would be codified but essentially hollow, because presidents are, in fact, reliant on the Congress for legislation to implement international agreements. Provisions within executive agreements—such as the nuclear deal between President Bush and Indian prime minister Manmohan Singh, mentioned previously—often must be processed through the House and Senate because they alter existing statutes, require funding, or are a result of Congress having delegated the initial authority to negotiate the agreement to the president while maintaining a two-chamber approval process. When pursuing approval for NAFTA, the Central American Free Trade Agreement (CAFTA), and other recent multilateral and bilateral trade agreements, presidents have had to personally lobby members of Congress. Agreements involving foreign aid require the Congress to appropriate funds. Moreover, formally ratified treaties often require implementation legislation from Congress to provide funding, authorizations, and changes in domestic law.[8] If the Senate were being subverted on a regular basis by presidential use of executive agreements, we would expect at least one senator to stand up and filibuster the accompanying attempt to pass implementation or funding legislation.

Additionally, what incentives are there for the chair of the Senate Foreign Relations Committee to allow presidents to run roughshod over their constitutional prerogatives? That the Senate does not regularly throw executive agreements back in the president's face suggests two possible scenarios. First, Congress might completely defer to the president on international agreements generally. Given the propensity of the Senate to quibble with the president on the content of submitted treaties (Auerswald and Maltzman 2003) and the wherewithal of some members, such as long-serving senator Robert Byrd (D-WV), to guard their constitutional prerogatives, this scenario is highly unlikely. Evidence from our in-depth interviews around Washington bolsters this unlikelihood. One senior Senate staffer working for the Senate Foreign Relations Committee said, "If there was an end run around the Senate and the Senate was divided on the matter, there would be a backlash." A senior State Department official working as a Senate liaison concluded, "I've never gotten a phone call or my boss hasn't with someone with Senate Foreign Relations saying, 'Why is something an executive agreement and not a treaty? What are you guys trying to do to us?' That just hasn't happened."[9]

Second and alternatively, the Senate (and Congress more generally) may, more or less, be a willing party in this trend. We posit that this is indeed the case. We argue that in the area of international agreements, the president and Congress participate in what Richard Neustadt (1960: 26) calls "a government of separated institutions *sharing* power." Along these lines, Mark Peterson (1990: 2), describing his "tandem institutions" perspective, speaks of "the symbiotic relationship of the president and Congress in the legislative arena and of the elaborate contexts in which the institutional interactions are carried out." Peterson posits a decision-making system consisting of the White House and Capitol Hill, which together are responsible for collective solutions. Peterson's framework fits well with Neustadt's framework built around the power of persuasion. To Neustadt, the Congress is one of several constituencies that the president must seek to influence through persuasion, because formal powers only get a president so far toward their desired outcomes. As the president needs the Congress for implementing and funding the provisions of international agreements, we find this perspective helpful here. Approaching the topic of presidential-congressional relations on international agreements from this perspective leads to a very different interpretation of the rise of executive agreements than the conventional understanding that emphasizes unilateral action at the expense of the Senate in the domestic politics of international agreements.

While Neustadt emphasizes persuasive power and Peterson points to the propensity of the institutions to work in tandem to solve policy problems through the legislative process, the unilateral options provided presidents by the use of executive agreements differs considerably, as presidents are able to make policy outside of the legislative process. Their ability to do so, however, hinges on the degree to which the legislature is willing to grant discretion to the executive. Theories of delegation that emphasize the degree to which Congress grants discretion to the executive therefore allow us to gain traction in explaining why the Senate (and Congress more generally) might allow presidents greater authority when completing international agreements than is set forth in the Constitution. The legislative delegation of power to the executive is a common feature of modern American government. Delegation to the executive branch by Congress hit its stride during the massive expansion of the federal government during the FDR years, at about the same time that executive agreements became the primary mode for completing international agreements. Trade legislation, for example, a delegation of Congress's commerce power, provides important benefits for congressional influence on trade politics while maintaining strict legislative oversight and the need for legislative approval (O'Halloran 1993).

Epstein and O'Halloran, in their book *Delegating Powers*, outline the reasons Congress delegates authority to the executive. The two most obvious reasons, they argue, are that "Congress delegates to reduce its workload and to take advantage of agency expertise" (1999: 48; see also Ripley and Franklin 1984). A less obvious reason still critical to explaining delegation is that Congress delegates to promote political and institutional efficiency. Epstein and O'Halloran (1999: 230) posit that, to promote policy making and political efficiency, Congress will delegate greater authority to the executive when the informational content of an issue is high and complex and where the ratio of political benefits to costs are low. Foreign policy fits both of these conditions quite well, as the executive tends to maintain informational advantages and as the electoral payoffs and district-level benefits for members of Congress are minimized (Canes-Wrone, Howell, and Lewis 2007; Wildavsky 1966). When the legislative benefits of delegation are given full consideration, this mode of policy making fits well the logic of a system of separation of powers, rather than an abdication of power on the part of the legislature. This is especially the case should Congress take its oversight role seriously and maintain checks on the authority it delegates (Epstein and O'Halloran 1999). In the realm of war powers, for example, Fisher (2000: xiv) argues that congressional quiescence has amounted to an abdication of constitutional power rather than delegation, because Congress has failed to maintain significant checks on presidential actions.

Institutional Incentives for System Efficiency

In terms of institutional incentives for the two branches, it is clear that the president benefits from having the ability to forge executive agreements. Such agreements enter into force much more quickly than would occur under the constitutional process. But what is in it for the Congress? Few scholars have considered congressional thought on these developments; most focus almost exclusively on the rise of executive agreements from the president's perspective. How does a balanced, interbranch system produce an extraconstitutional policy tool for one branch (executive agreements for the president) while seemingly slighting the constitutional process of the other branch (Senate treaty consent)? Is this not the executive power grab that troubles contemporary observers of presidential politics? We contend that it is not and that the Congress is complicit in this policy evolution. This becomes apparent as we begin to explore reasons why the Congress would be willing to allow the rise of executive agreements.

We see the rise of executive agreements as a fundamental, rational response by the president and Congress to the challenges faced by the United States during the daunting complexity brought on by the emergence of its international leadership in the twentieth century. In an increasingly complex world, the Senate is willing to allow presidents and their administrations to deal with the logistical challenge of annually processing hundreds of such agreements. Processing such a workload through the Article II process would grind the presidential-congressional system to a halt, at least in regard to foreign policy, at both ends of Pennsylvania Avenue. To gain the two-thirds majority needed, presidents, their White House staff, and State Department officials would spend constant time coordinating with the Senate Foreign Relations Committee. One high-level and long-serving official in the State Department's Office of the Legal Advisor reflected, "The treaty process is a drain on the president's time. There are issues of economy and efficiency, which is why we have the rise in preauthorized executive agreements."[10]

For its part, if all international agreements were completed as Article II treaties, the Senate agenda would be inundated with foreign policy minutiae. Even the Congressional Research Service's Louis Fisher, who, in his many writings, has long disdained the increasing power of the presidency vis-à-vis the Congress, allows for the possibility that the growth of executive agreements can be accounted for by "the sheer increase in volume of the amount of business and contacts between the United States and other countries"; he adds, "Many observers believe it would be impractical to submit every international agreement the United States enters to the Senate as a treaty" (2001: 40). It is striking that, when asked about the issue, key legislative staffers and executive bureaucrats in the process focus on executive agreements as a mechanism of efficiency rather than strategic evasion. One staffer in the State Department's Office of the Assistant Legal Adviser for Treaty Affairs stated, "No one's looking to evade; they're looking to streamline the process." A senior staffer on the Senate Foreign Relations Committee concluded, "It's just an efficiency matter. The reality is, as the Senate's plate gets fuller and fuller, the process is cumbersome . . . [and] delay can be substantial." The staffer maintained that executive agreements are "a quicker way of doing things."[11]

If all international agreements were sent to the Senate for advice and consent, the Senate Foreign Relations Committee would become primarily a treaty processing plant. Given the goals senators pursue, which include reelection, effective policy making, and institutional prestige (Fenno 1973), it is difficult to imagine that much would be gained in service of those goals if the committee's primary job was to rubber-stamp the president's treaties. Furthermore, if the committee were to faithfully exercise its institutional responsibility of vetting the agreements, it would get nothing else done. The likely outcome is that treaties would be given consent en masse, as committee members leaned on the diplomatic expertise of the executive branch and those that initially negotiated the agreements. The treaty approval process would become a farce. A more practical solution for the Senate would be to delegate much of the treaty-making power to the president, by allowing for executive agreements for the vast majority of cases, while maintaining the Article II consent process for the truly significant commitments and those agreements that alter domestic law (e.g., tax treaties).

In addition to practitioners, a few scholars have also suggested that executive agreements provide an efficient mechanism to get things done in a busy international system. In examining two centuries' worth of aggregated time series data, King and Ragsdale (1988: 113) speculated that this may be the case: "Presidents and a growing executive branch engage generally in more activities to keep up with the constant expansion of foreign policy. In their attempts to supervise foreign policy, presidents use executive agreements as convenient devices that accommodate the intricacies and details of the foreign policy environment rather than as political devices to circumvent the Senate." Edward Corwin's conclusions (1984: 243) are similar: "It is evident that if an executive agreement is a convenient instrument for carrying out a conceded executive power or if an executive agreement, in the broader sense of the term, is a convenient instrument for effectuating a power of Congress, or merged powers of President and Congress, then the employment of this method of reaching an understanding with another government cannot be warrantably characterized as an 'evasion' of the treaty-making power in which the Senate participates." Our theory, then, rests on the reduced costs incurred by senators when they allow executive discretion by delegating authority on international agreements.

In addition to eschewing the evasion hypothesis and thus the conventional understanding that executive agreements are part and parcel to the imperial presidency, our logic leads to a very different view of the Senate treaty consent process. In exchange for allowing the president some leeway in utilizing executive agreements, we expect that the most important international agreements will be submitted as treaties per the original process designed in the Constitution. Executive agreements do not replace the Article II treaty process altogether, especially when significant international commitments are considered. The Senate is a willing partner in the policy innovation of the executive agreement, provided that the Senate still processes the most salient international agreement issues of the day as treaties.

The exception to this institutional bargain on treaties occurs when the Congress gives its formal consent, through legislation, for presidents to enter into a certain type of international agreement as an executive agreement, rather than as a treaty. When Congress delegates to the president its constitutional prerogative to regulate foreign commerce, for example, it does so by requiring that presidents submit their trade agreements to the Congress (not just the Senate) for approval. An example of such legislation includes the Omnibus Trade and Competitiveness Act of 1988, which requires bicameral approval of trade agreements. Hence, whereas the Senate stands to benefit from this bargain in terms of institutional efficiency, the House of Representatives also stands to benefit from the use of executive agreements, as it becomes a full partner in giving consent (or delegating authority) on international agreements. If, for instance, we find a very active House as a result of the executive agreement innovation, then that chamber, specifically, has gained from this important institutional change.

If, in order to maintain this bargain, presidents submit consequential and controversial international agreements as treaties, the remaining treaty process should be highly political, not pro forma, because it provides the political theater and struggle we would expect of shared power. In addition to explaining the rise of executive agreements, a second main purpose of this book is to take the reader inside the politics of treaty advice and consent in the U.S. Senate. As we will show, politics abound in the treaty consent process.

We by no means intend to argue that this bargain between branches is sustained without conflict. A strong element of self-institutional interest is certainly present, as we would expect to see in all vibrant democratic political systems. Individual presidents, for example, often elevate their executive agreements through public statements in pursuit of their foreign policy agendas (Caruson and Farrar-Myers 2007). Moreover, battles can occur between the branches on international agreements, particularly when boundaries are pushed and players believe the bargain struck either is a poor one or is being abused. At two key junctures in the post–World

War II era, presidents became too aggressive in their use of executive agreements, and in both cases, Congress responded strongly to reel in presidents who were pushing the proverbial envelope. As we describe in some detail in chapter 1, the proposal of the Bricker Amendment, pursued as an amendment to the U.S. Constitution during the 1950s, was a reaction to the overuse of executive agreements by Presidents Roosevelt and Truman, and Congress's Case-Zablocki Act in the 1970s lodged a statutory protest of presidential overuse of executive agreements, particularly secret agreements. In both cases, presidents obliged, and the institutional bargain was maintained.

Presidents, of course, are not the only plausible abusers of the international agreement process. At other times, Congress has pushed the envelope, making it difficult for presidents to maintain a modicum of foreign policy rationality. Such congressional recklessness provided the impetus for the rise of executive agreements on the part of internationalists in both the legislative and executive branches prior to World War II (see Ackerman and Golove 1995). During the late nineteenth and early twentieth centuries, the Senate would routinely reject significant treaties after years of U.S. negotiation, prompting critics to look for an alternative, which President Franklin Roosevelt found in the executive agreement mechanism. In the modern era, on occasion, the rules of the Senate have been exploited to block consideration of a treaty that has widespread support and to delay or reject ratification, placing the United States in an untenable diplomatic position. As we profile in chapter 4, this was the case with the Genocide Convention in the 1980s and the Comprehensive Nuclear Test Ban Treaty in the 1990s. However, both branches have an incentive to work things out. As long as the branches work in conjunction and maintain boundaries, this interbranch adaptation to a changing environment will work well as a self-correcting system.

Constitutional Construction

Some scholars have been critical of the Article II treaty process. James Sundquist (1992), for example, laments the two-thirds requirement, which effectively killed a number of majority-supported pacts between World Wars I and II. Among these failures was the Treaty of Versailles, which ended World War I, and the League of Nations. We acknowledge that the Article II treaty power was not as clearly conceived as it could have been and that practitioners of foreign policy recognized this problem following the foreign policy failures of the late nineteenth and early twentieth centuries. However, such criticism is only useful to a degree and not especially productive given the barriers to constitutional amendment. The founders had only a handful of countries in mind when they wrote the rigorous treaty process of Article II; they did not envision the vast international system in which the United States now participates. The executive agreement serves as a tool to provide flexibility in the Constitution where a strict interpretation finds none.

Tying the discussion back to unilateral theory and the imperial presidency, this institutional change and constitutional evolution of executive agreements appears intellectually consistent with at least the front end of both Howell's (2003) and Rudalevige's (2005) frameworks. Both scholars set up their theories with the governing context having outgrown the general framework provided by the Constitution. Indeed, that occurred in the case of international agreements. It would be virtually impossible, as we discussed earlier, to process through the Senate treaty process the hundreds of international agreements that presidents pursue each year. Hence, the need for a policy tool like the executive agreement is not that far off from theoretical assumptions of unilateral scholars. The executive agreement mechanism also permits the president to act unilaterally at times—without the Congress joining in—through so-called sole executive agreements (though these are a small minority of all executive agreements), which derive not from congressional delegation but from the president's Article II powers. Moreover, executive agreements (and treaties, for that matter) provide the president with a first-mover advantage and antecedent power when congressional approval is not required. This is an important characteristic of unilateral powers generally (Howell 2003).

The key difference between the institutional change in the rise of executive agreements and the assumptions of unilateral theory and the imperial presidency is that the president and Congress shared in and benefited from crafting systemic responses to environmental changes that could not be dealt with by original design. The president did not simply step into a vacuum and engage in a power grab, leaving the Congress (and the separation of powers) waving in the wind. In the face of uncertainty about constitutional processes, the branches together formed a new constitutional process in order to adapt the system to a changing international environment, which had outgrown the original document. The difference is that the separation of powers, not just the president, framed the institutional change. Louis Fisher's insights on constitutional dialogues and constitutional development are helpful here: "What is 'final' at one stage of our political development, may be reopened at some later date, leading to revisions, fresh interpretations, and reversals of Court doctrines. Through this never-ending dialogue, all three branches are able to expose weaknesses, hold excess in check, and gradually forge a consensus on constitutional issues" (1988: 275).

The type of institutional evolution exhibited by the rise of executive agreements fits especially well with Keith Whittington's (1999) theory in *Constitutional Construction: Divided Powers and Constitutional Meaning.* Whittington posits that the Constitution has a dual nature. The first and best-known dimension is constitutional interpretation, or the extent to which the Constitution acts as a binding set of rules enforced by the courts against government actors. However, Whittington argues that the Constitution also permeates the political arena, to guide and constrain political actors in the public policy process. In so doing, the Constitution also depends on political actors, "both to formulate authoritative constitutional requirements and to enforce those fundamental settlements in the future" (Whittington 1999: 1). Whittington characterizes this process, by which constitutional meaning is shaped within politics at the same time that politics is shaped by the Constitution, as one of construction, rather than interpretation. He further argues that constitutional ambiguities and changes in the political situation push political actors to construct their own constitutional understanding. Hence, the U.S. Constitution constrains institutional behavior while at the same time empowering officials, through political practice, to alter its practical meaning. According to Whittington's framework, the U.S. Constitution both binds and empowers government officials.

This framework works quite well with the interbranch nature of the rise of executive agreements. The Article II process had created significant ambiguities as the international environment faced by the American national government changed fundamentally in the twentieth century. This context set the stage for constitutional construction—in this case, a new process for international agreements. Still, Whittington writes about the binding nature of the Constitution. In the case of the rise of executive agreements, the separation of powers constrained what was possible and required a presidential-congressional adaptation (or bargain, to use our language from earlier), not a unilateral construction by the president.

Theoretical Implications

In summary, presidents increasingly utilize executive agreements rather than submitting treaties for ratification by the Senate. Political observers in Washington and academia point to the rise of executive agreements as one of the most important changes in the way foreign policy is constructed in the modern presidency era. According to these observers, the rise in the use of executive agreements, supplanting Article II treaties, is a cornerstone of presidential dominance in foreign policy and the imperial presidency more generally, and executive agreements are often cited as a unilateral power of the president. They cite the power of presidents, seemingly at will, to complete their international agreements as executive agreements rather than treaties, thus evading the constitutional requirements of a formal treaty. To continue the conventional wisdom, with politically controversial matters accomplished via executive agreements, it is easy to understand why floor defeats of treaties over the last half century can be counted on one hand. Treaty consent in the Senate becomes pro forma.

Our theoretical framework of the rise of executive agreements views the change and the presidential-congressional relationship in a very different light. While treaties and executive agreements are, for the most part, legally interchangeable, they are not politically interchangeable. Hence, we argue that in the arena of international agreements, the president and Congress participate in a system of separated institutions sharing power (Neustadt 1960). While a strong element of self-institutional interest is certainly present and while battles can occur, the president and Congress need one another to accomplish their diplomatic and policy goals (M. Peterson 1990). In the face of uncertainty about constitutional processes, the branches have formed a type of self-correcting system via the executive agreement so that they may adapt to a changing international environment.

As is the case for empirical work addressing the politics of shared power, the theoretical argument of this book has important normative implications. The undertone of the literature on imperial presidency is that presidents have usurped the separation of powers—or at least that Congress has not effectively curtailed presidents' aggrandizement of power. While it is quite apparent that presidential powers in foreign affairs have increased during the modern era, what remains unclear is whether or not the change in how the treaty power is applied in practice is outside the boundaries of theories of constitutional change. Our theory suggests that the change is well within the system of shared powers. The rise in executive agreements has afforded the U.S. political system, in the making of international commitments, an opportunity to respond rationally to a volatile international system. Furthermore, if Congress has been complicit in the rise of executive agreements and if presidents are attuned to congressional constraints, their use may not be as problematic as is assumed by the concerns voiced throughout much of the literature.

Plan of the Book

The interview evidence, case studies, and quantitative analysis in the chapters of this book significantly bolster our theoretical perspective. In chapter 1, we trace the historical change in how presidents complete international agreements and seek congressional consent. Readers will see that the treaty process has changed remarkably since the early days of the republic. In addition to discussing the evolution of the treaty power, we introduce many important concepts and processes, providing important grounding for the specific case studies and analyses that come later in the book. We discuss at length the treaty process and its evolution, in terms of both constitutional construction and practical politics. We also emphasize describing the rise of executive agreements as an alternative to traditional treaties, as well as the legal and political arguments underpinning this important innovation.

In chapter 2, we ponder and test several specific research questions regarding the rise of executive agreements. What factors contribute to the explosion of executive agreements vis-à-vis treaties? Do presidents increasingly turn to executive agreements because the political environment has become tougher in the last few decades, making it harder to get treaties through, or do presidents increasingly turn to them (and Congresses allow them) for efficiency reasons related to the increasingly complex international environment? In chapter 2, we develop more explicitly the theoretical framework outlined in this introduction. In doing so, we derive several testable hypotheses and attempt to assess how well the competing perspectives explain the rise of the use of executive agreements in the modern era. Our across-time analysis suggests that partisan political concerns are not as important as conventional wisdom suggests and that factors relevant to the Senate Foreign Relations Committee and the international environment are of primary importance. In the analysis, we examine all international agreements from 1948 to 1998, as well as the subset of major international agreements. Consistent with our theoretical framework, the evasion hypothesis, which emphasizes partisan and strategic explanations, receives next to no support. The analysis supports our theoretical claim that efficiency drives the process, but it also suggests that for the most significant treaties, political strategy may play a role, though in ways different from the standard partisan theories of separation of powers. Instead, ideological considerations matter most in structuring interbranch relations on this topic.

Chapter 3 engages directly the topic of presidential decision making by exploring the choices that presidents face in determining the form their international agreements will take in terms of domestic law. Presidents are unconstrained legally in their choice. However, clear political constraints remain. We discuss how strategic politics and our efficiency perspective might play a role in the process, and we add to this familiar discussion the important role of international politics. Building on the work of Lisa Martin (2000), we argue that agreement partners are also interested in the president's choice; hence, their decisions have international ramifications. Through a combination of quantitative evidence and interviews with Washington practitioners, we find that the process of agreement classification is institutionalized in the State Department on all but major international agreements. On the major ones, we still find little evidence of the evasion hypothesis, while institutional efficiency considerations continue to be robust in their significance. This dovetails with interview evidence that suggests that congressional leaders are willing to allow presidents to use executive agreements in many cases so that their agendas remain uncluttered.

We next turn to the treaty consent process in the Senate. Our theoretical framework would suggest that presidents would still send many major items through as treaties. These major items should not be expected to be entirely pro forma, as the strategic implications of presidential evasion suggest. Indeed, we expect that there should be some element of politics on major items sent through as treaties. In chapter 4, we present case studies of the U.S.-Soviet Consular Treaty, the Panama Canal Treaties, the Genocide Convention, and the Comprehensive Nuclear Test Ban Treaty. Our primary and secondary evidence is based in part on work in congressional archives and is suggestive of the costly politics and significant delay that can arise when presidents send their important international agreements to the Senate for formal consent.

Moving beyond case studies, we next turn to a more comprehensive examination of treaty politics and the delay that commonly occurs as presidents battle for their treaties. Our purpose in chapter 5 is to explain the delay or speed of treaty consideration and to explain why some treaties falter in the consent process. We examine all treaties before the Senate from 1949 to 2000 and test whether treaties stall due to strategic-political reasons or if gridlock in the Senate treaty process is due to other institutional considerations. We reveal some environmental and treaty-specific factors that make passing treaties difficult, that support a shared powers framework, and that are explained by interesting political considerations, which are primarily ideological rather than partisan. In the final analysis, we do find that politics are significant in the Senate treaty process, as the framers intended. The process, rather than being pro forma, is indeed political and presents difficult problems for modern presidents when they seek Senate approval of their international agreements.

We move to the other side of Capitol Hill in chapter 6. Naturally, most analyses of international agreements focus on the Senate-president relationship, as the House of Representatives is explicitly excluded from the treaty process by the Constitution. The rise of executive agreements, however, has altered the original constitutional landscape and provided for a significant role for the House. Our theory provides that the House stands to gain significant benefits as it legislates on executive agreements and exercises its institutional role of oversight. Typically, scholars point to the requirement of appropriations and implementation of treaties—roles the House has traditionally played. We find, however, through examination of congressional hearings on international agreements since the 1970s, that the House is fundamentally interested in the many facets of the international agreement process. For example, the House, when compared to the Senate, is especially significant in the oversight of international agreements. Hence, the rise of executive agreements, the most common variety being the congressional-executive agreement, has altered the bicameral relationship in foreign policy, allowing for direct involvement by the House of Representatives, which a strict reading of Article II of the Constitution does not afford. The House, not just the Senate, has something to gain through presidential use of executive agreements. The lower chamber is not so forgotten after all.

We begin the conclusion of this book by highlighting the answers to our core research questions, which on balance provide a wide sweep of support for our theoretical argument. In so doing, we incorporate two of President George W. Bush's agenda items involving international agreements: the Law of the Sea Treaty and the recent twenty-billion-dollar arms pact with Saudi Arabia and its neighbors. We then contemplate what our theoretical argument and these answers mean for theories of presidential power and presidential-congressional relations and for models of institutional change. We finish the conclusion and the book with a discussion of the key normative implications of our findings.

1 | Treaties and Executive Agreements: A History

The power to enter into international agreements is a fundamentally important power of the American presidency. Historically, international agreements have played a prominent policy role—from the creation of important alliances and the ending of major wars to the emergence of critical international organizations and global trade structures. As discussed in the introduction, a new policy innovation emerged during the twentieth century that enabled the president and Congress to effectively deal with the increased diplomatic demands of America's new leadership role: the executive agreement. Executive agreements do not require supermajority support in the Senate as do formal Article II treaties. Since the 1940s, the vast majority of international agreements have been completed by presidents as executive agreements rather than as treaties. This major policy evolution occurred without changes to the Constitution, though Supreme Court decisions and practice by the political branches have validated the change. This has led some scholars to conclude that the treaty power "has become effectively a Presidential monopoly" (Franck and Weisband 1979: 135; see also Corwin 1984).

This important innovation has created a conundrum for practitioners of foreign policy and students of separation of powers. Has the presidency usurped power and made unilateral what was intended by the framers to be shared? Are presidents routinely evading the Senate (and the Constitution's supermajority requirement for treaty consent) and completing consequential agreements as executive agreements rather than as treaties, while sending the less controversial agreements to the Senate as treaties? Or is the emergence of executive agreements a natural response to the complexities of the twentieth century by the American system of separate institutions sharing power, with the Congress complicit by allowing the evolution of the executive agreement as a policy tool? The framework we developed in the introduction clearly points to the latter conclusion. As the reader will come to see, historical practice also supports the latter conclusion. However, to make a strong case challenging the received wisdom of a presidential monopoly in treaty making, we must first provide some historical context.

In this chapter, we trace the change in how presidents complete agreements with other countries and seek congressional consent. Recent treatments of the politics of international agreements often lack this historical perspective and proceed from a set of unfounded assumptions. Readers will see that the treaty process has changed remarkably since the early days of the republic and America's first consequential treaty, the Jay Treaty, completed with Britain in 1794. In addition to discussing the evolution of the treaty power, we introduce many important concepts and processes, providing important grounding for the specific case studies and analyses that come later in the book.

The Treaty Power in Constitutional Perspective

We begin at the most logical place: the U.S. Constitution. It is clear that the authors of the Constitution intended that the president share the treaty power with the Senate. They wrote into Article II, Section 2, that the president "shall have power, by and with the advice and consent of the Senate, to make treaties, provided two-thirds of the Senators present concur." While this passage in Article II is most important regarding our interest in the separation of powers, the Constitution also mentions treaties elsewhere. In Article I, Section 10, the Constitution provides that the treaty power is clearly in the domain of the national government, by prohibiting states from entering into treaties: "No state shall enter into any treaty, alliance, or confederation . . ." The Constitution provides a role for the judiciary when it states, in Article III, Section 2, that "judicial power shall extend to all cases, in law and equity, arising under this constitution, the laws of the United States, and treaties made, or which shall be made under their authority." Finally, the Constitution clearly states, in Article VI, that "all treaties made, or which shall be made, under the authority of the United States shall be the supreme law of the land," further eroding any claim to states' rights in regard to treaty compliance and firmly establishing the legal significance of treaties (Dalton 1999).

Under the Articles of Confederation, America's first constitution, all treaty powers were vested in the Congress and the various states. Article VI states, "No State, without the consent of the United States in Congress assembled, shall send any embassy to, or receive any embassy from, or enter into any conference, agreement, alliance or treaty with any King, Prince or State." Other restrictions on states' entry into international agreements were peppered throughout the Articles of Confederation (e.g., Articles VI and IX provide restrictions but do not completely disallow states from entering into international agreements). That states could enter into international agreements, with the consent of Congress, was disconcerting to the framers. One goal of the Constitutional Convention was to centralize the treaty-making process and, more broadly, control over diplomacy and commerce, in the new national government (O'Brien 2003: 71).

Originally, the founders placed the treaty power squarely in the hands of the Senate. This is unsurprising given the lack of an executive in the Articles of Confederation and the Constitutional Convention's early lack of clarity about how the executive would be shaped (Milkis and Nelson 1999). However, late in the convention, the framers agreed to include the president in the process. Excluding the House from the process was defended by Alexander Hamilton and John Jay in the Federalist Papers (Nos. 64, 69, and 75). Though controversial, it was argued that the Senate's smaller size and lengthier terms would facilitate secrecy, which was considered valuable in the exercise of diplomacy, and that the supermajority requirement would protect minority interests (Ackerman and Golove 1995: 10; Franck and Weisband 1979: 135; Lindsay 1994: 78; Spitzer 1993: 195).

The language of Article II and the historical record are clear that the intent of the framers was to share the treaty power between the president and Senate. The authors of the Federalist Papers wrote extensively about the dangers of executive prerogative in making international agreements. Alexander Hamilton, an advocate for broad interpretation of executive power, expressed in Federalist No. 75 his belief that the legislature should be included in making international agreements. Moreover, in Federalist No. 69, Hamilton cites several versions of treaties and "every other species of convention usual among nations," which require joint action by the president and two-thirds of the Senate. In Federalist No. 64, John Jay argued against delegating the treaty power to the president; and as Michael Glennon notes, James Madison "considered treaty making more of a legislative function" (Glennon 1990: 181–82).

It was not long, however, before the extent of executive power granted in Article II served as a subject of dispute. In his arguments on behalf of

President Washington's Neutrality Proclamation, Alexander Hamilton reasoned that the executive vesting clause, which states that "the executive Power shall be vested in a President," was a much broader grant of power than what was subsequently enumerated in Article II (see Corwin 1984: 208–10). The treaty-negotiating power is an executive monopoly, given the president's role as chief diplomat, with the Senate playing a veto role. This is the argument used by proponents of executive power in the international realm, such as Hamilton, and furthered by future jurists, such as Justice Sutherland, who wrote that the president "alone negotiates" (quoted in Corwin 1984: 488). Under this view, presidents negotiate treaties and then receive advice and consent once the treaty has been made. Corwin (1984: 210) explains, "Ordinarily this means that the *initiative* in the foreign field rests with [the president]. . . . He is consequently able to confront the other departments . . . with *faits accomplis* at will. On the other hand, Congress is under no *constitutional* obligation to back up such *faits accomplis*."

The other view is that the framers expected the Senate to be involved in the treaty-negotiating process from the beginning, providing advice and then consent to the final treaty. The Senate would then play an important role in advising presidents regarding their diplomatic initiatives (Franck and Weisband 1979: 135). James Madison disputed Hamilton's claim for additional executive prerogatives stemming from the vagueness of the executive vesting clause, arguing that the president's diplomatic powers were limited in their range of discretion (Corwin 1984: 210). To be sure, the famous exchange between Hamilton and Madison over the extent of executive power involved primarily the war power, rather than the treaty power, but their argument set the stage for a century and a half of debate, of which the treaty power was a central bone of contention.

While the view of the treaty power as a presidential monopoly has clearly won out in terms of constitutional practice, Louis Fisher (1985: 253–58; 1998: 182–84) persuasively argues that the view providing for direct Senate involvement is much closer to the intent of the framers. While the framers clearly delineated a two-step process for advice and consent on executive branch appointments, which has been verified through historical practice (Sollenberger 2006), Fisher (1998: 183) notes that "no such two-step division of labor . . . exists for treaties." Rather, Senate advice is appropriate throughout the process, according to this line of argument. It is not uncommon and is politically wise, as Fisher demonstrates, for presidents to include members of the Senate in the treaty-negotiating process; however, they are not required to do so. The greatest treaty failure of all time, the Treaty of Versailles, may be explained by Senate opposition as a result of President Wilson's exclusion of senators from the negotiating process, presenting the Senate with a fait accompli, which it rejected.[1] Fisher (1985: 256–57) cites several cases where legislators were part of the negotiation team on significant international agreements during the twentieth century. However, Franck and Weisband (1979: 136), in their pointed critique of the modern treaty process in practice, point out how, as early as the Jay Treaty of 1794, presidents began to skirt senatorial advice during the negotiation stage.

Why the presidential monopoly view dominates legal thinking remains an interesting question for scholars. However, it is beyond our task here to enter into the debate. It is instructive that such a view continues to dominate at both ends of Pennsylvania Avenue.[2] Some scholars argue that the early exclusion of the Senate in the negotiating process was a sign of things to come—the exclusion of the Senate from the process in its entirety, through executive "cooption and circumvention" of the Senate's role, most notably in the form of the rise of the modern executive agreement (Franck and Weisband 1979: chap. 6; see also L. Johnson 1984; Margolis 1986). Corwin (1984) and Ackerman and Golove (1995) do not see the rise of executive agreements as quite so problematic; rather, they see it as a process that has evolved with the general consent of Congress (see also Spiro 2001). Later in this chapter, we turn to the rise in the use of executive agreements, but we first address the classic process of treaty ratification that presidents must traverse today.

The Classic Ratification Process

For purposes of theoretical clarity, we adopt the view that there is a presidential monopoly on treaty negotiation, the first stage of the treaty process. We assume presidents are unitary actors when negotiating and signing international agreements. The Senate's own documents clearly point to the first stage of the process as an executive prerogative. The second stage includes formal consideration by the Senate, which may or may not include amendments, reservations, understandings, or declarations.[3] The final stage includes ratification of the final treaty document by the president.[4] In the first stage, the executive branch initiates negotiations; the president appoints negotiators (appointments that may be subject to advice and consent by the Senate if the appointees are not already ambassadors or officers in foreign service), delegates powers to negotiate on behalf of the United States, and concludes the treaty through signing the document.

Maintaining the initiative, presidents also begin the second phase, when they formally transmit treaty documents to the Senate.[5] Treaties, once transmitted, are automatically referred to the Senate Foreign Relations Committee in accordance with Senate Rule XXV. The committee must act on a resolution of ratification—with conditions, if applicable—before the full Senate can take up the treaty for advice and consent.[6] According to Rule XXX, should the committee fail to report a treaty before the end of a Congress, the treaty remains on the calendar during the next Congress.

Once the committee reports a treaty, the full Senate can act. A two-thirds vote of those present is required for the Senate to give its advice and consent to ratification of a treaty. Amendment and reservations require only majority approval. A treaty that fails to receive the necessary support in the Senate is returned to the committee, where it sits on the committee calendar indefinitely until the committee reports it to the full Senate again or until the treaty is returned to the president by simple resolution. According to Rule XXX, should the full Senate fail to act on a reported treaty, the treaty is recommitted to committee, and the committee must report it again before the full Senate can give its advice and consent (see Rundquist and Bach 2003).

Should the Senate give its consent to a treaty, the treaty then awaits final presidential action (ratification). It is a widely held misperception that the Senate ratifies treaties. Rather, the Senate consents to the treaty, as amended, and ratification awaits presidential action (Crabb, Antizzo, and Sarieddine 2000: 196–97). Again, the president retains the initiative; he is free to decide whether or not to formally ratify the treaty, as amended, by signing the instrument of ratification. If, for example, the conditions placed on the resolution of ratification by the full Senate are too onerous for the president (or U.S. treaty partners), the president may decide not to ratify the treaty. Finally, the instruments of ratification are exchanged between treaty partners, thus entering the treaty into force for U.S. law.

A Role for the House of Representatives

While many treaties are self-executing, should the treaty require implementing legislation or obligate the United States to spend sums of money, then the House of Representatives also plays a role after ratification (Vasquez 1995).[7] Through normal legislative channels, Congress must appropriate the funds necessary for carrying forth the treaty's provisions. Moreover, if the treaty involves commercial interests or the disposition of territory (as did, e.g., the treaty purchasing Alaska from Russia in 1867), the House has retained the right to act jointly with the Senate, requiring the passage of legislation (Fisher 1998: 186–87). To be fully implemented, treaties often require appropriations—a fundamental power of the House (Corwin 1984: 243; O'Brien 2003: 71). Following ratification of the Jay Treaty in 1794, the House asserted its constitutional prerogatives in carrying forth duly ratified treaties (see Fisher 1998: 185–86). More recently, once Senate consent to the Panama Canal Treaties was won by the Carter administration, the tense legislative battle over implementing and funding the provisions of the treaties moved to the House. The House only narrowly approved the implementing legislation required to put the treaties into effect (Public Law 96-70).

The House is also involved in the process of legislative approval for congressional-executive agreements, which often require congressional approval. Examples of such agreements include most agreements involving major trade (e.g., NAFTA), nuclear cooperation, and fisheries. Finally, the modern House of Representatives has shown a keen interest in the treaty process through oversight and investigatory hearings, as we demonstrate in chapter 6.

The Executive Agreement Process

The formal treaty process is indeed cumbersome, is often politically untenable due to the supermajority requirement in the Senate, and can ultimately require involvement by the House. As a result, modern presidents have more often opted for the more efficient policy alternative of executive agreements. A comparison of the modern executive agreement process with the formal treaty process previously outlined clearly shows the attractiveness of the former to the executive branch: in the case of executive agreements, the second and third phases are cut from the process, as many such agreements enter into force upon signature of executive branch negotiators. However, to focus on this benefit alone would be a gross oversimplification. In most cases, an executive agreement is pursuant to a statutory grant of power to the president or requires ex post congressional approval (through joint resolution) before the agreement enters into force. Executive agreements of this sort are typically referred to as "congressional-executive agreements," whereas the rarer executive agreements that rely entirely on the executive's plenary powers in foreign policy are referred to as "sole executive agreements" (Klarevas 2003: 394). Moreover, if the executive agreement requires budgetary outlays (as would, e.g., a military assistance agreement), Congress remains involved through its control of the purse strings.

Other Presidential Treaty Powers

Presidents maintain two other important treaty powers beyond their negotiation and choice of form: treaty interpretation and treaty termination. Presidents do not appear to be constrained legally in their decision to terminate treaties.[8] To be sure, the unilateral termination of a treaty by a president is uncommon in practice and raises serious domestic and international political questions;[9] however, the Supreme Court has concluded that treaty termination is a power of the executive, which can be checked by the legislature through statute (*Goldwater v. Carter* 444 U.S. 996 [1979]; see O'Brien 2003), something congressional opponents have been unable or unwilling to do (Rudalevige 2005: 208).

The law is also murky when it comes to treaty interpretation. The constitutional text is unclear about which branch is responsible for interpreting a treaty once it is ratified. Presumably, the executive maintains this authority when a treaty provision is unclear, but that does not necessarily mean that presidents are free to reinterpret treaties in force (Kennedy 1986). The constitutional matter remains largely unsettled, however, allowing presidents and proponents of executive power to argue that interpretation is largely an executive prerogative (see, e.g., Yoo 2001), though the recent decision in *Hamdan v. Rumsfeld* (126 U.S. 2749 [2006]) is a blow to this school of thought. Finding, in that case, that the military tribunals set up through executive order by the Bush administration violated the Geneva Conventions, the Court suggested that the executive and legislative branches together interpret the meaning of treaties.[10]

The Treaty Power in Practice: A Brief Political History

In the wake of the Constitutional Convention, it was clearly understood that the treaty power was shared between the president and Senate. Most convention delegates agreed with Pierce Butler of South Carolina that treaties should "be gone over, clause by clause, by the President and Senate together" (Franck and Weisband 1979: 136). This is evidenced by President Washington's famous dealings before the Senate regarding a treaty negotiated with the Creek Indians in August 1789. In a situation that proved embarrassing to both Washington and the Senate, the president sent the Senate thirteen questions for guidance during treaty negotiations and appeared in person on the Senate floor but was faced with significant delay, as the Senate was reluctant to discuss the treaty with him. Washington felt insulted enough to vow that "he would be damned if he ever went there again" (quoted in Milkis and Nelson 1999: 75). While Washington continued to seek the written advice of the Senate on future treaties, he set the stage for the elimination of the advice portion of the process of advice and consent (Edwards and Wayne 2006: 477–78; Lindsay 1994: 78).

Following Washington's experience, presidents were inclined to complete negotiations of their treaties prior to seeking the advice and consent of the Senate, effectively shutting the Senate out of its shared role in treaty negotiation. The first such case where a treaty was negotiated without prior advice was the Jay Treaty of 1794. According to Franck and Weisband (1979: 136), a new practice gained steam: presidents would negotiate treaties, only rarely would Senate advice be sought in any meaningful way during negotiations, and then the president would submit the treaties to the Senate for an up or down vote, essentially limiting the Senate's role of advice and consent to simply consent.

Naturally, in a system of shared powers, the Senate did not stand idly by and allow the president to unilaterally usurp its advice role. Instead, the Senate retaliated through the amendment phase of the treaty process. In some cases, this proved disastrous for U.S. foreign policy, as presidents would negotiate treaties only to have significant changes made in the Senate, prompting treaty partners to reject the eventual treaty as amended. Examples include the King-Hawkesbury Convention of 1803 and the Hay-Pauncefote Treaty of 1900, which proposed a canal through Panama (Franck and Weisband 1979: 136). Between 1789 and 1992, forty-three treaties given consent by the Senate were rejected by the president or U.S. treaty partners as a result of changes made by the Senate. The practice of significantly amending treaties in the Senate increased following the Civil War, when the Senate changed its rules to ditch the two-thirds requirement to amend treaties, instead going with a simple majority vote, which it retains today (Lindsay 1994: 79–81). The Senate was protecting its treaty power with its only available tool. Senator Lodge (R-MA) famously stated "that a treaty sent to the Senate is not properly a treaty but merely a project" (Holt 1933: 179). The practice was so onerous for presidents and their advisors that it led Richard Olney, secretary of state, to conclude that defeat of the president's treaties was preferable to allowing wholesale changes by the Senate (Franck and Weisband 1979: 137).

In fact, defeat on the floor of the Senate became commonplace in the late decades of the nineteenth century and early decades of the twentieth. While the most notable treaty defeat was the Treaty of Versailles (the peace treaty ending World War I), it should not have been a surprise to observers of the time that the treaty failed in the Senate. The Senate had failed to give its consent to every significant treaty between 1869 and 1898 (Holt 1933; Lindsay 1994: 15). Of the twenty-one outright Senate rejections of proposed treaties (indeed a rare occurrence over the scope of history), fourteen occurred between 1860 and 1935 (O'Brien 2003: 74, table 4.1). Teddy Roosevelt once complained, "individual Senators evidently consider the prerogatives of the Senate as far more important than the welfare of the country" (quoted in Holt 1933: 178). President McKinley placed three senators on the negotiation team of the peace treaty formally ending the Spanish-American War. The treaty made it through the Senate in 1898—the first major treaty victory for a president in thirty years (Lindsay 1994: 15–16). Both of these presidents served when their party controlled the majority of seats in the Senate.

Why were presidents' treaties so endangered in the Senate during this period of U.S. history? Early studies of the treaty process suggest that presidents faced problems inherent in a system of shared powers. The Senate jealously guarded its role of advice and consent, and senators firmly believed they had an important role to play in shaping American diplomacy, no matter the complaints of the executive branch or foreign powers. One reason treaties were so endangered, then, is the fact that the Senate was prodded to defend its foreign policy prerogatives through the only real means available to it, since presidents had so often excluded the Senate from the first phase of the treaty process.

Moreover, fights over treaties during this period were marked with partisanship (Dangerfield 1933; Holt 1933; Fleming 1930), especially during periods of partisan polarization, where a large gulf existed between the median ideologies of Senate Republicans and Democrats. Senate polarization scores derived from Poole and Rosenthal's NOMINATE data and party voting scores clearly show that the two political parties were highly polarized during the 1880s through the early 1900s (Aldrich, Berger, and Rohde 2002; Poole and Rosenthal 1997). Such high levels of polarization and partisanship exacerbate any effects that separate partisan control of the presidency and Senate may have had on interbranch relations.[11] Since treaties require a supermajority for consent in the Senate, it is not surprising that early twentieth-century presidents had difficulty with their treaties. Holt's (1933) analysis of the Treaty of Versailles clearly shows that the battle in the Senate was primarily based along party lines, as President Wilson, a Democrat, faced off against the Republican Senate.

The Treaty of Versailles was not just a major political defeat for President Wilson but a significant setback for an internationalist foreign policy. A major part of the treaty included Wilson's brainchild the League of Nations, a world organization designed in the wake of World War I to prevent the calamity of another world war. That the United States was not a member of the league limited the organization's claim to legitimacy (Bennett and Oliver 2002: 44; Jentleson 2000: 101, 222). Prominent isolationists in Congress learned a different lesson from the experience of World War I than did the internationalists: America could avoid world war by keeping the internationalist tendencies of the executive in check. While the United States participated widely in armament and financial accords during the interwar years (e.g., the Kellogg-Briand Pact of 1928 and the Washington Naval Conference of 1921–22), the domestic popularity of isolationism contributed to protectionist trade policies (e.g., the 1929 Smoot-Hawley Tariff) and, in 1935, to the defeat of the World Court treaty. The last floor defeat of a treaty during this era occurred despite the fact that both political parties had endorsed the World Court treaty in their 1932 platforms (Lindsay 1994: 16–17).

Treaties in the Modern Era

Since 1935, the Senate has only formally rejected three treaties, prompting many scholars to refer to the modern process of treaty consent as pro forma and to the Senate as "a most compliant partner" (Hastedt 2000: 162).[12] Most accounts focusing on floor failures fail to mention treaties ignored by committee or blocked procedurally on the floor (e.g., the Genocide Convention),[13] those withdrawn from consideration by the president for political reasons (e.g., the Strategic Arms Limitation Talks [SALT] II in 1980), or other obvious treaty consent failures. Other scholars, drawing from case studies, paint the modern process as a tangled web of domestic and international politics rife with partisan and ideological conflict. Examples include studies on the Nuclear Test Ban (Divine 1978), SALT II (Caldwell 1991a; Talbot 1979), the Panama Canal Treaties (Furlong and Scranton 1984; Jorden 1984; Moffett 1985), the Chemical Weapons Convention (Evans and Oleszek 2003; Hersman 2000), and the Comprehensive Nuclear Test Ban Treaty (Evans and Oleszek 2003).

Which is it? Is the process pro forma or rife with political conflict? In chapters 4 and 5, we are able to demonstrate that politics play an important role in the defeat of treaties, as well as contributing to significant delay to Senate consent to treaties in the modern era. The process is not pro forma, especially in regard to the most significant treaties. For example, 7.4 percent of the treaties transmitted by the president to the Senate from 1949 to 2000 failed to ever receive Senate consent.[14] Those treaties that received consent often faced significant delay. Among the treaties that made it through, the median number of days from the date when the president transmitted the treaty to the date of Senate consent is 216, or seven months.[15]

These statistics notwithstanding, most treaties sail through the process rather smoothly, albeit with some delay. It is clear that the Franklin Roosevelt administration witnessed a sea change in the treaty consent process. Subsequent presidents no longer faced the high degree of uncertainty attributed to the treaty process in the earlier period. To be sure, on some treaties, attaining consent requires the expenditure of a great deal of political capital, but not to the degree faced by Roosevelt's predecessors. In addition, the Senate appears to have reduced its practice using reservations to provide its advice during the consent phase, as only one in five treaties given Senate consent between 1947 and 2000 had reservations or amendments attached (Auerswald and Maltzman 2003: 1102).

The obvious explanation for this shift in treaty politics since Roosevelt is the marked rise in the use of executive agreements, rather than formal Article II treaties. Rather than submit their treaties to the Senate for consent, modern presidents have the option available to treat their international agreements as executive agreements. What contributed to this important policy evolution? Was it a result of executive overreach and unilateralism, or did the branches accommodate to more effectively pursue American foreign policy?

Treaty Termination and Interpretation

Treaty termination and interpretation also involve unsettled constitutional issues and represent areas of treaty practice where presidents have seized the initiative. Modern presidents maintain the prerogative to terminate and interpret treaties. In 1978, President Carter announced that the United States would withdraw from the 1954 Mutual Defense Treaty with Taiwan in order to facilitate full diplomatic recognition of the People's Republic of China. Carter was sued in federal court by several senators, led by Barry Goldwater. Senator Goldwater claimed that the unilateral termination represented "a dangerous precedent for executive usurpation of Congress's historically and constitutionally based powers" (Rudalevige 2005: 206–7). Goldwater won in district court, but that decision was reversed by the D.C. Circuit. On appeal to the Supreme Court, Goldwater's case was dismissed as a political question (Adler 2004; O'Brien 2003). If Congress opposed the president's action, concluded the Court, they were within their power to legislate (*Goldwater*, 444 U.S. 996).

More recently, President George W. Bush unilaterally withdrew the

United States from the Anti-Ballistic Missile (ABM) Treaty of 1972. Again, members of Congress brought suit, only to have their case dismissed in district court as a political question (*Kucinich v. Bush*, 236 F. Supp. 2d 1 [D.D.C. 2002]). However specious and unsatisfying these decisions are to some (see, e.g., Adler 2004), they represent the sum total of court rulings on the topic.[16]

Until very recently, the Court has left unsolved the thorny legal issues around treaty interpretation, leaving an opening for the claim of executive prerogative. Two high-profile cases of treaty interpretation have emerged in recent decades. The first instance dealt with the Reagan administration's reinterpretation of the ABM Treaty in 1985 to allow for development of Reagan's Strategic Defense Initiative (SDI)—a clear violation of the treaty as originally interpreted. The matter became a political football, as proponents of SDI and, in later administrations, national missile defense argued for reinterpretation of the treaty, while opponents argued that reinterpreting it would require the assent of the Senate (see Kennedy 1986). The Senate responded by including language, known as the "Biden Condition," prohibiting such unilateral reinterpretations in the ratification documents attached to the Intermediate-Range Nuclear Forces Treaty. Legally, this condition, part of the treaty ratified by President Reagan, became part of the treaty and therefore is binding on the executive (Glennon 1990: 138–44). Further language was added to the Flank Document Agreement to the Conventional Armed Forces in Europe Treaty in 1997, conditioning ratification on the president submitting amendments to the ABM Treaty for Senate approval (Auerswald 2006: 83). Events (i.e., the collapse of the Soviet Union) eventually overtook the controversy, and President George W. Bush withdrew from the treaty in 2001.

More recently, President George W. Bush has claimed to hold inherent war powers, as commander in chief, that allow him to hold enemy combatants indefinitely, set up military tribunals, and participate in "extraordinary rendition," whereby U.S. officials deliver terrorist suspects to third-party nations for interrogation (Weaver and Pollitto 2006). A question emerged as to whether or not the president's military tribunals were prohibited by the Geneva Conventions. In 2006, in *Hamdan v. Rumsfeld* (548 U.S. 507), the majority, absent statutory authorization from Congress, applied the Geneva Conventions to the tribunals, demonstrating the Court's preparedness to defend treaties against unilateral presidential action in interpreting treaties. Later that year, Congress enacted the Military Commissions Act of 2006 (Public Law 109-366), providing legislative guidance to the executive in the use of tribunals to try "unlawful enemy combatants" and declaring that the Geneva Conventions are not a source of rights for detainees.[17] Additionally, the Bush administration has been assailed for narrowly interpreting the Convention against Torture in its prosecution of the War on Terror (see Nowak 2006). When the president signed into law a defense appropriations measure that had an antitorture provision attached to it, he used a signing statement to reassert his authority to interpret treaties as a power inherent to the commander in chief (Savage 2006).[18]

The Rise of Executive Agreements

As internationalist foreign policies dominated post–World War II Washington, foreign policy makers looked to executive agreements as an efficient means to complete important diplomatic ends. In their treatise on behalf of the constitutionality of executive agreements, Ackerman and Golove (1995) look to the historic moment provided by World War II as an explanation for this significant constitutional change. According to their story line, it is during such moments of American history that significant constitutional evolutions occur, including broader interpretations of executive power (Ackerman 1991). Their argument hinges on the notion that as a result of political practice, consent by the legislature, and popular support, the Constitution was effectively amended to allow for alternatives to the formal Article II treaty. That the increase in the use of executive agreements preceded World War II (Ackerman and Golove's "constitutional moment") complicates their constitutional story considerably. It is clear, however, that the use of executive agreements became the dominant method for completing international agreements during the 1940s.

Many looked to the Senate and its obstruction in the treaty process as a serious problem facing American foreign policy. Such obstruction, they argued, led to the U.S. rejection of the League of Nations, undermining the organization's ability to check war and contributing to the rise of fascism. Even public opinion had turned against the Senate's treaty power. By 1944, the Gallup Poll reported that 60 percent of the public favored a major change in the treaty consent procedure, preferring to give it to majorities in both the House and Senate. Even so, public support for executive unilateralism remained scant. In 1945, the House approved a constitutional amendment that would have made the treaty consent procedure the prerogative of both chambers, but unsurprisingly, the Senate never took up the amendment (Ackerman and Golove 1995: 63–65).

Contemporary scholars and members of the foreign policy establishment sympathetic to this argument of Senate obstruction began to look for alternative methods by which to complete international agreements (Ackerman and Golove 1995: 66–73). They asked how the United States could enter into an international accord as long as America's treaty partners did not know whether the United States would keep its word. They believed that the system of separated institutions sharing the treaty power in the manner that had developed, where presidents would submit their treaties to the Senate for them to be considerably altered and possibly vetoed, had proven dysfunctional. How, they asked, could the system adjust to the requirements of emerging international realities and remain within the confines of the Constitution? The "constitutional moment" needed for such a major reinterpretation of the Constitution was provided by the violence of World War II and the triumph of internationalism among the American political elite (Ackerman and Golove 1995). Spiro (2001) doubts the significance of Ackerman and Golove's "constitutional moment," instead arguing that the executive agreement emerged incrementally as a viable option for completing international agreements over a period of several decades. According to Spiro, the executive agreement mechanism is a natural response to a more complex global environment by political institutions that shared the treaty power.

The solution championed by some academics (see, e.g., McClure 1941) and adopted by President Franklin Roosevelt was the modern executive agreement. The constitutional support came in the form of several Supreme Court decisions that dealt with foreign affairs and favored the executive over Congress, opening the door to the exponential rise in executive agreement usage. Executive agreements were not new to presidents, as they had been an alternative in use since the earliest days of the republic.[19] The use of executive agreements had risen considerably during the early decades of the twentieth century, however, when the United States entered into a greater number of trade agreements as it industrialized (see Spiro 2001).

Many of the first major executive agreements during the industrialization period consisted of reciprocal trade agreements negotiated by the president as a result of congressional delegation of power (e.g., the McKinley Tariff Act of 1890 and the Reciprocal Trade Agreements Act of 1934). Many of these early executive agreements, then, were derived "immediately from a delegation of power by Congress to the President" (Corwin 1984: 245).[20] Such delegations of the commerce power were found constitutional in *Field v. Clark* (143 U.S. 649 [1892]). Indeed, President Roosevelt held an expansive view of powers delegated to the president by Congress, particularly in the area of trade. He completed the 1933 Silver Agreement and Wheat Agreement without submitting them to the Senate as formal treaties, even though they involved issues that are legislative in nature rather than solely executive. Roosevelt looked to the Agricultural Adjustment Act of 1933 for justification and later used the Gold Reserve Act of 1934, on tenuous grounds, to enter into a series of agreements for currency stabilization. Congress did not effectively resist Roosevelt's expansive view regarding international economic agreements, probably because the New Deal Democrats had overwhelming control of both the Senate and the House (Ackerman and Golove 1995: 46–50).[21] Nor did Roosevelt bother submitting the agreements to Congress for approval by joint resolution (Spiro 2001), as is common practice today for such agreements.[22]

The judicial nod given in *Field* in favor of executive agreements led presidents to pursue this avenue in a variety of areas, including military and diplomatic, well beyond any clear delegation of authority by Congress (Margolis 1986: 55; O'Brien 2003: 73).[23] However, the more expansive view adopted by Roosevelt toward the end of the 1930s was met with significant resistance in the legislature. For example, the Congress passed the Neutrality Acts (1935–40), which imposed arms embargoes on nations at war. International events overtook congressional resistance, however. As the Roosevelt administration mobilized for war, the justification for the interchangeable use of executive agreements and treaties in matters other than trade gained steam. Despite congressional resistance (Paul 1998), Roosevelt completed one of "the most controversial sole executive agreements ever concluded," the Destroyers for Bases Agreement of 1940 (Ackerman and Golove 1995: 52–56, especially n. 251), which, along with subsequent executive agreements with Britain and Denmark, "virtually assured" America's "later entry into the war" (Spiro 2001: 985). The bases agreement "violated a 1917 statute prohibiting the transfer of warships to a belligerent nation and also the 1940 Neutrality Act" (Rudalevige 2005: 49).

The U.S.-British agreement exchanging destroyers for bases is often cited as an example of President Roosevelt running roughshod over congressional prerogatives (Crenson and Ginsberg 2007; Paul 1998; Rudalevige 2005; Spiro 2001). Arthur Schlesinger's account (1973: 105–8) of the internal White House debate on the agreement indicates that Roosevelt wrestled mightily with the decision, because he initially believed he was prohibited from completing the agreement without congressional assent. In responding to the initial plea of Britain's prime minister, Winston Churchill, for the destroyers, Roosevelt wrote, "A step of that kind could not be taken except with the specific authorization of the Congress, and I am not certain that it would be wise for that suggestion to be made to the Congress at this moment" (quoted in Schlesinger 1973: 105). It was clear that the Senate would reject a treaty, given the high hurdle required for consent. A month after this initial request, in June 1940, the Senate amended a naval appropriations bill denying the president authority to transfer war matériel to a foreign nation unless the chief of staff or chief of naval operations first certified that it was essential for the defense of the United States (Schlesinger 1973: 106).

Schlesinger writes, "Contrary to the latter-day view that a strong President is one who acts without consultation and without notice, Roosevelt proceeded with careful concern for the process of consent. He consulted with his cabinet. He consulted with congressional leaders. He consulted through intermediaries with the Republican candidates for President and Vice President. For some time Roosevelt's view remained that he could not send destroyers to Britain without legislation" (1973: 106). The impasse ended when Republican senators, most notably the Republican candidate for vice president, Charles McNary (R-OR), indicated that while they could not support such a deal publicly through a vote in the Senate, they would not move to block it should Roosevelt complete the deal as an executive agreement, provided sufficient justification were made on the grounds of national security requirements. Roosevelt's attorney general, Robert H. Jackson, in writing a memo supporting the president's action, looked to tenuous statutory grounds rather than resting his case entirely on the plenary constitutional powers of the executive. Indeed, the situation for Britain was dire, and fast action was necessary in order to avert disaster (Schlesinger 1973: 106–8).

In concluding his discussion of Roosevelt's decision, Schlesinger (1973: 108) writes, "Roosevelt paid due respect to the written checks of the Constitution and displayed an unusual concern for the unwritten checks on presidential initiative. Though the transaction was unilateral in form, it was accompanied by extensive and vigilant consultation . . . To have tried to get destroyers to Britain by treaty route was an alternative only for those who did not want Britain to get destroyers at all." The more expansive use of the executive agreement in areas not clearly related to congressional statute proved a significant challenge to the separation of powers in terms of treaty making. The prevailing view among scholars is that President Roosevelt essentially interpreted the executive power to allow him to enter into binding international agreements and to complete those agreements without the required two-thirds consent of the Senate and, in many instances, where presidential power was plenary (based in Article II), without any interference from the legislature. After all, the destroyers deal was just the tip of the iceberg. As the situation in Europe deteriorated, Roosevelt completed executive agreements with Denmark that allowed American forces to occupy Greenland and defend Iceland. This move put the U.S. Navy in direct conflict with German U-boats and resulted in several clashes in the Atlantic, prompting Roosevelt to order the navy to sink Axis submarines—all several months prior to the Japanese attack on Pearl Harbor in December 1941 (Rudalevige 2005: 49).

Such an expansive view of the president's powers in foreign policy is consistent with the Supreme Court's majority opinion in *United States v. Curtiss-Wright Export Corporation* (299 U.S. 304 [1936]), where Justice Sutherland concluded that the president's powers in the international realm were "plenary and exclusive."[24] Although *Curtiss-Wright* did not address executive agreements directly, the opinion allowed for vast delegations of power from Congress to the executive in the international realm (Ackerman and Golove 1995: 58). Moreover, where Congress was silent, presidents were essentially authorized to complete executive agreements (see Glennon 1990: 178–79). It did not take long, however, before the Court gave executive agreements the same legal weight as formal Article II treaties. In two cases involving settlement disputes flowing from the Litvinov Agreement of 1933, a sole executive agreement where President Roosevelt officially recognized the government of the Soviet Union (O'Brien 2003: 79), the Court addressed the issue more directly. In *United States v. Belmont* (301 U.S. 324 [1937]) and *United States v. Pink* (315 U. S. 203 [1942]) the Court's opinion essentially elevated the legal status of executive agreements to treaties consented to by the Senate.[25] Margolis (1986: 61) summarizes, "Like its more formal counterpart, the executive agreement was now the law of the land."

The complete overhaul of the Senate's treaty role in terms of ex post consent would not be solidified until the 1940s, when the American people began to doubt the wisdom of keeping such an important power in the hands of such a small minority (it only takes a small minority in the Senate to kill a popular treaty). As a result of historic changes in the wake of World War II, executive agreements became the normal method in completing most international agreements. Figure 1 charts the use of executive agreements as a percentage of all international agreements completed by U.S. presidents through 1989. The data are clear: in the modern era, the vast majority of agreements (nearly 95 percent) are completed as executive agreements rather than as treaties.[26]

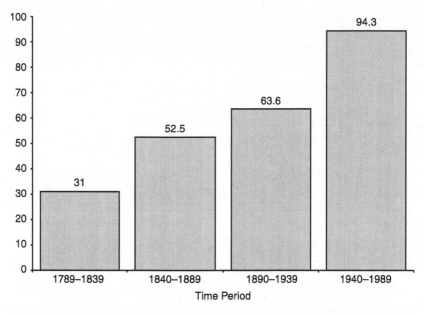

FIG. 1.   Executive agreements as a percentage of all international agreements, 1789–1989. Executive agreements refer to all international agreements other than treaties. (Data from Fisher 2001: 39 [table II-1].)

Types of Executive Agreements

Modern executive agreements come in several types. The State Department's Office of the Assistant Legal Adviser for Treaty Affairs categorizes Article II treaties as formal treaties and all other international agreements as "agreements other than treaties." The Legal Office further divides these "other agreements," which we call "executive agreements," into three subcategories that have important distinctions bearing on our discussion here: (1) congressional-executive agreements, which are pursuant to a previous act of Congress and sometimes require congressional approval (usually through a joint resolution of approval);[27] (2) agreements pursuant to a treaty; and (3) presidential agreements concluded pursuant to an Article II power of the president (J. Grimmett 2001: 78–95), often termed "sole executive agreements."

Most political scientists do not distinguish between the types of executive agreements (see, e.g., Margolis 1986; Martin 2000, 2005).[28] Among political scientists, only Loch Johnson (1984) makes distinctions between these forms of executive agreements, noting that a large percentage (87 percent) are what he terms "statutory agreements," fitting with the first category just mentioned. Those who point to executive agreements as an example of a unilateral presidential power (see, e.g., Howell 2003; Rudalevige 2005) fail to note that a large percentage of executive agreements involve congressional delegations of authority to the president, often with strings attached or ex post congressional approval by joint resolution (Epstein and O'Halloran 1999).

Modern examples of congressionally authorized executive agreements (including both ex ante and ex post authorization) include trade, arms control, and fishery agreements (Fisher 1991: 242–43). For example, the 1961 law establishing the Arms Control and Disarmament Agency also "states that any agreement to limit U.S. armed forces or armaments must be approved by legislation or treaty" (*CQ Almanac* 1992: 622). We discuss these types of agreements in greater detail in chapter 6. Executive agreements pursuant to U.S. treaty obligations are rarely controversial and are generally considered well within the domain of the executive as chief diplomat (J. Grimmett 2001). Presidential agreements, or sole executive agreements, however, have met with some degree of controversy in the modern era, as many secret military and intelligence agreements fit into this category (L. Johnson 1984).

Treaties and Executive Agreements in the Modern Era

The policy evolution whereby executive agreements became the dominant form of international agreement reached its high point immediately following World War II. Several consequential agreements were completed as congressional-executive agreements rather than as treaties, including the agreement considered the foundation of international economic policy: the Bretton Woods Agreement of 1945, committing the United States to the World Bank and International Monetary Fund (Spiro 2001). Despite this available option, presidents did not abandon the treaty altogether, even for their controversial international agreements. This fact suggests that presidential choices over the form of an international agreement are political rather than legal. Given the strength of isolationists in the Senate following World War II, it is not surprising that President Truman would tread delicately when deciding how to handle such critical international agreements as the UN Charter, which the president submitted as a treaty.[29]

The Bricker Revolt

Soon after Truman left office, a pitched institutional battle between the president and Senate over the treaty power emerged, the outcome of which could have curtailed the constitutional use of executive agreements in place of Article II treaties. Conservative senators threatened the use of executive agreements by proposing the so-called Bricker Amendment, an amendment to the Constitution that would have eliminated or limited (depending on the version of amendment) the use of executive agreements. In their attempt, conservatives retained the support of the American Bar Association and a public lobbying effort that led to lopsided congressional mail in favor of the amendment (Tananbaum 1988).[30] Congressional foreign policy historian Robert Johnson (2006: 61) cites the Bricker revolt as the greatest opportunity to alter the treaty power as set forth in the Constitution. The compromise version (the George Amendment) failed by just a single vote in the Senate in February 1954.[31]

The Bricker Amendment, named for Senator John Bricker (R-OH), originally stated that "executive agreements shall not be made in lieu of treaties" (Tananbaum 1988: 221). However, this provision was later dropped in order to retain Republican support as the amendment faced vigorous opposition from President Eisenhower. The president was "unalterably opposed" to the Bricker Amendment, even after several attempted compromises (R. Johnson 2006: 60). In several letters to his brother, Edgar Newton Eisenhower, the president indicated his unabashed opposition to the amendment. In one letter, the president stated, "Never have I in my life been so weary of any one subject or proposition." At one point during the controversy, President Eisenhower mused, "If it's true that when you die the things that bothered you most are engraved on your skull, I am sure I'll have there the mud and dirt of France during invasion and the name of Senator Bricker" (Galambos and van Ee 1996: doc. 707).[32]

Various versions of the amendment sought to restrict the breadth of the treaty power under the Constitution and to require direct congressional input on executive agreements. The George Amendment, which substituted for the Bricker Amendment during the Senate debate in January 1954, stated, "An international agreement other than a treaty shall become effective as internal law in the United states only by an act of Congress" (Tananbaum 1988: 225).[33] President Eisenhower, however, was unwilling to accept this compromise, as it altered the Constitution to erode presidential power vis-à-vis executive agreements. President Eisenhower was well aware of the advantages provided for in using executive agreements, and his intransigence in the face of opposition from his own party led to the eventual defeat of the Bricker revolt (Tananbaum 1988: 166).

Conservatives, led by Senator Bricker, assailed the treaty power, arguing, "American sovereignty and the American Constitution are threatened by treaty law" (quoted in R. Johnson 2006: 58). This was particularly the case when it came to human rights agreements, as conservatives feared that such treaties as the UN Universal Declaration of Human Rights might require states to alter social and economic programs (R. Johnson 2006: 58). Senator Bricker sought to "close 'a loophole in our Constitution' through which the American people could be subjected to 'a tyrannical world government and a Marxist covenant on human rights'" (Tananbaum 1988: 157).[34] Subsequent renditions of the amendment focused on other aspects of the treaty power that conservatives found problematic. For instance, conservatives found fault with the supremacy of treaties in domestic law and included a provision that would require valid legislation before ratified treaties or signed executive agreements could go into effect. Others were inclined to seek limitations on presidential use of executive agreements, as they viewed their use as a usurpation of congressional power in foreign affairs.

While Senate coalitions for and against the Bricker Amendment and its various relatives were fluid in early 1954 (see Tananbaum 1988: chap. 5), the sixty votes in favor of the George Amendment was but a single vote shy of the Senate going on record as formally endorsing a constitutional amendment restricting the president's use of executive agreements. What is more, given that the revised amendment would have formalized a role for the House of Representatives in international agreements, it is likely that it would have received the support necessary in the House to send it to the states for ratification. Indeed, the Bricker revolt was a significant broadside on the president's use of executive agreements and put the White House on notice that the Senate clearly preferred formal Article II treaties when completing significant international agreements. It is also important to consider that the fight over the Bricker Amendment was not a partisan one but, rather, institutional. Most of the thirty-one senators that sided with President Eisenhower against the George Amendment were liberal Democrats, with the remainder being Republicans that shifted their original positions as a result of pressure from the president (Tananbaum 1988: chap. 5).

The underlying suspicions inherent in the Bricker revolt were maintained decades after the amendment's defeat. For example, more recent Senate opposition to various human rights accords was based on arguments similar to those made by Senator Bricker regarding the sovereignty of domestic and state law in regard to personal rights (Henkin 1995; Kaufman 1990; Kaufman and Whiteman 1988). The Brickerites were suspicious not only of international entanglements but also of unbridled executive and federal power, which they believed were best exhibited by the transformation of the treaty power (L. Johnson 1984: 108; Tananbaum 1988: 47–48). We see these oppositional themes continued throughout the modern era of treaty politics, as we demonstrate in our analysis of treaty politics in chapters 4 and 5. Despite this loss by conservatives, the closeness of the Bricker defeat sent a clear message to the executive: the Senate wanted its say when it came time to enter into significant international agreements, especially those that may trump congressional statute and the rights of the various states.

The Case-Zablocki Act

Over time, the total number of international agreements (both executive agreements and treaties) entered into by the United States continued to increase, and presidents continued to use executive agreements much more than they did treaties. Accounting for the number of executive agreements vis-à-vis treaties became problematic, as the executive failed to keep an accurate accounting of international agreements other than treaties. During the 1960s, as the Vietnam War dragged on, congressional mistrust of the executive in foreign policy increased. Presidents Johnson and Nixon completed several secret executive agreements, committing the United States to significant security requirements without even the knowledge of the legislature (Edwards and Wayne 2006: 479–80; Fisher 2000; L. Johnson 1984; Shull 2006). Senator Henry Jackson (D-WA) characterized the Nixon-Kissinger strategy of back-channel diplomacy as "obsessive secrecy," as these agreements constituted significant commitments on the part of the United States (Rudalevige 2005: 125). A new revolt emerged as a result, but this time it was among internationalists, such as Senator Fulbright (D-AR), who shared the Brickerites' suspicion of unilateral executive power in the realm of international security commitments (L. Johnson 1984; R. Johnson 2006).

The legislative product of this more recent opposition to presidential unilateralism in the field of international agreements was the Case-Zablocki Act of 1972 (Public Law 92-403). The Congress used this act to broadcast to the executive branch that they wanted to be more involved in this area. A forerunner to the ultimate act was passed by the U.S. Senate in 1969 and expressed the sense of the Senate through resolutions in two respects. First, the Senate stated its opinion that the making of national commitments involving military obligations should involve joint action by the legislative and executive branches (S. Res. 85, 91st Cong., 1st sess. [1969]; see Fisher 2000: 58–62). A more specific resolution in 1972 (S. Res. 214, 92d Cong., 2d sess.) stated that agreements regarding military bases should take the form of treaties (Glennon 1990: 180–81).[35] Members of the Senate Foreign Relations Committee continued to press the Nixon White House to submit basing agreements as treaties. Senator Frank Church (D-ID) remarked that it was time for the Senate to "reassert itself in the treaty making area" (quoted in Finney 1972). The Senate stopped short of requiring a direct legislative role in executive agreements, though two pieces of more restrictive legislation were considered. One of the bills would have required Senate confirmation of executive agreements (S 3475, 92d Cong., 2d sess. [1972]), while the other bill (S 3637, 92d Cong., 2d sess. [1972]) would have disallowed funding for basing agreements that did not have the consent of the Senate.

In its final form, the Case-Zablocki Act requires that all international agreements other than treaties be reported to the foreign affairs committees of both the House and Senate within sixty days of their entering into force (McCormick 2005). As a result of lax implementation of the original act, it was further amended in 1977 and 1978 to require executive departments to transmit to the State Department the text of any new executive agreement, including oral agreements, so the agreements could be expeditiously reported to Congress (L. Johnson 1984). There were several additional attempts in the Senate during the 1970s to further limit the executive agreement option (Rudalevige 2005: 125). Several bills introduced in the mid-1970s for an Executive Agreements Review Act (e.g., S. Res. 24, 95th Cong., 1st sess. [1977]; see Glennon 1990: 181) would have provided "for congressional review of executive agreements by requiring they be transmitted to Congress, to become effective sixty days after transmittal unless disapproved by congressional resolution." Hearings were held in both the Senate Judiciary Committee and the House Foreign Affairs Committee.[36]

In summary, with the Case-Zablocki efforts (the 1969 Senate resolutions, the 1972 statute, and the 1977 and 1978 amendments), the Congress went on record as wanting to see more treaties rather than executive agreements and as wanting to know more generally about what was happening on U.S. international commitments. Despite these efforts to reign in the president, executive agreements vastly outnumber treaties and remain the dominant form of international agreement. During the 1980s and 1990s, for example, the United States completed 6,796 international agreements, of which only 415, or 6.1 percent, were treaties submitted to the Senate for advice and consent. Additionally, the State Department has been lax in reporting executive agreements. It is not uncommon for there to be significant delays in the reporting of new agreements (Caruson 2002; L. Johnson 1984; Shull 2006). Additionally, when justifying an executive agreement, the links made by presidents to statutes for ex ante legislative authority to complete agreements are often decades old, precluding much legislative involvement (Caruson 2002; Rudalevige 2005: 206). Presidents persist in completing major agreements outside of the formal treaty process. For instance, most important trade agreements today are completed as congressional-executive agreements, including NAFTA, the General Agreement on Tariffs and Trade, and the Central American Free Trade Agreement.

The Practical Effects of Bricker and Case

While Senator Bricker's efforts to amend the Constitution were repelled and while the Case-Zablocki Act is largely procedural, the two events have contributed to the way recent presidents account for how the Senate might respond when they consider the form their significant international agreements will take. Presidents often consider treating major agreements as executive agreements rather than as treaties; however, evidence suggests that presidents consider domestic and foreign politics when doing so (see Martin 2005). This is especially the case when precedent points to the use of a treaty rather than an executive agreement, as is the case with international agreements dealing with arms control, alliances, and human rights. For example, in 1990, President George H. W. Bush openly discussed treating an agreement with the Soviet Union on chemical weapons reduction as an executive agreement instead of a treaty, prompting a written rebuke by the Senate Foreign Relations Committee. Despite their mistreatment by the Senate historically, human rights agreements have always been submitted to the Senate as treaties. Presidents simply do not challenge the Senate's role in these cases, even though the Senate has routinely turned aside or eviscerated human rights conventions signed and submitted by presidents (Kaufman 1990; Spiro 2001: 1000–1001). We explore the alternative use of executive agreements and treaties systematically in chapters 2 and 3.

Conclusion

The fact that presidents consider the likely opposition in the Senate prior to deciding whether to submit an international agreement as a treaty or to treat it as an executive agreement lends credence to the evasion hypothesis, an important plank of the received scholarly wisdom that presidential use of executive agreements is strategic (Margolis 1986; Lindsay 1994) and is evidence in support of the imperial presidency (Crenson and Ginsberg 2007; Rudalevidge 2005). For example, Lindsay (1994: 81–82) writes, "Presidents facing strong opposition in the Senate have an incentive to negotiate a treaty that reflects senatorial views . . . But presidents need not always heed their critics. Presidents can skirt a truculent Senate through the use of executive agreements." Lindsay explains that even when agreements require congressional approval, "presidents prefer it to a treaty because they usually find it far easier to round up majority support in both chambers than a supermajority in the Senate."

Why have legislators allowed for this shift in power, with the president now committing the United States to significant binding international agreements, sometimes without legislative consent and rarely through the standard treaty process? Our response to this question rests on the benefits provided to both the executive and legislature under the current treaty-making regime: efficiency and international faith in agreements signed by U.S. presidents. The benefits for the executive are obvious: their agreements are completed more quickly and with less interference from the legislature. Congress stands to gain in two general ways through the use of executive agreements. First, the Senate's agenda remains uncluttered with the hundreds of agreements completed outside of the formal treaty process. This allows members to focus on the more significant diplomatic issues and those foreign policy issues more likely to provide direct personal and electoral benefits. Second, executive agreements provide an important role for the House of Representatives in diplomacy. By excluding the House from a formal role in the treaty process, the framers significantly diminished the influence of the lower chamber in diplomacy and foreign policy more broadly. Executive agreements, therefore, have increased the foreign policy influence of the House significantly, as we document systematically in chapter 6.

Hence, while much of the conflict that results over the treaty-making power points to the conclusion that presidents have usurped this power and routinely "evade" the Senate, our reading of history leads to a very different conclusion. While much of its early expansion may be rooted in evading an isolationist legislature, the modern executive agreement has emerged as an efficient policy-making tool that has largely replaced the untenable treaty process on most routine matters and in some areas of significant policy. This significant change evolved as a result of constitutional construction through political practice. The political branches, encouraged by a complex policy context and unrestrained by the Supreme Court, altered the practical meaning of the Constitution to allow for international agreements other than treaties.

Informal boundaries exist, however, which serve to constrain presidential actions on international agreements. When presidents overstep their prerogatives on international agreements, Congress responds with attempts to reign in the executive, as exemplified by the Bricker revolt and the Case-Zablocki Act. Outside of these two high-profile instances of congressional opposition, the legislature has largely allowed—and in many cases encouraged—the policy evolution of executive agreements. While the responses of Congress to increased presidential power on treaties are limited in scope when they succeed, they send clear signals to the executive regarding what could happen should presidents continue to push the envelope of executive power. This logic suggests that presidents behave in a manner that will preserve this policy tool. Additionally, this logic suggests that Congress will be more inclined to allow greater discretion on international agreements when the majority's policy preferences coincide with the president's. In chapters 2 and 3, we examine the historical record of treaties and executive agreements more systematically, through quantitative analysis, and find substantial support for the logic of institutional efficiency and only limited support for strategically evasive behavior on the part of the presidency.

2 | Explaining the Rise of Executive Agreements in the Modern Era

As outlined in chapter 1, modern presidents since Franklin Roosevelt have more regularly used executive agreements, rather than treaties, to complete important diplomatic action. The usage rate for executive agreements is astounding, as 94 percent of international agreements completed by American presidents today are executive agreements rather than treaties. This increase has alarmed scholars and policy makers who believe that it upsets the delicate balance of shared powers between Congress and the president. The use of executive agreements is another arrow in the quiver of those who argue that the modern presidency is imperial (Rudalevige 2005; Schlesinger 1973). The argument hinges on the logic that executive agreements provide presidents yet another unilateral power that affords them the opportunity to act in lieu of constitutional constraints important in maintaining a system of shared powers (Crenson and Ginsberg 2007; Moe and Howell 1999).

The logic that underlies the conventional wisdom on executive agreements suggests that presidents are strategic in their use. Scholars conclude that presidents often seek to evade the constitutional process when completing their executive agreements, making treaties less important in the modern era (Crenson and Ginsberg 2007: 194–95; Lindsay 1994: 131). The evasion hypothesis states that presidents skirt the Senate treaty process because of difficult political hurdles that are exacerbated by partisan politics (Lindsay 1994; Margolis 1986). Rather than expending the political capital necessary to get Senate consent for their treaties, modern presidents have instead avoided the Senate on most agreements (Moe and Howell 1999: 163–64). The conventional wisdom posits that modern presidents use the executive agreement as a means to enter into binding international agreements while avoiding the political uncertainty of the treaty process.

Our framework suggests an entirely different explanation for the rise of executive agreements: the president and Congress have developed an important policy tool to allow for the completion of international agreements more efficiently than is prescribed by the constitutional treaty process. As a result of this efficiency, international agreements go into effect sooner. If law demands that Congress has a say, executive agreements only require majority approval in both chambers, rather than the supermajority approval in the Senate that is required for formal treaties. Moreover, executive agreements that require congressional approval allow for the House to have direct input on agreements that directly effect the Article I powers of Congress, such as international commerce. Our framework, outlined in the introduction to this book, suggests that the increased use of executive agreements is an evolutionary response by the presidency and the Congress to the greater diplomatic demands of the modern era. Therefore, Congress is largely amenable to the rise of executive agreements and plays an important role in maintaining checks on the executive's treaty-making power.

In this chapter, we address the following question in a systematic fashion: why are executive agreements, rather than treaties (which require a two-thirds vote of support by the U.S. Senate), increasingly used as a means to formalize U.S. relations with other countries? We examine this question from two perspectives. In the first, it is assumed that presidents behave strategically when using executive agreements, a view held by the lion's share of scholars (Crenson and Ginsberg 2007; Fisher 1991; Lindsay 1994; Margolis 1986; Moe and Howell 1999). Hence the use of executive agreements is driven by the desire of presidents to circumvent the Senate when governing circumstances are difficult. Second and alternatively, we envision organizational efficiency at the heart of the use of executive agreements. In general, conducting foreign affairs has become increasingly complex in the modern era, necessitating the reliance of the executive branch and Congress on an efficient mechanism to get things done in a busier international system.[1]

We begin by developing hypotheses for these two alternative explanations of this important institutional change: political strategy and institutional efficiency. We then offer an explanation of our procedures for data collection, followed by a description of our dependent and independent variables. We next present our findings, and we conclude with a discussion of the broader implications of our results and with an analysis of how the results fit with our overall argument.

Executive Agreements as a Policy Innovation

The pattern of presidential behavior in completing international agreements over time is instructive regarding the institution's response to changing domestic political environments as well as changes in the international context—all within the constitutional framework set out by the framers. Despite their constitutional significance, very little systematic study, outside of the historical research we cite heavily in chapter 1, has focused on the process of forging executive agreements rather than formal Article II treaties. We do know that the use of executive agreements took off during the Franklin Roosevelt administration. Roosevelt completed several executive agreements with Allied powers prior to U.S. entry into World War II, avoiding the treaty process altogether.[2] While Congress was not always skirted in Roosevelt's efforts, persuading a majority of both houses to approve funding bills (in fulfillment of the executive agreements) might prove more likely than gaining the approval of two-thirds of the Senate.

Citing the evasion hypothesis, Margolis (1986) finds a greater propensity for presidents to use executive agreements over treaties during divided government. He concludes that presidents routinely evade the Senate when completing significant international agreements and are especially more likely to do so when their party is weak in the Senate. More recently, however, Martin (2000) has argued that presidents are incapable of evading the Senate through the use of executive agreements. While her findings question the conventional wisdom, she stops short of providing a rival explanation for the trend; that is, she does not provide empirical evidence directly answering why presidents have more readily utilized executive agreements over treaties in the postwar era, if not for strategic political reasons. Her research does suggest, however, that Congress maintains "mechanisms for influence over international agreements" and that presidents behave in a constrained fashion for that reason (Martin 2000: 71).

Other studies have questioned the political use of executive agreements that underlies the evasion hypothesis. For example, Loch Johnson (1984) points out that the vast majority of international agreements are completed pursuant to congressional statute or approval.[3] While his analysis suggests that presidents share international agreement responsibility with Congress, he does not provide an explanation for the rise of executive agreements. He does note that sole executive agreements have been used more routinely to complete major military commitments abroad, with 99 of the 131 agreements he examined fitting into that category (L. Johnson 1984: 59). However, this statistic makes sense given the plenary power presidents enjoy when agreements can be directly linked to their role as commander in chief, as is the case for military agreements. Johnson's analysis suggests that disaggregating in terms of the important agreements is useful for disentangling why modern presidents have chosen the more expedient alternative and that doing so may provide a more effective test for presidential motivations.

A major flaw in the literature is the way scholars account for the difficult governing circumstances that may lead a president to evade the Senate. Margolis (1986) relies on simple measures of divided government and the size of the president's party in the Senate, whereas Martin (2000) also considers presidential support scores.[4] Divided government is often considered a major culprit in legislative gridlock (Edwards, Barrett, and Peake 1997). However, recent research suggests that institutional preferences (Binder 1999) and the preferences of pivotal players in the process (Krehbiel 1998) best explain legislative gridlock. These latter factors may matter more because the modern era has not featured Senate majority coalitions sizable enough to overcome supermajority requirements on partisan issues. Neither Margolis nor Martin account for the institutional preferences or pivotal players that are likely to emerge as important when there is a two-thirds requirement to ratify a treaty. In addition, the Senate Foreign Relations Committee (SFRC) can be a major roadblock in the treaty process, as most treaties that fail die there, yet no previous study has taken into account the views of this important committee.[5]

Research in this area has also focused on the implications of the Case-Zablocki Act of 1972 (Public Law 92-403), which we discussed in chapter 1. Congress did not stand idly by and allow presidents to circumvent the constitutional treaty process without trying to reign in the president (see L. Johnson 1984; Martin 2000). With the Case-Zablocki efforts, Congress went on record as wanting to see more treaties rather than executive agreements and as wanting to know more generally about what was happening on U.S. international commitments (U.S. Senate Committee on Foreign Relations 2001). It is possible that this attempt to reign in the president served to check presidential behavior in this realm, encouraging presidents to consider congressional wishes when deciding how to complete an international agreement. Thus we account for the significance of Case-Zablocki in the analysis in this chapter.

The current state of knowledge on the topic has texts claiming the treaty process as pro forma, with presidents primarily getting their way. This argument raises the following question: if the treaty process is pro forma, why use executive agreements instead of treaties? It is possible that the treaty process is murkier than conventional understanding suggests (Auerswald and Maltzman 2003), so strategic-political incentives may drive presidents to use executive agreements instead of treaties. Or, as we argue, the alternative perspective of efficiency may be the best explanation. In this chapter, we more carefully address this question through a systematic examination of international agreements in the modern era, specifically the use of executive agreements as an alternative means to formalize relations with other countries.

Explaining the Rise of Executive Agreements: Political Strategy or Efficiency?

Domestic politics might drive presidential decisions of whether to submit an international agreement to the Senate as a treaty or alternatively treat the agreement as an executive agreement. The president is not bound legally to go the treaty route, and for the most part, treaties and agreements are legally interchangeable. As demonstrated in chapter 1, major international agreements have commonly been completed using executive agreements. Scholars have posited similar behavior related to the politics of executive orders. Deering and Maltzman (1999: 768) describe the strategic model as related to executive orders: "According to this strategic model, executive orders are instruments used by Presidents to circumvent the constitutionally prescribed policymaking process." Executive orders, they conclude, therefore enable presidents to "pursue policy goals in an efficient and alternative manner" circumventing the legislature. Lindsay (1994) suggests that the "law of anticipated reactions" is likely to govern executive behavior in terms of treaties and executive agreements. Strategic-minded presidents facing stiff opposition in the Senate are inclined either to negotiate treaties to reflect senatorial views or to circumvent the Senate altogether by employing the executive agreement rather than the treaty. The assumption underlying the evasion hypothesis is that presidents are more inclined to take the latter approach.

Little in the way of empirical evidence has been forwarded to support the claim that presidents behave strategically when completing executive agreements. Anecdotal evidence suggests that political strategy may play a role in certain high-profile decisions. When presidents openly consider completing an important agreement as an executive agreement instead of a treaty, they may come under pressure from members of the Senate to respect the constitutional design. For example, in 1979, President Carter floated a trial balloon suggesting that he might submit SALT II to Congress as an executive agreement, requiring majority approval in both chambers, rather than as a treaty, as President Nixon had done with the original SALT agreement. Carter recognized that opposition in the Senate would be difficult to overcome and stated that "if a SALT agreement were blocked or emasculated in the upper chamber," he would ask for approval of both the House and Senate by simple majority (quoted in Burns 1979, cited in Caldwell 1991a: 64).

In 1990, President George H. W. Bush signed a major agreement on chemical weapons with the Soviet Union and considered submitting the agreement for congressional approval. Administration officials cited concerns about getting the necessary two-thirds vote in the Senate if the agreement was treated as a treaty. In response, in June 1990, the SFRC held public hearings on the acceptability of this practice, with a formal protest issued by eighteen of the nineteen committee members. Bush still opted for the executive agreement route, but he never asked Congress for official approval, and international events overtook the process (Lindsay 1994: 83; CQ Almanac 1990: 709).[6] Anecdotal evidence thus suggests the importance of the SFRC in the presidential decision to complete an agreement by executive agreement or treaty.

That presidents use executive agreements strategically, in order to avoid a hostile Senate, is consistent with much of the recent literature on institutional change. Scholars posit that the design of institutions bubbles up from the battle of politics (Binder 1997; Katz and Sala 1996; Schickler 1998). While there is some disagreement among scholars about the tenor of that change, they proceed from the same underlying assumption that the formal and informal design of institutions reflects the desires of purposive and self-interested political actors. These actors seek to craft institutions and develop policy mechanisms that will better enable them to enact their policy preferences. The use of executive agreements as a strategic avoidance device appears consistent with this point of view. Their rise may indeed be the result of shifting political coalitions and the creative strategy of political actors (namely, the president) to avoid major fights over international commitments.

While the idea that presidents skirt Senate prerogatives by using executive agreements instead of treaties makes some sense, there are theoretical reasons to question the assumption that they do so as a result of difficult governing circumstances. If the practice were common, we would expect the Senate to respond with efforts to curtail the use of executive agreements more than it has in the modern era. Additionally, what incentives are there for the SFRC chair to cede influence to the executive on a power as significant as treaty making? Such behavior is especially unlikely if the chair is from the opposite party and is generally hostile to the president's policies. Additionally, presidents do not get a free pass by using this approach; with the use of an executive agreement, presidents get around the two-thirds requirement in the Senate, but they still must put together a Senate (and House) majority to pass the budgetary and implementation particulars of executive agreements, should that be necessary. Furthermore, Congress has signaled its concern over the use of executive agreements with the passage of the Case-Zablocki Act in 1972 and further amendments thereafter.

If the Senate was opposed to the presidential use of executive agreements, it could simply refuse to fund the accompanying provisions, forcing presidents to employ the treaty. That the Senate does not regularly refuse presidents on their executive agreements suggests two possible scenarios.[7] First, senators might completely defer to the president on international agreements. Given the propensity of the Senate to quibble with the president on treaties (see Auerswald and Maltzman 2003) and the tendency for Senate members to guard their constitutional prerogatives, this is highly unlikely. A senior bureaucrat in the State Department's Office of the Assistant Legal Adviser for Treaty Affairs concluded, "If the Senate really wants to do something, wants the president to do it with a treaty, it is not without some power. It may not prevail, but it can tell the president if and when it wants a treaty."[8]

Alternatively, the Senate may be amenable to the rise in executive agreements during the modern era. In a system of separated institutions sharing power (Neustadt 1960), it is unlikely that there will be a major evolution in the way international commitments are completed—and hence an increase in the power of one branch—without the acquiescence of the other branch. Congressional agreement to the policy innovation does not mean that the legislature has abdicated its power to the executive.

Should the Congress maintain boundaries and provide checks on presidential behavior, the institutional bargain that we describe in the introduction to this book provides for a better explanation for the rise in executive agreements.

This second scenario leads to an alternative view of executive agreements that is consistent with the organizational view of institutional change. The organizational approach to institutional change posits that Congress adapts itself in concert with changes in its external environment. For example, Polsby (1968) found that as the country grew in size and complexity, the Congress gradually aligned itself with that change by adopting respect for seniority and a stricter division of labor. Another adaptation in response to increased complexity, especially in the realm of foreign affairs and commerce, was the expansive use of congressional delegation during the twentieth century (Epstein and O'Halloran 1999).

The growth of executive agreements can therefore be accounted for as an adaptation by the Congress and president to "the sheer increase in volume of the amount of business and contacts between the United States and other countries" (Fisher 2001: 40). Along these lines, Richard Grimmett (2001: 22) suggests that the Senate has accepted the use of executive agreements on most international agreements because reliance on the formal treaty process for most agreements would overwhelm the Senate or make the approval process perfunctory. The SFRC, responsible for processing treaties, has a wide array of responsibilities that it would otherwise have to sideline. When asked about the process, key legislative staffers and executive bureaucrats involved directly in the process focus on executive agreements as a mechanism of efficiency rather than political strategy. A State Department staffer in the Senate Liaison Office reported: "In any given year there are 50 to 65 ambassador nominations processed by SFRC; in a new administration year, it's 125. Therefore there is only so much time and interest to do other things. I've never seen it [using executive agreements] as a problem [in the eyes of the Senate]." The view from Capitol Hill is similar. One senior SFRC staffer related, "The advice and consent role is something we take seriously. But we are conscious of the cumbersome nature of the process." He described it as "fairly a collegial sort of process," adding, "To do all executive agreements as treaties would increase our workload substantially." A staffer from the other party stated that the use of executive agreements is "typically not [seen as] a desire to make an end run around the Senate."[9] Hence, while it is clear why the use of executive agreements has increased relative to the evolution of the presidency, the Senate's general acquiescence to the process also makes sense.

Hypotheses

To assess systematically the assumptions underlying each of the perspectives discussed in the preceding section, we here analyze the propensity of presidents to use executive agreements in a given Congress. The strategic-political perspective suggests that presidents more often turn to executive agreements when Senate consent to a treaty is less likely or would take greater effort on behalf of the president, owing to the particular set of governing circumstances. The efficiency perspective, however, suggests that presidents will accrue increased discretion on foreign policy when governing circumstances are improved and when the Senate is more likely to grant the president leeway. With increased discretion, presidents are more likely to use executive agreements. More directly, the efficiency perspective indicates that presidents should increase their use of executive agreements in response to an increasingly complex international environment.

Our analysis starts with several propositions. First, the evasion hypothesis underscores the strategic-political perspective, which suggests that presidents in a weak position relative to the Senate are more likely to avoid the treaty route. Stated more formally, *presidents with fewer fellow partisans in the Senate are more likely to use executive agreements than treaties.*

Second, it is probable that policy preferences, not just partisan differences, play a role in the process (Krehbiel 1998). Although previous tests of the evasion hypothesis emphasize the partisan nature of evasive behavior, it is clear that the degree to which presidential policy preferences differ from the policy preferences of key players in the treaty process is likely to matter. It is more challenging for presidents to enact their policy preferences when the pivotal senator's policy preferences differ significantly from the president.[10] Therefore, we test the proposition that *presidents are more likely to use executive agreements when the "pivotal" member of the Senate is further from the president on an ideological continuum.*

Third, the SFRC plays an important role in the treaty ratification process, so its preferences are likely critical when presidents assess the political landscape of the Senate. It is likely, then, that the SFRC chair is a pivotal player in the Senate, as Senate rules require that treaties must first get through the committee before they can be considered on the floor. A conservative SFRC chair may be less willing to rubber-stamp a president's treaties, because "conservatives have traditionally had a greater distrust for international agreements than their more liberal colleagues" (Auerswald and Maltzman 2003: 1101). Therefore, the strategic-political perspective suggests that *presidents utilize executive agreements more often when the SFRC chair is conservative.* Alternatively, when the chair of the committee is more conservative, he or she may be more likely to object to presidential skirting of the treaty process. To keep intact the efficient mechanism of executive agreement use, presidents may avoid skirting the Senate when the chair objects. This suggests an alternative hypothesis based on the efficiency perspective: *presidents utilize fewer executive agreements when the SFRC chair is conservative.*

These ideological hypotheses go beyond the standard partisan hypotheses of previous analyses, as it is likely that ideology plays a role in structuring the SFRC chair's beliefs regarding international agreements, irrespective of the president's political party. To illustrate, conservative senators have been suspicious of international entanglements historically, so a highly conservative chair (e.g., Jesse Helms, cited by one of our interviewees at the State Department as a problematic SFRC chair) might oppose certain treaties on principle, no matter which president submits the treaty. A historical example of conservative ire for treaties would be the Bricker Amendment of 1954 (discussed in chapter 1), which would have amended the Constitution, curtailing the president's use of executive agreements. The episode, a direct assault on the authority of the president, was led by conservatives, with a Republican (Eisenhower) in the White House. Conservatives have also been suspicious of human rights treaties (Kaufman 1990) and have been more likely than liberals to oppose arms control agreements (DeLaet and Scott 2006). These conservatives, however, could be protecting the institutional prerogatives of the Senate. In the words of one SFRC staffer, when conflict arises between the Senate and White House over the use of executive agreements, the argument primarily involves "an institutional struggle, not a political one."[11]

Finally, the broader domestic political context may play a role in presidential decisions to use executive agreements rather than treaties. Presidents may believe that getting a treaty through the Senate would be less difficult when they are popular than when their popularity is low. Therefore, the strategic-political perspective predicts that *as presidential approval declines, presidents utilize more executive agreements.* However, a popular president might be granted greater discretion by the Senate when conducting foreign policy. When the president's approval falters, senators may be more likely to challenge the president on foreign policy. Thus just the opposite relationship could emerge.

If the rise in executive agreements is primarily a response to the complex international system, our expectation is that presidential behavior will differ considerably from what is predicted by the strategic-political perspective. More directly, the efficiency perspective suggests that the use of executive agreements rises as the international system grows in terms of size and complexity. The closest measurable concept to this posited relationship is the number of potential countries with which the United States intends to formalize international agreements. Our most direct test of the efficiency explanation includes a test of the hypothesis that *as the number of nations with whom the United States has relations increases in a given period, the president is more likely to utilize executive agreements.* Indirectly, however, the broader international context may play a role in presidential decisions to use executive agreements. During the Cold War, for example, presidents may have been given greater discretion from the Senate to pursue international agreements through the executive agreement process rather than the more formal treaty process. For example, Auerswald and Maltzman (2003) found that the Senate was more likely to attach reservations to treaties, and DeLaet and Scott (2006) found a greater propensity for conservatives to vote against arms control agreements in the post–Cold War era. Similarly, Auerswald (2006) found that the Senate more commonly attached critical and nongermane reservations on arms control treaties after the Cold War ended. Because the Cold War structured much of U.S. foreign policy during the time period under discussion and because Congress was then more inclined to grant leeway to the executive in conducting foreign affairs, the efficiency explanation suggests that *presidents are more likely to utilize executive agreements during the Cold War period.*

Another proposition flows from the circumstance of the Case-Zablocki Act of 1972. In that act, the Senate (and the House) went on record with the demand that presidents submit more treaties to the Senate, rather than relying on executive agreements to codify international agreements. In a system of separated institutions sharing power, the branches have an incentive to respond to such strong signals. Hence we expect that, controlling for other factors, *presidential use of executive agreements would be lower as a proportion of all international agreements after the passage of Case-Zablocki than before.* However, as explained by the Congressional Research Service (U.S. Senate Committee on Foreign Relations 2001: 226), the State Department liberally reported executive agreements in the wake of Case-Zablocki—even reporting more executive agreements (those of little significance) than was determined necessary by the Congress. As a result, this relationship could very well be positive, reflecting the increased propensity of the State Department in reporting executive agreements in the wake of the reform. No matter the expected relationship, the Case-Zaclocki Act is likely to affect the number of executive agreements, and hence its effects should be controlled.

Data Sources

Because data sets from earlier analyses of international agreements are fraught with problems,[12] we sought out other sources of data that have not previously been used by scholars.[13] We found an internal accounting of international agreements provided by the State Department to the Congressional Research Service in the Library of Congress for a study prepared for the SFRC (U.S. Senate Committee on Foreign Relations 2001). More specifically, the list was compiled by the State Department's Office of the Assistant Legal Adviser for Treaty Affairs.[14] The agreements on this list represent the universe of international agreements that were concluded by the executive branch on behalf of the United States. As we are examining the change in issue processing on international agreements, we believe studying all those concluded by the United States during a particular Congress, which is consistent with the State Department list, is the proper set.[15]

A Subset of Major International Agreements

Legally, the determination on whether to treat an international agreement as a treaty or executive agreement is at the discretion of the White House, unless prescribed by statute.[16] However, the process of agreement classification is a good deal more institutionalized than has been previously suggested. An overwhelming majority of these decisions are made without any input by the White House, based on the institutionalized State Department process, which is informed by traditional practice and statute.[17] Many executive agreements, because of their relative insignificance, are unlikely to approach the "radar screen" of the White House or the Senate. As we are interested in presidential behavior on executive agreements, it makes sense to narrow our analysis to include only those agreements where the president might actually take an interest. We therefore depart from previous quantitative analyses on international agreements by narrowing our analysis to examine the important international agreements separately.

To narrow our focus on the important international agreements, we rely on Congressional Quarterly's *American Treaties and Alliances*, compiled by Alan Axelrod (2000). This source catalogs the five hundred or so historically significant international agreements in which the United States has taken part since its early history. While this data source does not provide information on all treaties and executive agreements, Axelrod has used both secondary and primary sources to compile a list of what he considers most significant.[18] Given that our questions are focused on the politics surrounding presidential decisions on international agreements, we focus on the important agreements, as they are more likely to deal with salient issues. The State Department data discussed earlier and used in much of the analysis that follows makes no such distinction. Our analyses utilize both the broader list and the subset of important agreements (as defined by Axelrod), to allow a full test of the explanations of international agreement behavior.

Dependent Variables for the Aggregate Analysis

We coded two dependent variables based on the two different sets of international agreements. First, for the broader list of all international agreements, the dependent variable is the number of executive agreements over the total number of international agreements (executive agreements plus treaties). This variable measures the degree to which presidents choose the executive agreement option over the treaty option in a given two-year Congress, and the data are based on the date the United States entered (signed) the agreement.[19] We also express the second dependent variable, using the Axelrod "important" cases of international agreements, as the number of executive agreements over the total number of international agreements (executive agreements plus treaties) for each two-year Congress, based on the date each agreement was signed.[20]

Independent Variables

The primary independent variables include the number of presidential partisans in the Senate,[21] the distance between the CS-NOMINATE score of the president and the pivotal senator,[22] the ideology score (CS-NOMINATE) of the SFRC chair, and the average level of presidential approval for the two-year period. As presidents are faced with tougher political circumstances (fewer partisans in the Senate, a pivotal senator who is further away from the president, a conservative SFRC chair, and lower presidential approval), the strategic-political perspective predicts that use of executive agreements will increase. We also include a dummy variable for the Case-Zablocki Act, with all years after 1972 receiving a code of 1. Our variables to test for the efficiency perspective include the number of new UN member countries in the most recent Congress (to account for the growth in new nations)[23] and a dummy variable to control for whether or not the Congress convened during the Cold War.[24] As new nations become part of the United Nations, the efficiency perspective posits that the United States is more likely to complete executive agreements, as a means of getting more done in a busier international system.

Findings

The results of our analysis of executive agreements as a percentage of all international agreements are presented in table 1. To test the hypotheses, we employ multivariate regression analysis, while accounting for the autoregressive trends in our data. The analysis provides little support for the strategic perspective. None of the relationships representing the political context is as expected given the propositions. The political situation, as explained in conventional partisan terms, does not appear to play a role in determining whether presidents more regularly go the route of executive agreements when entering into international agreements. Interestingly, popular presidents use executive agreements more often vis-à-vis treaties;

TABLE 1. Explanation of the Percentage of Executive Agreements per Congress, 1949–98

Independent variable	Coefficient	Standard error	$|t|$
Growth in UN members	0.087**	0.047	1.86
Cold War	3.839**	0.458	8.39
Distance from president to pivotal senator	1.002	1.555	0.64
SFRC chair	−3.034**	0.757	−4.01
Number of presidential partisans	−0.023	0.020	−1.15
Presidential approval	0.162**	0.020	8.07
Case-Zablocki Act	3.176**	0.531	5.98
Constant	80.350**	1.592	50.46

$N = 25$
Model F statistic $= 27.9$**
Adjusted $R^2 = 0.98$

Note: The dependent variable was the percentage of all international agreements that were executive agreements. The Prais-Winsten AR(1) regression technique was utilized because the Durbin-Watson d statistic indicated a potential autocorrelation problem. The analysis was conducted in Stata 9.0.

*$p < .1$ **$p < .05$ (one-tailed)

as approval rises, presidents are more likely to use executive agreements instead of treaties. This finding is counterintuitive to the strategic perspective, which suggests that presidents who are hurting politically (as shown by their low approval) rely more on executive agreements as a way to get around a tough battle in the Senate. The finding does, however, support the logic that when presidents are unpopular, they are inclined to avoid upsetting the Senate by using executive agreements, perhaps to protect the option for future use.

Also, the variable for the Case-Zablocki intervention is significant and positive. We would expect presidents to use fewer executive agreements after that act (1972), since a major feature of it was the demand from Congress that presidents utilize more treaties. The multivariate findings suggest that aggregate use of executive agreements actually increased after Case-Zablocki, perhaps indicating their acceptability to Congress as long as it was kept informed. This finding may just be a measurement artifact, however. The positive relationship may instead reflect the increased propensity by the State Department, in the wake of the reform, to report more extensively than was finally required by future amendments to the act (see U.S. Senate Committee on Foreign Relations 2001: chap. 10).

The efficiency perspective receives support in the first analysis. The greater international context of U.S. foreign policy appears to impact presidential usage of executive agreements considerably. Presidents used a greater number of executive agreements vis-à-vis treaties during the Cold War than since the Cold War's end. Additionally, the variable of the growth in UN members is significant and in the posited positive direction, suggesting that as new nations emerge, presidents use executive agreements as a means of forging new agreements in an efficient manner. Finally, when the SFRC chair is more conservative, presidents use executive agreements less often. The chair's ideology structures the process in a way that is counter to the strategic-political perspective but more in line with the efficiency perspective and the logic that when the SFRC chair is likely to challenge presidents in the treaty area, presidents give more consideration to the backlash that might result should they rely on executive agreements.

The Important International Agreements

Table 2 shows the results of our analysis of the proportion of important international agreements that are executive agreements. Here we find mixed support for the strategic rationale of executive agreement use, but the efficiency hypothesis again receives solid support. The variable measuring the ideological distance from the president to the pivotal senator is again insignificant when we analyze only the important international agreements. While the variable of the number of presidential partisans is significant, it is in a direction counter to what is expected if presidents routinely evade the Senate based on partisan calculations. As presidential partisans are present in higher numbers, presidents more readily use executive agreements when completing important international agreements. If presidents routinely evade the Senate on treaties due to partisan calculations, we would expect the opposite relationship. This finding suggests that the Senate, as a body, might grant the president greater leeway to use executive agreements to complete important international agreements when the president's party dominates the institution. Presidents therefore appear to act with greater discretion on their significant international agreements precisely when the Senate is most likely to accommodate presidential policies.

The findings for the SFRC chair and presidential approval, however, are significant and in the direction posited by the strategic-political perspective. The more conservative the chair, the more likely it is that the president will use executive agreements when completing major international agreements. Presidential approval is again significant, but this time in the direction suggested by the strategic model. As presidents see their approval ratings take a dive, they rely more on executive agreements when

TABLE 2. Explanation of the Percentage of Important Executive Agreements per Congress, 1949–98

Independent variable	Coefficient	Standard error	$|t|$
Growth in UN members	2.63**	0.77	3.42
Cold War	10.85*	8.01	1.35
Distance from president to pivotal senator	−8.21	26.84	−0.31
SFRC chair	31.24**	12.62	2.48
Number of presidential partisans	0.71**	0.34	2.06
Presidential approval	−0.60**	0.34	−1.77
Case-Zablocki Act	2.12	9.28	0.23
Constant	33.90	27.75	1.22

$N = 25$
Model F statistic = 3.42**
Adjusted $R^2 = 0.41$

Note: The dependent variable was the percentage of all international agreements that were executive agreements. The Prais-Winsten AR(1) regression technique was utilized because the Durbin-Watson d statistic indicated an autocorrelation problem. The analysis was conducted in Stata 9.0.
$*p < .1$ $**p < .05$ (one-tailed)

completing important agreements. Interestingly, these findings are just the opposite of what we found when we examined the broader set of all international agreements. It is plausible to conclude, in part, that the politics surrounding important international agreements, as opposed to the broader set of all agreements, are different and somewhat more in line with the strategic perspective when their political significance is taken into account. Pitched political battles are more likely when we consider the significant agreements, and presidents appear to behave more strategically as a result.

The variables representing the efficiency perspective work well in the more narrow analysis of important agreements. The growth in UN members is statistically significant and in the anticipated direction. As new countries emerge, presidents rely more on executive agreements to speedily complete diplomatic action. Also, presidents used a greater number of important executive agreements vis-à-vis treaties during the Cold War than since. Finally, the results indicating the significance of the Case-Zablocki Act disappear when we narrow our attention to the significant international agreements.

Discussion

In summary, our systematic analyses of aggregate trends in the usage of executive agreements since 1949 offer strong support for our theory that the use of executive agreements during the modern era reflects a concern for institutional efficiency. We find only mixed support for the strategic perspective, which is based on presidents strategically evading Senate treaty-making prerogatives. When we examine international agreements in the aggregate, making no distinction in terms of importance, we find no meaningful support for strategic evasion but substantial support for the efficiency perspective. In fact, as the SFRC chair becomes conservative and as the president's political capital (as expressed by public approval) decreases, presidents are less likely to evade the Senate. Under these difficult circumstances, presidents use fewer executive agreements as a proportion of all international agreements.

This is the exact opposite of what the strategic perspective hypothesizes. A conservative senator may be more inclined to voice opposition to a president's use of executive agreements in place of treaties, as the process skirts historic constitutional procedures. Moreover, senators are more inclined to challenge a president on institutional processes when the president is unpopular. That presidents appear attuned to this is instructive. Rather than seek to evade a conservative SFRC chair and possibly endanger their future use of executive agreements, presidents have been more inclined to include the Senate in the process under these conditions. We believe the reason for this behavior on the part of presidents is to protect the executive's institutional prerogative—the policy innovation of executive agreements. To do otherwise and inflame Senate opposition might threaten the very existence of this vital institutional arrangement.

When we narrow our analysis to include only important international agreements, we find that some of the strategic political explanations for trends in aggregate usage of executive agreements become significant. Presidents are more likely to use executive agreements when completing major international agreements when they are unpopular and when the SFRC chair is conservative, as hypothesized by the strategic perspective. Partisan explanations, however, receive no support. When compared to the findings when we analyze all international agreements, it follows that presidents appear more willing to behave strategically—and perhaps to risk opposition to executive agreements as a policy innovation—when the international agreement is a major one. Relative to previous research on the topic, however, it is interesting that the standard measures of partisan political roadblocks (e.g., the number of presidential partisans) do not coincide with the expectations of the evasion hypothesis. In fact, our findings suggest that presidents more readily use executive agreements when the Senate has more of their fellow partisans—a finding in the opposite direction. The significant variables guiding strategic behavior on the part of presidents are ideological, not partisan, when we consider major agreements.

The efficiency perspective, which runs counter to the conventional wisdom of a strategically evasive president, offers a worthwhile addition to our understanding of aggregate usage of executive agreements. As the world becomes more complex, we see presidents utilizing more executive agreements when completing international agreements, particularly when considering important agreements. Moreover, as the number of presidential partisans increase in the Senate, the leeway granted to the president by that body is likely to increase, leading to the president using a greater number of executive agreements vis-à-vis treaties to complete important international agreements.

This apparent leeway is an important consideration, given the framework we set out in the introduction to this book. Presidents are freer to pursue important international agreements through executive agreements when their partisans control the Senate. Given this finding, evasion for partisan reasons holds little water as an explanation for aggregate usage of executive agreements. Rather, it appears that if a president were to routinely and strategically evade a Senate controlled by the opposition party on significant international agreements, they may risk the policy innovation their predecessors developed through use of executive agreements and, as a result, sufficiently weaken the presidency as an institution and its ability to prosecute foreign policy.

The differences in our findings between the larger set of all international agreements and the smaller set of important agreements are interesting. Important international agreements are much more salient in terms of the media coverage they receive and the attention they garner in Congress. Additionally, these are the very agreements where the president and important advisors may take a close interest. It thus makes sense that the strategic perspective receives some support when examining the more important agreements. However, the ideological variables have more power than the traditional partisan variables. As the SFRC chair is less inclined to grant leeway to the president on highly salient foreign policies, this provides greater incentive for the president to circumvent the Senate in order to complete a major international agreement. Finally, the efficiency hypothesis receives strong support even in the subset of important agreements, further crystallizing its importance as an explanation of this institutional change.

Conclusion

Overall, the increased use of executive agreements vis-à-vis treaties to complete international agreements primarily reflects concerns for efficiency by the presidents and the U.S. Senate in completing diplomatic action. The role of partisan politics has been emphasized in previous analyses and in textbook accounts of the process. We believe that this emphasis is misplaced and that the efficiency perspective, which dominates descriptions given to us by participants in the process, has not received due attention. However, our findings suggest that politics matter in ways left unconsidered by previous research. The ideological preferences of pivotal players in the process, particularly the chair of the SFRC, structure presidential decisions to use executive agreements. The president's domestic political capital, as measured by approval ratings, appears to play a role as well.

However, these relationships are not always in the direction suggested by the strategic perspective, and they change depending on the set of international agreements examined. This is important both methodologically and theoretically. It makes sense, theoretically, that political strategy plays more of a role with the subset of important international agreements examined in the aggregate. Methodologically, the findings suggest that future scholarship should account for the importance of international agreements when examining presidential behavior using this policy mechanism. As we proceed in our examination of international agreements in the next several chapters, we narrow our focus on the important international agreements.

More broadly, our findings suggest that the greater use of executive agreements vis-à-vis treaties does not necessarily support the perspective that presidents dominate U.S. foreign policy—the notion of an imperial presidency (Rudalevige 2005; Schlesinger 1973). Instead, the evolutionary change is more of a reflection of changing political circumstances for both the president and the Senate, which cause them to want to get diplomatic action completed sooner rather than later. That the Senate has acquiesced to this change in policy making is not surprising given the sizable number of international agreements completed by the executive branch each year and the benefits that accrue to the legislative branch when it delegates. When the issues involved are significant, however, politics are more likely to play a role in presidential decisions on international agreements. We suspect, as Martin (2000) argues in her work, that presidents cannot evade the Senate at will. The behavior is contingent upon discretion granted by the Senate to the executive.

Because they are aggregate in nature, our analyses in this chapter only indirectly speak to actual presidential decisions to use executive agreements vis-à-vis treaties. Where presidents make decisions regarding whether or not to complete international agreements as treaties or executive agreements, it is likely that characteristics of the individual agreement, as well as the political factors previously outlined, might influence the process. Until recently, research has been handicapped by its focus on aggregate counts of the usage of executive agreements versus treaties.[25] In chapter 3, we disaggregate the analysis to include a cross-sectional case-by-case analysis of the important international agreements. Our findings there lend more support to the efficiency rationale and further question the conventional understanding of political use of executive agreements.

3 | Presidential Decision Making: The Alternative Use of Treaties and Executive Agreements

On May 24, 2002, President George W. Bush signed the only major arms control agreement with Russia to be completed during his first term, the Moscow Treaty, also known as the Strategic Offensive Reductions Treaty, or SORT. The treaty was remarkable because of its brevity and vagueness; as such, it was a departure from past standard agreements on arms reduction. Moreover, the treaty took only about a year to negotiate (Trachtenberg 2004). The shortness of the negotiations and the brevity of the three-page document mask significant disagreement between the signatories of the international agreement. President Bush preferred a loosely worded document, what he liked to refer to as a "gentleman's agreement," which allowed for flexibility. President Putin of Russia, however, preferred a more specific document with "legally binding" language on force levels (Woolf 2003: 8). One bone of contention that arose while negotiations proceeded was the form that the final agreement would take under American law.

In line with his informal preferences, Bush considered completing the agreement not as a treaty but as an executive agreement. While either form is legally binding under international law, President Putin clearly preferred that Bush submit the agreement to the Senate for formal ratification as an Article II treaty. Putin wanted a "full-blown treaty" to provide "certainty" (Martin 2005: 448). Internally, U.S. administration officials struggled with the decision. Defense Department officials preferred the flexibility provided under a more informal agreement, and during hearings before the SFRC in February 2002, they stressed that legally binding language should be limited to verification requirements and not force levels. But Colin Powell, secretary of state, believed that completing the treaty as a more formal agreement with some limitations on force levels was the preferable approach. Part of his reasoning was that doing so would provide political cover for President Putin when it came to ratification of the treaty in the Russian Duma, as a formal treaty carried more weight with the Russians. At the same hearings, he indicated that the president "could complete the agreement as an executive agreement, whose approval would be subject to a majority vote of both houses of Congress, or a formal Treaty, which would require the consent of two-thirds of the Members of the Senate." President Bush endorsed Secretary Powell's approach and agreed that a formal agreement on force levels was appropriate; however, he still was unsure about which form the final agreement would take (Woolf 2007: 4). Bush noted, "There needs to be a document that outlives both of us" (quoted in Pincus 2002: 19).

That the president was openly considering completing the important arms control agreement as an executive agreement, rather than as a treaty, caught the attention of members of the Senate. By convention, presidents tend to submit significant arms control agreements as formal treaties, but the Arms Control and Disarmament Act specifically allows presidents to go the route of a congressional-executive agreement. Doing so had precedent, as President Nixon chose to forgo formal Senate consent of the original Strategic Arms Limitation Talks (SALT I) in 1972, instead submitting the agreement to both chambers of Congress for majority approval. In March 2002, Senators Biden (D-DE) and Helms (R-NC), the senior Democratic and Republican members of the SFRC, sent a joint letter to the president "demanding" that he submit the eventual arms control agreement with Russia as a treaty. In their letter defending the institutional prerogatives of the Senate, the senators noted that "significant obligations by the United States regarding the deployment of U.S. strategic nuclear warheads . . . constitute a Treaty subject to the advice and consent of the Senate" (Shanker 2002: 16; see also Woolf 2007: 5). Though reluctant, the president announced in May that he would treat the agreement as a treaty and submitted the agreement to the Senate for formal ratification on June 20, 2002 (Treaty Doc. 107-8). Press accounts suggest that the Biden-Helms position helped push the administration to its final decision (Woolf 2007: 5).

As reported in the *Congressional Record,* during floor debate on the Moscow Treaty on March 5, 2003, Senator Biden reflected on his efforts to get the president to go the formal treaty route.

I remind everyone who may be listening—and I know my colleagues on the floor fully understand this—the President started off with a flat assertion that this would not be a treaty, the Moscow agreement. As a matter of fact, . . . I was up on the stage, and the President . . . walked up on the stage, grabbed my arm, and said: "You owe me one, Joe." I looked at him joking and said: "How is that, Mr. President?" He said: "You got your treaty."

During his argument on behalf of the treaty and against amendments that the president might oppose, Biden suggested that if the treaty were bogged down by amendment, the president might prefer to leave the amended treaty unratified and instead "keep the verbal agreement, the executive agreement with Mr. Putin, rather than have it as a treaty and have to accept these conditions."[1] On March 6, 2003, after rejecting six floor amendments, the Senate voted (ninety-five to zero) to ratify the Moscow Treaty, with only a few minor conditions placed on the president's implementation of the agreement. Why did President Bush complete the Moscow agreement as a treaty and not as an executive agreement? The preceding discussion suggests that Bush was responsive to both the concerns of senators and the Russian president. If Bush had ignored the pleas of Biden and Helms, he might have endangered other international agreements (given the significance of the SFRC in the approval process) or possibly even the expediency afforded him through executive agreements.

On July 18, 2005, President Bush and Indian prime minister Manmohan Singh announced a bilateral agreement that would allow for full civil nuclear cooperation between India and the United States. A second agreement, completed on March 2, 2006, helped facilitate the cooperation by separating civilian and military nuclear facilities in India, which would allow for the International Atomic Energy Agency (IAEA) to inspect India's civilian facilities (see Squassoni 2006). These international agreements were significant for several reasons. First, they represented a significant step forward in cementing a friendlier relationship between the United States and the world's largest democracy, India. Second, they opened nuclear facilities inside India for international inspection for the first time, a significant step lauded by IAEA leaders (VandeHei and Linzer 2006). Finally and most controversially, the agreements represented a significant departure from American policy on nuclear nonproliferation: under the agreements, the United States would supply nuclear fuel and technical know-how to a nation with nuclear arms that had not signed the Nuclear Nonproliferation Treaty (NPT).

That U.S. companies could now supply technology for civilian nuclear power to India, a nation of 1.1 billion people with vast energy needs, was a significant boon for American businesses, and the business lobby mounted a significant effort on behalf of the deal (Schatz 2006). However, many in the arms control community were distressed by the agreements and lobbied against them (Hutcheson and Landay 2006), prompting several press reports foretelling a difficult fight to approve the agreements in Congress (Associated Press 2006; Cirincione 2006; Pant 2006). While the president was free to treat the agreements as a treaty or a congressional-executive agreement, he chose the latter, and the administration forwarded to Congress legislation intended to amend the Atomic Energy Act to allow for U.S. cooperation with a nation that had not signed the NPT, having the effect of approving the agreements.

The Republican-controlled Congress moved quickly on the legislation, and there was no discussion in the media or among members of the administration or Congress on the form the agreement would take (Ku 2006), despite its controversial nature. To approve the deal, however, Congress had to amend existing law, which required the president to waive certain conditions that India clearly had not met (e.g., complete safeguards on all if its nuclear facilities) and then to submit any future cooperation agreements to Congress for a joint resolution of approval (Squassoni 2006). At first, the administration attempted to get the law changed to allow the president to further negotiate nuclear cooperation agreements with India without additional approval needed by Congress. But the version of the law that finally passed (HR 5682, Public Law 109-275) kept Congress in the loop by requiring a joint resolution of approval within sixty days of the agreement, certain conditions on the part of India, and significant consultation between the president and Congress as agreements were negotiated and export licenses were granted. Despite the predictions of difficulty for the agreement's acceptance by Congress, its approval was passed overwhelmingly in the House, by a vote of 359 to 68, and in the Senate, by a vote of 85 to 12 (Monaghan 2006b).

In his signing statement issued on December 18, 2006, President Bush brushed aside several of the consultation requirements and conditions, ordering the executive branch to consider them "advisory" or to construe them "in a manner consistent with the President's constitutional authority to protect and control information that could impair foreign relations." It is unclear whether or not the president plans to ignore these consultation requirements and what effect doing so would have on the approval of future agreements in Congress (Squassoni 2006: 24). However, if the president had gone the treaty route, nuclear cooperation could have occurred between the United States and India without future consultation with Congress and ex post approval of future agreements: a duly ratified Article II treaty would supersede the limitations set forth by the Atomic Energy Act, and future agreements could be completed pursuant to the treaty. This, of course, assumes that the Senate would give its consent to such a treaty.

Why, then, did President Bush go the route of an executive agreement, when a treaty might have given him more of what he wanted? It is likely that the executive agreement affords the president greater flexibility. He could issue the signing statement and then assure the Indian government that future agreements required only majority approval in each chamber of Congress, something Bush and future presidents could easily muster, given the support nuclear cooperation has among business groups. Also, if the Senate had attached similar conditions to a treaty, the deal might have been irreparably damaged, prompting the president or the Indians to refuse to ratify the amended treaty, because treaty conditions carry the force of law (Auerswald 2006). Furthermore, given Bush's low approval ratings,[2] his diminishing political capital on Capitol Hill, and the vocal opposition the agreement attracted, Bush may have calculated that gaining consent to a treaty may have taken longer than approval of the agreements and that mustering a supermajority in the Senate may have proven too difficult. That no senator stood up and expressed dismay that the president treated the agreement as an executive agreement, despite heated opposition to the legislation during floor debate (Monaghan 2006a), suggests that senators have largely acquiesced to the use of executive agreements when completing significant international agreements under some circumstances.

Conclusions drawn from the cases of the Moscow Treaty and the U.S.-India Civil Nuclear Cooperation Initiative appear to support our theory (laid out in the introduction to this book) that the rise of executive agreements is an evolutionary response by the presidency and the Senate to greater diplomatic demands of the modern era. Moreover, the cases suggest that presidents consider both domestic and international political concerns when making their decisions on how to complete their executive agreements. In his decision to complete the Moscow Treaty as a formal Article II treaty, President Bush acceded to Russian and Senate requests in order to send a signal of commitment to Russia and to not needlessly reject the desires of two powerful senators. That a formal treaty was not considered for the Indian deal also indicates the significance of international considerations, as well as the acquiescence of the Senate to the use of executive agreements under certain circumstances and the efficiency afforded by the executive agreement mechanism. Interesting insights can be drawn from these cases, but to properly test our theory, we now turn to a systematic examination of presidential decisions on the form of their international agreements.

Insights on Presidential Decisions regarding International Agreements

Few formal constraints exist on presidential decisions on international agreements (Setear 2002); hence presidents have wide latitude in choosing the form their international agreements will take under domestic law. As a result, since World War II, there has been a marked rise in the use of executive agreements in order to complete international agreements efficiently and perhaps to avoid the politicized treaty process in the Senate. In chapter 2, we explored reasons for the rise of executive agreements vis-à-vis treaties in the modern era. We found that presidents, rather than seeking to evade the Senate based on partisan political calculations, increase their use of executive agreements in an efficient response to a complex international environment. However, we found some support for strategic considerations when we narrowed our examination to the subset of significant international agreements. Now we turn our attention to a question largely ignored by political scientists:[3] what agreement-level factors encourage presidents to use an executive agreement instead of a treaty? This is an important decision by presidents, and in this chapter, we seek to explain, at the level of individual agreement, why presidents might bother even pursuing the treaty route—and hence face significant hurdles and delay—when the executive agreement option is open to them.

Also missing in the scholarly debate is recognition of the degree to which decisions on international agreements are institutionalized within the executive branch. Hence another goal of this chapter is to elucidate the process whereby decisions are made on the form an international agreement will take. We find that the White House is largely removed from the process in the vast majority of cases. While it is generally assumed by scholars that these decisions are primarily presidential,[4] the process rarely involves the White House. Instead, most of these decisions are made in the Office of the Assistant Legal Adviser for Treaty Affairs, within the State Department. Additionally, many of the decisions are made as a result of tradition[5] or law,[6] which suggests that when the White House becomes involved, it is primarily only on the international agreements of consequence. Caruson and Farrar-Myers (2007), in a recent study on executive agreements, show that presidents "elevate" only about 4 percent of their agreements and that they tend to do so on agreements relevant to their priorities in foreign policy.[7] Of the thousands of international agreements completed in the modern era, a great percentage involves technical agreements, tax or extradition treaties, agricultural agreements, and so on, which are unlikely ever to reach the "radar screen" of the White House. As a result, we focus our attention on the treaties and executive agreements of significance, where presidents (or their aides) are most likely to become directly involved.[8]

A Significant Presidential Decision

As illustrated by the Moscow Treaty, presidents sometimes grapple with deciding whether to formalize their significant international agreements as treaties and hence submit them to the Senate for consent or to treat their agreements as executive agreements, which do not require supermajority consent in the Senate and might only require majority congressional approval.[9] The choice can have profound implications for both domestic and international politics. The penchant of President Franklin Roosevelt and his immediate predecessors for using executive agreements to commit the United States to important international commitments without significant vetting in the Senate[10] led to a domestic political struggle over an amendment to the Constitution.[11] Secret executive agreements initiated by Presidents Kennedy, Johnson, and Nixon further embroiled the United States in the conflict in Southeast Asia, prompting a backlash in the Congress that culminated in the enactment of the Case-Zablocki Act in 1972.[12]

Historical examples abound of modern presidents grappling with the decision on how to complete their important international agreements. Presidents routinely float trial balloons suggesting their intention to submit an important international agreement for congressional approval as an executive agreement, therefore requiring only majority approval in both chambers, rather than as a treaty. President Carter did so with SALT II in 1979 but backed down due to a negative response from his own partisans in the Senate (Caldwell 1991a). A similar case occurred during the Clinton administration (in the Flank Document Agreement to the Conventional Armed Forces in Europe Treaty), but the administration caved when the SFRC presented a unified front urging treaty action.[13]

Pressure to complete an international agreement as a treaty rather than as an executive agreement may come from international sources as well. International leaders value the surety provided by formal treaties—presidents are less likely to renege on an agreement in the future when domestic ratification for the agreement levels significant political costs on the president (Milner 1997). The political hurdles of securing the Senate's consent to an Article II treaty are clearly higher than is the case for executive agreements in the vast majority of cases. Lisa Martin (2005: 447–48) outlines several historical cases where other nations pressured American presidents to complete their international agreements as treaties rather than as executive agreements, given the greater significance afforded formal treaties. For example, in the case of SALT II, Carter was pressured by the Soviets to pursue Senate consent for a formal treaty because they believed an executive agreement would have "inferior status" to a treaty.

Modern presidents do not always back down to pressure over the form their international agreements will take. President Franklin Roosevelt, with his famous pre–World War II executive agreements committing the United States to helping the Allies against the Axis powers, resisted political pressure to go the treaty route. President Nixon submitted the original SALT agreement to Congress as an executive agreement rather than as a treaty. In 1972, in response, the Senate approved two nonbinding "resolutions urging President Nixon to submit agreements governing American bases abroad as treaties," but Nixon ignored both resolutions (Lindsay 1994: 83). Despite objections to Nixon's treatment of SALT as an executive agreement, the agreement was approved overwhelmingly by both chambers. The vote in the House was 308 to 4, and the vote in the Senate was 82 to 2 (*CQ Almanac* 1972: 622).

In 1990, President George H. W. Bush completed an agreement with the Soviet Union on chemical weapons reduction. Both nations agreed to halt production of chemical weapons and destroy existing stockpiles. James A. Baker III, the secretary of state, hailed the agreement as "trailblazing" and as a "precedent-setting accord" between the superpowers (Felton 1990b: 1664). Bush considered submitting the agreement for approval from both chambers of Congress, citing concerns about getting the necessary two-thirds vote in the Senate for a treaty. The SFRC issued a formal protest by eighteen of the nineteen members of the committee. The administration considered the senators' request but decided to stand by its initial decision to go the executive agreement route, citing requests by

House leadership for a two-chamber approval process (*CQ Weekly Online* 1990; *CQ Almanac* 1990: 709; Felton 1990a: 1800; Lindsay 1994: 83).

Anecdotal evidence thus suggests that presidents may grapple with these difficult decisions with political strategy in mind. After all, Carter chose the treaty route with SALT II when his party controlled the Senate. Nixon, however, made the opposite choice with SALT I when the other party controlled the Senate. In this chapter, we move beyond such anecdotal evidence and examine this decision-making process systematically. Scholars disagree regarding the importance of domestic politics in these important presidential decisions. The evasion hypothesis rests on the belief that presidents will skirt the Senate because of difficult political hurdles evident in the Senate consent process, which are exacerbated by partisan politics (Lindsay 1994; Margolis 1986; Nathan and Oliver 1994). Our analysis in chapter 2, however, eviscerates the partisan basis for the evasion hypothesis. Presidents simply are not using traditional partisan calculations when making these decisions—at least in the aggregate. Strategic considerations, in the form of the president's political capital and the ideological predispositions of significant senators, appear to play an important role, however, when we consider only the significant international agreements.

In the analysis that follows, we build further support for executive agreement usage as an efficiency mechanism—a policy tool that evolved during the twentieth century within the executive branch with the acquiescence of the legislature. A perspective that fits with our argument is the idea that presidents may use the agreement classification process (deciding whether to complete an agreement as a treaty or executive agreement) to send partners in international agreements credible signals that the agreement has widespread support and that the U.S. government intends to comply with its terms (Martin 2005; Setear 2002). Treaties therefore provide agreement partners an indicator of credibility on the part of the U.S. government (Martin 2000). In this chapter, we further test hypotheses stemming from competing theories, by accounting for domestic politics, signaling theory, and the desire by presidents and legislators to keep the efficient mode of executive agreements intact.

First, we justify the basis of our inquiry: that treaties and executive agreements are legally interchangeable but not politically interchangeable. Then we outline the institutionalized process surrounding executive decisions on the classification of international agreements. Our discussion highlights the degree to which the process is institutionalized (and therefore less politicized), an important consideration that has been overlooked by previous scholarship. Therefore, we justify our focus on only the important international agreements, as it is the consequential agreements that are likely to attract the attention of the White House. Next we analyze the alternative use of treaties and executive agreements for 441 of the most significant international agreements completed between 1949 and 1999. We capture individual-level (agreement-specific) factors that may influence a president's decision, as well as variables measuring the domestic political and international context. We further reduce our set of agreements and analyze only those agreements that were salient at the time of signing. Our analysis suggests that both domestic politics (in ways previously unconsidered) and the rational desire of presidents to send credible signals to U.S. agreement partners help explain the alternative use of executive agreements and treaties. Furthermore, the efficiency perspective receives robust support. Thus we provide further systematic evidence in support of our theoretical framework.

Are Executive Agreements and Treaties Interchangeable?

Our first order of business is to justify the major assumption underlying the analysis in this chapter: that executive agreements and treaties are legally interchangeable. The president faces no formal constraints on his decision to complete an international agreement as a treaty or executive agreement. According to *Restatement of the Law Third, Foreign Relations Law of the United States* (American Law Institute 1987: 308, 218), "the prevailing view is that the Congressional-Executive agreement can be used as an alternative to the treaty method in every instance," and "which procedure should be used is a political judgment, made in the first instance by the President."

There is a good deal of argument among legal scholars regarding the legal interchangeability of treaties and international agreements, however.[14] To be sure, international law makes no distinction between executive agreements and treaties (Henkin 1996), but in domestic law, executive agreements cannot be inconsistent with existing legislation or violate the constitutional rights of American citizens (see *United States v. Guy W. Capps, Inc.*, 204 F.2d 655, 660 [4th Cir. 1953] and *Reid v. Covert*, 354 U.S. 1, 16 [1957]). Additionally, should the Congress decide to act, it retains authority to resist executive action where its powers are clearly delineated (*Dames and Moore v. Reagan*, 452 U.S. 656 [1981]), which suggests the political nature of the question. As a result, the constitutional issue regarding the president's power to choose between treaty and executive agreement has been framed by the Court as a nonjusticiable political question—one that must be determined politically by the Congress and the president (Klarevas 2003; O'Brien 2003: 72; Setear 2002: S7). In the words of a senior State Department staffer, the power to enter into executive agreements on behalf of the United States and the treaty power are "not mutually exclusive" but, rather, "alternative means to accomplishing a policy." The staffer emphasized, "The president can do either. The president has a choice."[15] Should it decide to, Congress plays the role of constraining these presidential choices, as it must fund agreements; legislate in order to implement them; and, in many cases, give its direct approval to the agreements.

Bruce Ackerman and David Golove (1995) make a persuasive case on behalf of the interchangeability doctrine in domestic law, especially in regard to congressional-executive agreements, where the legislature plays an important role. Modern practice is that the two-chamber procedure afforded in many congressional-executive agreements (e.g., NAFTA) can substitute for two-thirds of the Senate (Ackerman and Golove 1995: 14). This practice is how most trade agreements are completed today. Other forms of executive agreements, most notably presidential agreements, have proven more problematic legally. But in most cases, justification for these agreements stems from the president's Article II powers (e.g., as commander in chief)[16]—hence providing more leeway legally for the executive (Dalton 1999). The conventional wisdom, as expressed by most legal scholars, is that treaties and executive agreements (no matter their type) are legally interchangeable.[17] This conclusion proves an important simplifying theoretical assumption for recent work addressing presidential decisions to go the route of an executive agreement rather than the route of a formal treaty (Martin 2005; Setear 2002). Our subsequent analysis rests on this legal assumption.

The more interesting question, for our purposes, is whether or not treaties and executive agreements are politically interchangeable. Both our theory outlined in the introduction to this book and the examples presented at the outset of this chapter clearly point us to answer no to this question. The president's decisions to classify agreements as treaties or executive agreements are not politically interchangeable.[18] The president's decisions have clear political consequences in terms of both domestic and international politics. Domestically, presidents seek to maintain an important policy tool (the executive agreement) without too much legislative opposition, which could result in difficulties passing necessary implementing legislation or could threaten other elements of the president's legislative or foreign policy agendas (Vagts 1995: 41). Moreover, presidents may follow certain established practices—treating arms control agreements as treaties, for example—in order not to inflame protectors of Senate prerogatives and give rise to a significant constitutional crisis (Spiro 2001: 961). The Senate has gone on record stating its insistence that presidents use treaties to complete these agreements, even to the point of denying its consent to the Vienna Convention on the Law of Treaties "because it wished to entrench the proposition that any document called a 'treaty' in that Convention [which would include all international agreements] was a treaty in the sense of Article II of the Constitution" (Vagts 1995: 41).[19] Internationally, as argued by Martin (2005), partners in agreements with the United States may take into account the president's decision about the form of the agreement and may use it as a signal to indicate the degree to which the president (and his successors) intends to adhere to the agreement. Before we can account for these important presidential decisions, we first must assess the overall process of classifying international agreements.

The Agreement Classification Process

Some international agreements rise to a level of importance and garner attention by the White House. However, neither presidents nor their staffs are tuned in to most potential agreements. Instead, bureaucrats follow a predefined, institutionalized process in the State Department. The Office of the Assistant Legal Adviser for Treaty Affairs is primarily responsible for overseeing and processing treaties and executive agreements on behalf of the administration.[20] Through a process described in the *Foreign Affairs Manual* (Circular 175), first published in 1974, the legal advisor is responsible for providing legal advice regarding the classification of international agreements. For potential agreements, whichever bureau is involved in a region of the world that sees a need will first broach the discussion with the assistant legal adviser's office (also called the "Legal Office," "Legal," or just "L" for short). This initial contact may evolve into further discussions through which the given State Department bureau and the Legal Office keep each other posted on developments related to the agreement.

Before any agreements between the United States and an international entity are developed in terms of actual text, a particular legal document called for in the *Foreign Affairs Manual* must be in place. This next formal step is a two-part document that comes out of the State Department and is typically called a "C175" after the relevant section in the *Foreign Affairs Manual*. A C175 includes a section on funding and other matters and a section on legal aspects that speaks to the form the agreement will take— whether a treaty or a specific category of executive agreement. These two sections are the result of a process between the Legal Office and the State Department bureau and serve as precursors to the final C175. They are carried out through two memoranda: an action memo to the decision maker and a memo of law.

The action memo is required by the *Foreign Affairs Manual* and asks the bureau (decision maker) such questions as, What are the funding implications? Will the Office of Management and Budget play a role? Are there risk factors? Is Congressional consultation required, or has it occurred? On the rare, thornier cases, this action memo may go up to the level of the secretary of state before the C175 process begins. The memo of law discusses what form the agreement should take. Will it be a treaty or executive agreement? If it will be an executive agreement, which type will it be? Is it a congressional-executive agreement? Will it be a sole executive (or presidential) agreement? Is it a close call? As part of the memo of law, the legal advisors at the State Department, including lawyers and analysts, consult with one another in what is commonly called "scrubbing" the agreement. These two precursors (the feedback from the action memo and the opinion from the memo of law) form the particular C175 package.

On the vast majority of potential agreements, this process does not garner the attention of the secretary or the White House, either because the subject matter is noncontroversial or is not a presidential priority (Caruson and Farrar-Myers 2007) or because existing law or tradition provides specific guidance and precedence on what format an agreement should take given its subject matter (Vagts 1995: 41). For example, presidents are formally authorized by law to use executive agreements instead of treaties in certain areas, such as fisheries agreements and basing agreements. In other areas, such as certain tax and extradition treaties, agreements must be processed as treaties. Since the form most agreements will take emerges from this internal State Department process rather than from a conscious choice between treaties and executive agreements on the part of presidents or their closest advisers, it is important to find a way to focus on the most salient agreements that will attract the attention of the White House.

Given the process within the State Department, a large percentage of the vast numeric divide between executive agreements and treaties can be explained simply as a function of an institutionalized bureaucratic process where State Department staff members work closely with their counterparts in the Congress. When only significant international agreements are considered, the ratio of executive agreements to treaties is reduced considerably: 44 percent of these international agreements were completed as treaties, compared to 6 percent when all agreements are considered. Hence, in the analyses that follow, we focus our attention on the significant agreements, and then more narrowly on the significant agreements that are most salient.

The Politics of Choice

When we separate out the agreements on which presidents are likely to become involved, what factors might explain why a president would go the treaty route instead of using an executive agreement? To probe this question, we test three sets of hypotheses that flow from the competing perspectives previously discussed: those related to the strategic-political perspective, those related to international politics, and those related to the efficiency perspective. The latter two perspectives fit best with our theoretical framework as outlined in the introduction to this book: executive agreements are a policy innovation in response to an increasingly complex international and policy environment and have been evolved over time by a presidency constrained in a system of separate power-sharing institutions and seeking to effectively prosecute American foreign policy. The strategic perspective, in contrast, is largely in line with the conventional understanding of executive agreement usage—that presidents use such agreements to circumvent the Senate when governing circumstances are difficult.

Executive Agreements as Strategic Devices

The strategic perspective that guides conventional understanding of the process of deciding between treaties and executive agreements states that presidents avoid using formal treaties when governing circumstances prove difficult. Put more simply, presidents are prone to strategically evade the Senate (Moe and Howell 1999) and, as a result, have relied more and more on executive agreements to complete major international agreements (Crenson and Ginsberg 2007; Lindsay 1994; Margolis 1986). Hence our hypotheses testing the evasion argument are largely the same here as in chapter 2, but our analysis here is focused on a case-by- case basis rather than the longitudinal design employed there. Therefore, *when presidents must deal with a Senate where the opposition party outnumbers their own party, the strategic perspective posits that presidents are less likely to choose the treaty route over the executive agreement route.*

As outlined in chapter 2, the SFRC is the most prominent hurdle for a president seeking Senate consent on a controversial treaty. The committee's chair, therefore, could be a significant hurdle if he or she is predisposed ideologically to oppose entangling international treaties. Scholars generally agree that conservative senators best reflect these isolationist tendencies (see Auerswald and Maltzman 2003), so *when the SFRC Chair is especially conservative, the strategic perspective expects presidents to evade the Senate and be less likely to complete an important agreement as a treaty.* Finally, a president's political capital (e.g., approval ratings) may structure these presidential choices on important international agreements. This is consistent with the strategic perspective, as well-situated presidents may be further inclined to go the treaty route due to enhanced likelihood of success. Therefore, *when presidential approval is high, presidents are more likely to complete their significant agreements as treaties.*

International Politics—Signaling Theory

While domestic politics are important to presidential decisions on international agreements, it is also likely that presidents are cognizant of the fact that their decisions have international ramifications. Therefore, international politics are likely to play an important role. Signaling theory states that presidents are keenly aware of the importance America's agreement partners place on the level of U.S. commitment to its international agreements. Treaties, by their two-thirds requirement and the costs incurred by presidents to get them through the Senate, send clear signals of U.S. commitment to the agreement (Martin 2005), particularly when easier options (executive agreements) are open to presidents (Setear 2002). Moreover, treaties are constitutionally unambiguous, and leaders in other nations see that as significant in terms of U.S. commitment. Put simply, treaties provide agreement partners with more credible signals of commitment (Martin 2000). Therefore, *presidents are more likely to use treaties to complete high-benefit agreements, as well as agreements involving high-stakes issues* (e.g., arms control, security, or peace), because these are the types of agreements where presidents want to send the clearest signal of commitment on the part of the United States (Martin 2005). Additionally, salient agreements—those agreements that receive attention from the media—are more likely to involve significant international issues. When agreements are salient in the media, then, presidents are more inclined to complete them as treaties.

Executive Agreements as an Efficiency Mechanism

The final perspective, one of efficiency (developed in this book's introduction and supported in chapter 2), is driven by the desire to keep the policy evolution of executive agreement use intact on behalf of both the president and the Senate. Presidents rely on the latitude provided over the years by the Senate so they can complete important agreements more quickly than otherwise might occur using the Article II process, which is cumbersome and often rife with delay and gridlock (as we show explicitly in chapter 5). The increased use of executive agreements over the years generally comes with Senate acquiescence; however, presidents realize that salient agreements are more likely to attract the attention of the Senate. If presidents routinely completed these significant and salient agreements as executive agreements rather than treaties, they might embolden senators inclined to protect the Senate's institutional prerogatives. Moreover, salient agreements are more likely to gain the attention of individual senators, and as a result, senators will want their say because of the agreements' political ramifications. Anecdotal evidence suggests that presidents have succumbed to Senate pressure to use the formal treaty route when they have considered otherwise (e.g., George W. Bush did on the Moscow Treaty). As a result, *presidents may be more likely to go the formal treaty route when an agreement is salient in the media.*

Additionally, the efficiency perspective suggests that partisan politics are likely to structure decisions by the president in a manner opposite to the strategic perspective. When the other party controls the Senate, presidents may actually be less inclined to use executive agreements instead of treaties for two reasons. First, doing so might inflame senatorial opposition to their use and hence endanger their future use. When the opposing party controls the committee chairs and, as a result, has the ability to control the agenda of the SFRC, it is better positioned to challenge the president in an effort to curtail executive abuse of power. Second, the president's own partisans are more inclined to grant the discretion necessary for the president to use the executive agreement to complete a controversial international agreement. This logic suggests the following hypothesis: *when presidents must deal with a Senate where the opposition party outnumbers their own party, the efficiency perspective posits that presidents are more likely to choose the treaty route over the executive agreement route.* The same reasoning has been used by scholars to explain the negative relationship between divided government and executive orders, another policy evolution allowing for unilateral presidential action based to a certain extent on institutional efficiency and the discretion provided by the legislature (Howell 2003; Mayer 2001; Warber 2006).

Applying a similar logic to the ideology of the SFRC chair suggests the reverse hypothesis from the strategic perspective. Conservative SFRC chairs may be more inclined to oppose the executive agreement process and to expect presidents to submit more of their important international agreements as treaties so that the chairs can put their mark on the international agreement. Hence, *when the SFRC chair is especially conservative, presidents are more likely to complete an important agreement as a treaty*, in order to protect this policy innovation.

Finally, there is the part of our framework that assesses the significance of international complexity, which indicates that presidents responding to a more complex international environment more readily use executive agreements. We here employ the same efficiency hypothesis used in chapter 2: *as the number of nations with whom the United States has relations increases in a given period, it is less likely for the president to complete international agreements as treaties.*

The Significance of an Agreement's Salience

Both signaling theory and our efficiency framework point to the significance of an agreement's salience to the president's decision making on the form an agreement will take. Salience can be assessed in two ways. First, whether or not the media address the issue being considered in an agreement is an indication of salience. Second, whether or not the president addresses the issue in his public statements sends a signal that the White House considers an issue salient (Caruson and Farrar-Myers 2007; Eshbaugh-Soha 2006). Agreements whose issues are thus addressed are likely to attract the most attention by domestic and international political actors. Examining the important salient agreements therefore provides the best test of the theories related to the politics of presidential decisions on international agreements.

Data and Method

In chapter 2, we demonstrated that the rise in executive agreements is primarily a result of institutional efficiency rather than a concerted effort on behalf of the White House to evade the Senate. Our methods, however, were limited because they relied on aggregate, longitudinal data. Because of its aggregate nature, such analysis is unable to tap presidential decision making at the agreement level. In the subsequent analysis, we account for this problem by disaggregating the analysis to the agreement level. Moreover, the analysis in chapter 2 and others like it (e.g., Martin 2000) are limited because they do not differentiate between the run-of-the-mill international agreement and the truly significant international agreement. We have already argued that presidents are only likely to take an interest in and make a decision on the significant agreements.

To test the previously outlined hypotheses of presidential decision making on international agreements, we collected data on 441 of the most significant international agreements completed by presidents for the period 1949–99.[21] Of these agreements, 246 were completed as executive agreements, and 195 were completed as treaties. We further disaggregated our population of important international agreements to include only those agreements addressed by the *New York Times*[22] or publicly by the president up to the date the agreement was signed.[23] This allowed us to further narrow our analysis to those agreements that we can be more certain captured the attention of the White House. Moreover, this more effectively tests the political hypotheses stemming from the three frameworks, as it is these agreements that attract the most attention by political actors. Of the 441 international agreements, 197 (109 executive agreements and 88 treaties) met either of these criteria. Our unit of analysis is the agreement, and our dependent variable is whether a president pursues a treaty on the particular agreement (coded 1) or instead utilizes an executive agreement (coded 0).

With this set of important international agreements, we collected various measures related to the agreements, along with measures of the political and international context. We coded several dummy variables for each international agreement. The first accounts for whether or not the agreement is multilateral. The expectation is that multilateral agreements, coded 1 (bilateral agreements are coded 0), are more likely to be completed as treaties.[24] Multilateral agreements, by definition, involve more signatories than simpler bilateral agreements; therefore, the expectation from signaling theory is that they are more likely to be completed as treaties than executive agreements, as presidents must ensure several partners (rather than just one) of U.S. compliance (Martin 2005). We also coded for the type of agreement, including a dummy variable (coded 1) for agreements that deal with "high politics" (0 for "low politics"). The expectation is that "high politics" agreements (which involve alliances, diplomacy, peace, and arms control agreements) are more likely to be completed as treaties because of high diplomatic value and are more likely to attract the attention of the Senate, as well as demands from international parties for a strong show of commitment.[25] To be sure, laws requiring presidents to submit certain types of international agreements as treaties would frustrate any type of analysis, as there would be no variation on the dependent variable for such agreements. However, this is not a problem in our analysis because all such treaties (typically tax and extradition treaties) are excluded from it, as they are not coded as important in the first place.[26]

As discussed earlier, we also coded for the media salience of each international agreement. We used coverage by the *New York Times* (prior to the president signing the agreement) as an indicator of media salience. Our expectation is that agreements that are salient in the media are more likely to be completed as treaties, rather than executive agreements, because they are the agreements that are likely to attract the attention of international and domestic political elites. As a result, legislative and international pressure on the president to use the formal constitutional process may be greater for these agreements. We drop this variable from our subset of salient agreements, as that sample is defined by mention of an agreement either in the *Times* or in a public statement by the president prior to the signing of the agreement.

Our final set of variables is not agreement-specific but instead accounts for the domestic and international political environment that the president must deal with when completing international agreements. The variables are the same as those employed in chapter 2 and there shown to be significant. We include in the model a measure counting the number of presidential partisans in the Senate,[27] an ideology measure of the SFRC chair (using CS-NOMINATE), the average monthly presidential approval for the year in which the agreement was completed, and a measure to account for the complexity of the international environment: the growth in UN membership for the Senate in which the agreement was completed.[28] Additionally, we include a control variable for agreements completed during the Cold War, as the findings in chapter 2 suggest that presidents were marginally more likely to use executive agreements during that era. Finally, we include a control variable for the period since the passage of the Case-Zablocki Act (1972), an important event signaling increased Senate oversight of the international agreement process.

Statistically, we employ logistic regression, as our dependent variable is binomial. We give a code of 1 to all agreements completed as treaties. We give a code of 0 to all agreements completed as executive agreements.

Findings

We report the findings for all important international agreements in table 3. The findings offer support for our expectations that signaling theory and the efficiency framework help explain presidential decisions to complete important international agreements as treaties rather than as executive agreements. Only modest support is found for the strategic perspective. As expected, agreements involving multiple signatories (multilateral) were substantially more likely to be completed as treaties. The baseline probability of a bilateral agreement being a treaty is only .07, whereas the probability of a multilateral agreement being a treaty is .63. Agreements involving high politics are also more likely to be completed as treaties, though this relationship is not statistically significant.

TABLE 3. Logistic Regression Results for Probability of a President Completing an Important International Agreement as a Treaty

Independent variable	Coefficient	Standard error	|z|	Estimated pr(1)
Multilateral	3.32**	0.29	11.56	.63
High politics	0.36	0.32	1.15	
New York Times coverage	0.49**	0.29	1.65	.11
Growth in UN members	−0.04*	0.027	−1.44	.05
Number of presidential partisans	−0.01	0.02	−0.76	
SFRC chair	−0.76*	0.58	−1.32	.05
Presidential approval	0.01	0.01	1.18	
Cold War	0.53	0.43	1.24	
Case-Zablocki Act	0.14	0.31	0.44	
Constant	−2.85**	1.19	−2.40	

$N = 441$
Pseudo $R^2 = .36$
LR chi^2 = 219.3
Baseline Pr(1) = .07

Note: Dependent variable agreement completed as treaty (1) or executive agreement (0). *Pr(1)* is the estimated impact of the independent variable when going from its arithmetic mean to one standard deviation above its mean (or from 0 to 1 for dummy variables), while holding all other variables at their mean values (or 0 if dummy). The estimated probabilities were calculated using CLARIFY (King, Tomz, and Wittenberg 2000). The analysis was conducted in Stata 9.0.
*$p < .1$ **p $< .05$ (one-tailed)

Agreements that received coverage in the *New York Times* were also more likely to be completed as treaties, as expected by both signaling theory and our efficiency framework. Multilateral agreements that were salient in the media are estimated to be treaties at .73; bilateral agreements at .11.[29] This is an increase over the nonsalient agreements from .63 and .07, respectively. As we found in chapter 2, international complexity, here represented by the growth in UN members, appears to encourage the use of executive agreements in our set of significant agreements, lending support to the efficiency perspective. Presidents completing agreements when more international agreements are likely, given growth in the UN, are less likely to complete a significant agreement as a treaty.

The variables measuring the political context provide mixed support for the strategic perspective. The number of presidential partisans in the Senate appears to have no impact on the president's decision, at least when we consider all of the important agreements together. However, the ideology of the SFRC chair appears to matter significantly, as hypothesized by the strategic perspective. The presence of an ideologically conservative SFRC chair encourages presidents to evade the Senate—presidents are less

TABLE 4. Logistic Regression Results for Probability of a President Completing an Important International Agreement as a Treaty, Salient Agreements Only

Independent variable	Coefficient	Standard error	|z|	Estimated Pr(1)
Multilateral	2.32**	0.37	6.21	.62
High politics	0.54*	0.36	1.49	.25
Growth in UN members	−0.08**	0.03	−2.23	.12
Number of presidential partisans	−0.04**	0.02	−1.76	.13
SFRC chair	−0.76	0.74	−1.03	
Presidential approval	0.02	0.02	1.09	
Cold War	0.21	0.56	0.37	
Case-Zablocki Act	−0.30	0.41	−0.31	
Constant	−0.47	1.51	−0.31	

$N = 197$
Pseudo $R^2 = 0.22$
LR Chi^2 = 60.3**
Baseline Pr(1) = .17

Note: Dependent variable agreement completed as treaty (1) or executive agreement (0). *Pr(1)* is the estimated impact of the independent variable when going from its arithmetic mean to one standard deviation above its mean (or from 0 to 1 for dummy variables), while holding all other variables at their mean values (or 0 if dummy). The estimated probabilities were calculated using Clarify (King, Tomz, and Wittenberg 2000). The analysis includes the important international agreements in which the president issued a public statement or there was coverage by the *New York Times*, both measured prior to the signing of the agreement. The analysis was conducted in Stata 9.0.
*$p < .1$ **$p < .05$ (one-tailed)

inclined to go the treaty route under this condition. It does appear, however, that evasive behavior is more common when the SFRC chair is conservative, especially when an international agreement lacks salience or is bilateral rather than multilateral. This lends further support to our finding in chapter 2 that when completing important international agreements, presidents are more inclined to use executive agreements vis-à-vis treaties if the SFRC chair is conservative. While positive, as expected by the strategic perspective, the relationship between presidential approval and completing important agreements as treaties is not statistically significant. However, consistent with the results in chapter 2, evasion does not appear to occur as a result of partisan calculations.[30]

The Salient Agreements

In table 4, we present results for the subset of important international agreements considered salient—they were either mentioned by the president in a public statement or covered in the *New York Times*—and therefore most likely to rise to the level of presidential notice. As expected by signaling theory, among the salient agreements, multilateral and high politics agreements are more commonly completed as treaties. Presidents are more inclined to complete their high-value international agreements as treaties.

More interesting, however, is the change in findings regarding the variables accounting for political context. Among the salient agreements, greater support is found for the efficiency perspective, whereas no support is found for the strategic perspective. Among those agreements most likely to attract political attention, presidents appear more inclined to discount strategic evasive behavior, instead focusing on keeping the executive agreement intact by not employing the method as often when facing significant partisan opposition in the Senate. If the strategic perspective best explains presidential behavior, we would expect to see the opposite result, as controversial agreements are most likely to receive attention.

According to the results presented in table 4, presidents are significantly less likely to complete their salient important agreements as treaties when the partisan context in the Senate is favorable. For example, the baseline probability for a salient agreement being completed as a treaty is .17. The estimated probability is reduced to .13 for a president with sixty copartisans in the Senate. Put another way, when a president has only forty-two members of his party in the Senate (a poor political context, to be sure), the estimated probability of going the treaty route increases to

.23. Additionally, UN growth (representing international complexity) leads presidents to complete their agreements less often as treaties, and this relationship is even more significant when we narrow our focus to those agreements that are salient. While the results for the ideology of the chair and the president's popularity are in the direction hypothesized by the strategic perspective, they are not statistically significant predictors of treaties. In sum, factors related to the efficiency perspective and signaling theory are most effective in explaining presidential behavior in agreement classification when we narrow our focus to the salient agreements. The ideology of the SFRC chair is of limited importance here, suggesting perhaps that chairs are less inclined to block salient agreements, so as not to appear as inhibitors to the efficient making of foreign policy, or that presidents are less inclined to evade the Senate on salient agreements.

Conclusion

In chapter 2, using a macroanalysis, we examined the aggregate use of executive agreements vis-à-vis treaties over time and found only limited support for strategic political considerations on the part of presidents in choosing to use executive agreements. Our results instead pointed to the significance of policy-making efficiency. The analysis reported in this chapter is derived from a microanalysis, where we examine agreement-specific factors in addition to the political factors typically addressed by research. Our examination into the process and politics surrounding individual presidential decisions on the form of their international agreements further verifies the explanatory power of the efficiency perspective. Moreover, we find that presidents behave in a way that considers both the domestic and international political ramifications of their decisions. Presidential behavior suggests that presidents understand the significance of their decisions as signals to international agreement partners and the Senate.

More interesting, theoretically, presidents behave in a way that is helpful in preserving the important policy innovation of executive agreements. We find that presidents facing off against a Senate dominated by the opposing party complete more of their significant and salient agreements as treaties—the exact opposite prediction of the evasion hypothesis, but one well in line with the efficiency framework. If the president were to ignore Senate wishes on these types of agreements, they might spark the ire of a Senate majority controlled by the opposing party. When presidents govern with a Senate controlled by their own party, they are granted greater leeway to pursue their policy goals by extraconstitutional means—in our case, through the use of executive agreements. This represents presidential behavior geared toward a long-term institutional goal of protecting the policy innovation of the executive agreement, rather than the short-term political goal of winning a foreign policy victory more easily than would occur pursuing a treaty.

Combining our findings here with the findings in our aggregate analysis in chapter 2, our systematic examination of presidential use of executive agreements contributes to the broader discussion in the presidency literature on the use of unilateral powers by modern presidents. Most of the systematic research on unilateral powers focuses on executive orders, which are not dissimilar from executive agreements. Executive orders allow presidents to legislate without reliance on Congress, much like executive agreements allow for presidents to avoid the Senate when completing international agreements. Research has shown a positive relationship between unified government and the use of significant executive orders, similar to what we identify with executive agreement usage among the significant international agreements (Howell 2003; Mayer 2001; Warber 2006). Moreover, executive orders, like congressional-executive agreements, often stem from delegations of authority by statute (Warber 2006), rather than from the president's Article II powers. Given the acquiescence of Congress to the rise of executive orders, a similar evolution on the part of the presidency in expediting international agreements through the use of executive agreements is not surprising.

Placed in broader perspective, then, the use of executive agreements as an efficiency mechanism fits well with the adaptive qualities of a presidency trying to get a handle on a more complicated international context. These adaptations appear conditioned by the leeway granted by the other players in the constitutional system—in the case of international agreements, the U.S. Senate. As we demonstrated in chapter 1, however, this adaptation by the modern presidency did not come unopposed by members of the Senate keen on protecting senatorial prerogative or among the attentive public interest groups with isolationist or states' rights tendencies. The new presidential policy tool weathered two significant attempts to curtail its use—the Bricker Revolt and the Case-Zablocki Act. To be sure, presidents have historically been free in classifying their significant international agreements as treaties or executive agreements. That presidents regularly choose the executive agreement route, even on significant international agreements, contributes to the conventional understanding that the treaty process is typically pro forma. If the treaty faces significant opposition, presidents have other options available to complete their agreement. Hence this logic suggests that presidents send only those international agreements that are likely to garner Senate support for advice and consent as formal treaties. Yet the modern historical record is replete with cases where presidents submitted treaties to the Senate for advice and consent knowing full well that significant opposition would likely arise. It is to these interesting cases of treaty politics that we now turn.

4 | Far from Pro Forma: Politics in Treaty Advice and Consent

The conventional wisdom that presidents routinely evade the Senate and the Article II treaty process when completing their international agreements is premised on the notion that presidents, according to the U.S. Supreme Court, may legally use treaties and executive agreements interchangeably. Hence presidents are expected to use executive agreements, which are easier to codify, as a means to circumvent an unwilling Senate. As the definition of an unwilling Senate amounts to only one-third of the body needed to block a treaty, widespread use of executive agreements to evade the Senate would be expected, especially in a competitive era of party control. Additionally, with politically difficult matters accomplished via executive agreements, it is easy to understand why treaty floor defeats over the last half century can be counted on one hand. Treaty consent in the Senate, as understood by this logic, becomes pro forma.

The previous chapters of this book beat back much received wisdom on the rise of executive agreements. The evasion hypothesis receives little support. In terms of explanatory power, it is eclipsed by an efficiency rationale for the rise of executive agreements. Indeed, we begin to understand why the Senate would approve of presidential employment of executive agreements on a vast majority of international agreements. In this chapter and the next one, we turn to the other side of the conventional wisdom, the piece that suggests that treaty consent is largely pro forma. The theoretical framework presented in the introduction to this book predicts that presidents will still send many major items through as treaties in order to retain the Senate's blessing to continue to use the executive agreement mechanism. In other words, we expect that there should be a strong element of politics on these major items sent through as treaties. Our analysis up to this point suggests that the politics will be largely institutional and ideological, rather than partisan.

In this chapter, we illustrate the politics of the Senate process by profiling four prominent treaties sent to the Senate for advice and consent. As readers will see, each of these treaties faced a very different set of circumstances and unique obstacles. In chapter 5, we examine treaty consideration and delay systematically by analyzing the process for all treaties over more than five decades. In this chapter, before moving to the four case studies of Senate advice and consent, we begin with a discussion of previous literature on treaty advice and consent.

Previous Work on Treaty Advice and Consent

Through a process designed in the Constitution, presidents negotiate treaties with other countries and then submit them to the Senate for advice and consent. The treaty consent process formally starts when the president transmits the treaty to the Senate. The treaty is automatically referred to the Senate Foreign Relations Committee (Senate Rule XXV), which must act on a resolution of ratification, with conditions if applicable, before the full Senate can take up the treaty for advice and consent. At the floor stage, a two-thirds vote of those present is required for the Senate to give its advice and consent to the treaty. The House of Representatives has no formal role.[1] Amendment and reservations require only majority approval. Unlike legislation or nominations, treaties remain on the SFRC's calendar until action is taken. Therefore, treaties carry over from one two-year Congress to the next, and action in a previous Congress is valid in later Congresses. A treaty that fails to receive the necessary support in the full Senate is returned to the SFRC, where it sits on the committee calendar indefinitely until the committee reports it to the chamber again or until the treaty is returned to the president by simple resolution.[2]

Given the importance of treaties and the interesting subtleties that potentially exist as the Senate considers them, why have scholars tended to ignore the study of the treaty consent process? One reason why very little systematic research has been done on treaty consent may be because of the conventional wisdom that treaty advice and consent is pro forma and therefore politically uninteresting. Certainly, examples abound where the Senate has played an important role in shaping treaties through the consent process.[3] But for the most part, the modern treaty process is not largely political according to conventional understanding. Such an assumption proceeds from consideration of final outcomes of Senate floor votes on treaties, which rarely result in failure. Indeed, the Senate has rejected final passage on treaty consent only three times since 1949 (O'Brien 2003: 74). Because so few treaties actually fail on floor votes, a presumption of success dominates our current understanding of the treaty consent process. As a result, scholars routinely conclude that presidents dominate the process, as the Senate only rarely asserts its key power of advice and consent (e.g., Frye 1994).

Clearly, the senatorial politics of treaty consent deserves closer scrutiny than political scientists have given it. As the substantial diplomatic benefits "can be lost without Senate consent," the domestic politics of treaties are as important as the negotiations leading to the agreement (Krepon and Caldwell 1991: 1). The two processes (negotiation and ratification) are clearly intertwined (Putnam 1988),[4] yet we do not have a firm and generalizable understanding of the politics that occur in the Senate, as most systematic study has focused on the negotiation of agreements rather than on their domestic ratification (Krepon and Caldwell 1991).

The prevailing wisdom has been challenged by recent scholarship on the treaty process. As Auerswald and Maltzman's (2003) analysis of the Senate's propensity to attach reservations to treaties suggests, the Senate can use the treaty process to have important effects on American foreign policy (see also Auerswald 2006). Analysis of Senate voting on arms control treaties suggests that political considerations are often salient (DeLaet and Scott 2006). This recent work, however, by focusing on final outcomes on treaties, misses interesting prefloor activity and those cases that falter in committee.[5] To illustrate, treaties sometimes appear and reappear on committee agendas without ever receiving floor consideration, and numerous treaties languish on the calendars of the SFRC or Senate. Indeed, from 1949 to 2000, of the 850 treaties transmitted to the Senate, 46 were rejected, ignored, or left pending by the SFRC. An additional 17 treaties were reported by the SFRC and placed on the Senate calendar but failed at the floor stage due to inaction.

We have already shown that presidents do not routinely evade the Senate through the use of executive agreements on their most significant international agreements. When they do circumvent the Senate, the empirical record suggests that presidents are not doing so strategically. Rather, they are seeking an efficient conclusion to their international agreements. Hence the notion that the treaty consent process is pro forma is likely misinformed, since presidents send even their controversial treaties to the Senate for consent. The fact remains, however, that treaties are regularly given consent without much political fanfare. Despite this generalization, the historical record indicates that some treaties submitted for advice and consent do face stiff opposition and may require significant expenditures of political capital on the part of the White House to get through the Senate intact. We now turn to four such cases. Our evidence suggests that costly politics can arise when presidents take their important international agreements to the Senate for formal consent and that analyses of both Senate treaty outcomes as well as Senate delay can prove fruitful for our understanding of this complex interinstitutional relationship.

The U.S.-Soviet Consular Treaty

Our relations with the Soviet Union and Eastern Europe are also in transition. I have tried to differ quietly and with courtesy, and without venom. Our basic objective is not to continue the Cold War, but to end it.
>—President Lyndon Johnson in his State of the Union address of January 10, 1967

Extremist groups in our society fear Polish hams as much as they fear any new gesture toward world peace.
>—Senator Thruston Morton (R-KY) on the Senate floor on January 31, 1967

I'm not impervious to misconceptions.
>—Senate minority leader Everett McKinley Dirksen (R-IL) explaining his change of position to supporting the U.S.-Soviet Consular Treaty after being staunchly opposed just a few weeks prior

The highly salient battle that played out over Senate consideration of the U.S.-Soviet Consular Treaty in 1967 was as unlikely as it was fascinating. Just two months prior to the March 16 final floor vote on the resolution of ratification, the prospects for Senate passage of the first bilateral agreement between the countries looked quite bleak. In the wake of his January 10 State of the Union message, President Johnson and his congressional liaison staff resigned themselves to a continued shelving of the pact. It appeared that the president had nowhere near the two-thirds majority required for Senate consent. Indeed, there were isolationist tendencies within both political parties, leading to bipartisan suspicion on completing a bilateral pact with the Soviets.

In part, what transpired over the next several weeks was fascinating because of the long cast of characters. This treaty process had it all, from J. Edgar Hoover at the FBI to Senator Dirksen leaving his hospital bed to vote in favor, from the Liberty Lobby's "The Communist's Next Door" cartoon (Liberty Lobby 1967) to Senator Fulbright's criticism of President Johnson's Vietnam policy. Before describing the spectacle of Senate consideration, we first frame the context and background of the U.S.-Soviet Consular Treaty.

Background

In terms of substance, the U.S.-Soviet Consular Treaty pertained to consulates, which are distinct from embassies. Countries with formal diplomatic relations establish embassies within each other's borders to be the focal points for diplomatic relations. All through the Cold War, even when relations were at their chilliest, the United States and the Soviet Union each maintained an embassy in the other country, with an ambassador therein residing. However, as relations chilled after World War II, the two countries had long since abandoned jointly established consulates, locations around the partner country established in addition to the central embassy. Consulates exist to represent the nongovernmental aspects of a country, including individual citizens visiting that country and business interests (U.S. Department of State 2007).

The Soviet Union set up consulates in New York and San Francisco in 1934, and the United States established a consulate in Vladivostok in 1941. Over the ensuing few years, as the Americans and the Soviets fought together as allies during World War II, additional consulates were established in both countries. Then, relations between the United States and the Soviet Union (and the East and West more generally) quickly digressed as the Soviets closed the iron curtain, and the Cold War took off in the wake of World War II. As *Time* (1967) reported, a negative, catalyzing event occurred in 1948: "A Soviet Consul General kidnapped Oksana Stepanovna Kasenkina after her escape from Russia's New York consulate, where she was a schoolteacher. She later escaped again by leaping from the consulate's third floor, and became a U.S. citizen before her death in 1960." The next moves were swift; the Soviet Union removed all of its consulates in August 1948, and the United States followed suit one month later (*CQ Almanac* 1968).

The United States Moves Next, Then LBJ

After more than ten years of tension and suspicion between countries that did not want much at all to do with each other, the United States initiated talks with the Soviet Union to reestablish consulates and improve bilateral relations. The Eisenhower administration made the first such move, but ultimately the talks failed, as the Soviets were not interested in what they considered to be too big of a step. Relations cooled again early in the Kennedy administration, culminating in the Bay of Pigs Invasion and the subsequent Cuban Missile Crisis of 1962. The frightening standoff between the United States and the Soviet Union over missiles in Cuba and the skirting of World War III brought on by a clandestine deal between representatives of Kennedy and Khrushchev set the stage for improved subsequent relations.[6] Tragically, President Kennedy's assassination in late 1963 came before talks could progress further.

President Lyndon Johnson made improved U.S.-Soviet relations a priority early in his presidency. To Johnson, it made perfect logical sense to pursue a program to build bridges of understanding to Eastern Europe. He saw no incentive to continue the Cold War indefinitely; we had seen, after all, what the Cold War could lead to, when we almost went to war against the Soviets in 1962 over missiles in Cuba. Ending the Cold War was an explicit goal of Johnson's administration. Just a few months after taking over the presidency, he pursued talks regarding consular relations with the Soviets. These talks took place periodically in Moscow, until an agreement was announced by President Johnson on May 27, 1964. The formal signing of the treaty took place on June 1, 1964, also in Moscow.

In addition to representing the first-ever bilateral pact forged by the two Cold War adversaries, the U.S.-Soviet Consular Treaty sought to accomplish two main purposes. First, it provided a framework for the two countries to reestablish an exchange of consulates. While the matter of how many such consulates and where they would be located would be left to future negotiations, it was reported that the United States wanted to locate one in Leningrad and that the Soviets wanted to establish one in Chicago. Second, the treaty gave immunity to all consulate officials and employees. *Time* (1967: 2) reported of the treaty, "It requires the Soviet government to notify U.S. officials within three days of the arrest of any American (18,000 now visit Russia annually) and to permit a visit within four days." Contemporary scholars of international law hailed the convention as a significant step in improving relations between the two superpowers (see Lay and Lillich 1965).

The Johnson administration maintained that the pact would improve relations with the Soviets and the Eastern Bloc and would provide a means to view activity inside the closed doors of the Soviet Union. LBJ also argued that the notification provisions previously detailed would serve to provide a safer environment for Americans in the Soviet Union (*CQ Almanac* 1967). Many observers saw these two areas of provision (consulates and immunity) as minor and mostly symbolic of more things to come between the two superpowers (e.g., nuclear weapons agreements). *Time* (1967: 2) described the pact as "actually not more than a footbridge," drawing a size reference to LBJ's imagery of building bridges with the East. However, as will become quite clear through the subsequent discussion, many others in various walks of life in the United States saw any sort of agreement with the Soviet Union in the mid-1960s as a major step in the wrong direction and a very bad precedent to set with an enemy that could not be trusted, especially in light of increased conflict over Vietnam. The basic fear was that the Soviets would use the consulates to expand espionage activities and that communism would have an easier time spreading if there were multiple consulates (Liberty Lobby 1965, 1967; Dobriansky 1967).

Submittal to the Senate, Committee Action, and Then Stalemate

President Johnson submitted the U.S.-Soviet Consular Treaty to the Senate on June 12, 1964, eleven days after he had signed the pact in Moscow (*CQ Almanac* 1968). As are all treaties, it was referred to the Senate Foreign Relations Committee immediately. The committee did not hold hearings on the treaty in 1964, reportedly "because the Johnson administration feared that the Convention might become an issue during the 1964 presidential election campaign" (*CQ Almanac* 1968: 191).

After being elected to the presidency in 1964, LBJ pursued his vision of improved U.S.-Soviet relations with new vigor in 1965. The SFRC held hearings over the summer and reported the treaty to the full Senate on August 3, 1965. However, once the floor environment was surveyed, it was decided by Senate Democratic leaders and White House officials that there was simply too much opposition to attempt a floor battle that year. Conservative (and isolationist) Republican and Democratic senators were aligned against the treaty, including Senate minority leader Everett Dirksen (R-IL). Several right-wing groups mobilized against the convention.

The most salient of the right-wing opposition groups was the Liberty Lobby, which started a grassroots campaign as soon as the treaty was submitted to the Senate. While we will save most of our references to this group for later in the chapter (when we discuss the final push for the treaty in 1967), it is here worth exploring a few references that arose in 1965, after the initial SFRC report. In a fund-raising letter to 160,000 subscribers, the Liberty Lobby was aggressive from the start.

> These [consulates] are not ordinary offices! Behind their massive walls, the American Constitution DOES NOT APPLY! Through their doors, no American may enter—not even a policeman in pursuit of a murderer, rapist—or kidnapper. Within their chambers, the intelligence officers of the Soviet Union can plan the Communist assault on *your* freedom with complete immunity. (Liberty Lobby 1965)

The fund-raising effort worked, and a grassroots letter-writing campaign ensued that summer and fall of 1965 between thousands of citizens and their senators. Similarly dramatic claims were made in the resulting correspondence from constituents to their senators.[7]

In addition to this opposition, the Johnson administration's own FBI director, J. Edgar Hoover, expressed significant concerns about the pact, in a hearing before the House Appropriations Committee on the FBI budget. When asked about the potential impact of several new Soviet consulates on his job at the FBI, he said that such a development would make things more difficult. As all of this opposition continued into 1966, together with an escalating situation in Vietnam, the administration asked the Senate Democratic leadership not to move forward with floor consideration. *CQ Almanac* (1968: 188) reported, "The Administration feared that the treaty would not receive the two-thirds Senate majority needed for treaty approval and that failure to pass the treaty would unnecessarily aggravate U.S.-Soviet relations."

Breakthrough in 1967, Then an Opposition Lobbying Campaign

In his State of the Union address on January 10, 1967, President Johnson extolled the virtues of bringing the East and West closer together. He said that ratifying the consular treaty would be one important step toward achieving this goal (U.S. Government Printing Office 1968). At first, the speech did not seem to move anyone on the issue. Vote counts in mid-January continued to show the administration falling well short of garnering the numbers needed for Senate consent. However, while not directly changing senators' minds, the speech apparently mobilized an ally.

On January 31, Senator Thruston B. Morton (R-KY), an international-ist Republican who had been assumed, in previous years, to be against the treaty or, at best, undecided, rose on the Senate floor to give an impassioned speech about the importance of ratifying the U.S.-Soviet Consular Treaty. In so doing, he accused opponents of the treaty of spreading paranoia and called on American leaders to rise above the smoke and mirrors and support the treaty. Morton also called directly on President Johnson to be much more active in supporting the treaty, to no longer delay its consideration, and to "fight hard" for its passage (*Congressional Record* 1967, January 31). Morton's effort was independent. The White House was pleasantly surprised when his campaign for passage unfolded, and it did indeed motivate the president to press harder for passage.

During a press conference two days later, President Johnson made reference to being asked to make a statement about the treaty (U.S. Government Printing Office 1968), which one outlet said was a reference to the speech by Senator Morton two days earlier (*CQ Almanac* 1967). The president went on to make his strongest and boldest argument for the treaty to date.

> I feel very strongly that the ratification of this treaty is very much in our national interest. I feel this way for two principal reasons: First, we need this treaty to protect the 18,000 American citizens who each year travel from this country to the Soviet Union . . . Second, the convention does not require the opening of consulates in this country or in the Soviet Union. It does provide that should any such consulates be opened, the officials would have diplomatic immunity. (U.S. Government Printing Office 1967)

In the same speech, President Johnson attempted to allay concerns related to J. Edgar Hoover's earlier statement to the Senate that having several new consulates would make the FBI's job of Soviet surveillance more difficult. Hoover's thoughts on the treaty had been the subject of an SFRC hearing on January 23, though Hoover himself was not present. In his February 2 address, the president stated that only one consulate per country was likely and that ten to fifteen Soviets were to be employed in the consulate. President Johnson then finished the point by saying, "Mr. Hoover has assured me that this small increment would raise no problems which the FBI cannot effectively and efficiently deal with" (U.S. Government Printing Office 1968).[8]

After Senator Morton's floor pleas and after President Johnson strongly made his case to the Washington community and the public, the Senate process was once again jump-started. The SFRC held more hearings. While some debate between committee members transpired, the main component of both hearings was testimony by interest groups for and against the treaty. In this regard, the crescendo produced by Senator Morton and President Johnson produced what was arguably the largest ever amount of direct involvement by interest groups at a hearing on a treaty.

Those speaking against the treaty far outnumbered those supporting it. Almost all of the speakers against the treaty were invited by Senator Karl E. Mundt (R-SD), who was opposed to the treaty (*CQ Almanac* 1968). The opponents (those who were not themselves senators) included a Georgetown professor (Dobriansky 1967); the American Legion; the Liberty Lobby (the only group officially asked to speak by the committee); the *Manion Forum;* the *Dan Smoot Report;* the United Republicans of America; the *National Review;* the Mothers of American Servicemen of South Pasadena, California; and a retired chief of naval operations. Supporting the treaty were former president Dwight Eisenhower, the executive board of the American Automobile Workers, the American Veterans Committee, former senator and Republican presidential nominee Barry Goldwater (R-AZ), and the executive council of the AFL-CIO.

One of the most colorful characters at a February 17 hearing was W. B. Hicks, who represented the Liberty Lobby. As mentioned earlier, this organization opposed all efforts to establish relations with the Soviet Union or to surrender any U.S. sovereignty to other countries via any treaties of this sort. Hicks said, "The treaty is a blank check for Soviet spies as well as an invitation to Russia to import anything from narcotics to A-bombs to the United States under the cover of diplomatic immunity" (*CQ Almanac* 1968: 192). When Senator Eugene McCarthy (D-MN) pressed him on facts and evidence, Hicks admitted to his lack of objectivity but said, "It is inescapable that the emotional response of the people today wouldn't allow passage of the treaty" (*CQ Almanac* 1968: 192).

Constituent letters to U.S. senators—an admittedly nonsystematic measure of intensity of opinion on the treaty—appear to bear out Hicks's claim. *CQ Almanac* (1968: 188) reported, "Senators complained that they were swamped by mail, which was, to a large extent, generated by these [conservative] organizations. Opposition to the treaty far outweighed support for it." For example, in a letter dated January 26, 1967, Ms. Ethel Reynolds of Elk City, Oklahoma, wrote to Senator Fred Harris (D-OK), "I do not want Soviet spies living and working in our cities. I and my neighbors would find it very hard to understand how any senator could ignore the warning J. Edgar Hoover gave in his testimony before the House Appropriations Committee on March 4, 1965."[9]

One of the more important factors in inciting constituent action against the treaty was the Liberty Lobby's cartoon "The Communists Next Door" (Liberty Lobby 1967). In addition to sending a copy to its growing membership of more than 170,000 people, the group paid to have this cartoon printed as an advertisement in twenty-seven newspapers around the country. Other groups and individuals came forward with additional money to enable the cartoon to be printed in seventeen more outlets (*CQ Almanac* 1968). The sixteen-panel cartoon took up an entire newspaper page. It begins with background on how the Soviets misused their previous consulates, particularly the New York consulate in the Kasenkina case. The cartoon then jumps directly into persuasion: "By June 1964, the horror of the Kasenkina case had been forgotten by U.S. State Department officials. They signed with the Reds a Soviet Consular Treaty . . . an agreement to open new consulates in the U.S.A.!" The remainder of the cartoon includes references to J. Edgar Hoover's concerns about new consulates, the problem with granting full immunity to the enemy, and the potential for these consul employees to bring in arms: "Suitcase sized A-bombs weighing 70 pounds or more, and highly destructive, can be scattered across the U.S.A.!" At the end of the cartoon, the group urged all Americans to contact their two U.S. senators and listed the names of the local elected officials.

Reported from Committee Again, Then Final Passage

On February 28, 1967, eleven days after holding a hearing in which every person giving testimony to the committee spoke against the U.S.-Soviet Consular Treaty, the SFRC voted (like they did in 1965) to support the treaty. The vote was fifteen for the treaty and four against, a strong endorsement of Senate consent, despite the vocal opposition from interest groups and grassroots organizations. The committee formally reported the treaty to the full Senate on March 3, 1967.

In between the committee vote on February 28 and the floor vote on March 16, several key factors entered into the case. First, Senator Everett Dirksen, a Republican and the minority leader, came out in support of the treaty. This was a significant revelation because Dirksen had been quite vocal against the treaty only weeks prior. The Senator was apparently persuaded by the floor speech in which Senator Morton (R-KY) called on the Senate and the president to do the right thing and rise above the paranoia.

With Dirksen's support came several other like-minded senators—namely, Republicans about whom the administration was very nervous.

In addition to impacting Dirksen's change of mind, Senator Morton made another significant impact as well. He recommended to the Democratic leaders in the Senate and the Johnson administration that Senator Fulbright, chairman of the SFRC, not serve as the floor leader for debate and final consideration of the treaty. On treaties, it was common to have the committee chairman, not the majority leader, serve in such a capacity. Senator Morton thought that having the majority leader, Senator Mike Mansfield (D-MT), run the floor debate would be more persuasive to Republicans than having Fulbright do so. Senator Fulbright was a lightning rod at the time, because of his regular criticism of Vietnam (*CQ Almanac* 1968).

Floor consideration of the U.S.-Soviet Consular Treaty took eight days. When the Senate carries out its role of advice and consent on treaties, it is permitted to modify or qualify the treaty through simple majority vote. Doing so is typically not preferred by the president who pursues final ratification. Indeed, such changes can also be proposed in order to kill a treaty (so-called killer amendments). The Senate may also add reservations and understandings, all of which could complicate final ratification of the treaty.

During floor consideration of the U.S.-Soviet Consular Treaty, six such parliamentary challenges were made by opponents prior to the vote on final passage. The administration staunchly opposed all six maneuvers, arguing that adopting any of them would essentially render the treaty null and void. Of these six formal challenges, one was an amendment, four were reservations, and one was an understanding. On March 9, the Senate rejected an amendment by Senator Herman Talmadge (D-GA) to provide immunity to consular officials for misdemeanors but not for felonies. The amendment received forty-two votes, nine shy of the threshold needed to adopt the amendment. A series of four reservations were proposed and defeated on March 14 and 15. The first reservation, which was offered by Senator Karl Mundt (R-SD), a leading opponent on the SFRC, dealt with the idea of a free press and general information distribution. It only attracted twenty-two votes of support. The second reservation, also brought by Senator Mundt, required that the president delay ratification of the treaty until U.S. forces were no longer needed for combat duty in Vietnam. It failed as well, receiving only fifteen votes. A similar reservation pertaining to Soviet aid to the North Vietnamese, which was offered by Senator Carl Curtis (R-NE), also failed, garnering only twenty votes. Senator Strom Thurmond (R-SC) proposed the fourth and final reservation. His proposal held that nothing in the treaty is taken to mean that the United States does not retain the right to protect itself. It failed with only twenty-four votes in support. The last proposal to alter the treaty came as an understanding from Senator Margaret Chase Smith (R-ME). Senator Chase proposed that no consulates be allowed to open until the situation in Vietnam was settled. With thirty-eight votes, this proposal received more support than the four reservations but still fell well short of a simple majority. The treaty had remained intact after multiple days of formal attempts to gut it (*CQ Almanac* 1968).

While the resounding defeats of the reservations suggested a coalition willing to support final passage, the narrower defeats of the amendment and the understanding made floor leaders and the president wary of the final outcome. Still, they pressed on. The final floor vote was taken on March 16. Of the ninety-four senators present, sixty-six voted to support the resolution of ratification, and twenty-eight voted against it. Hence the U.S.-Soviet Consular Treaty, which had appeared dead in the water in mid-January, had passed the Senate by a three-vote margin three months later. President Johnson ratified the treaty on March 31.

Opposition to the treaties came primarily from the conservative (isolationist) wings of the political parties, suggesting the significance of ideology in the final outcome. While a major victory for internationalist foreign policy, the consular treaty presents a clear example of why domestic politics are critical to outcomes on international agreements in the U.S. setting. The treaty was indeed significant, and its delayed ratification proved frustrating for the Johnson administration and threatened to derail an important additional step toward improving U.S.-Soviet relations. Moreover, the case suggests the importance of prefloor activity, including committee politics and leadership on the part of the president and Senate leaders, to eventual Senate consideration and consent to a treaty.

The Panama Canal Treaties

These treaties are fair and equitable, and essential to assure the continued effective use of the canal for American commercial and security needs. I urge you to support the treaties and to help in laying the facts before the public . . . I ask this of you in what I truly believe to be our highest national interest. I need your help.

    —President Jimmy Carter in a handwritten personal letter to U.S. senator Dewey Bartlett (R-OK) on November 5, 1977

As you know, the proponents are likely to conduct the floor fight on behalf of the Panama Canal Treaties on an Article-by-Article basis. Accordingly, I would like to suggest that we also divide up so that each of us can concentrate his efforts for optimal, overall results . . . [I]t would insure that we have at least two knowledgeable opposition spokesmen on the floor to rebut proponents' arguments at all times.

—Senator Paul Laxalt (R-NV), leader of the opposition, in a personal letter to fellow opponent Senator Dewey Bartlett on February 7, 1978

As early as the Andrew Jackson administration in the 1830s, the United States recognized the strategic, commercial, and military advantages of building a canal across Panama or Nicaragua to connect the Pacific and Atlantic Oceans (Mack 1944). President Jackson sent a representative to survey potential routes across the isthmus connecting South and Central America (*CQ Almanac* 1979). Although a canal would have to wait until much later, the United States opened a railroad across Panama in 1855 to run goods from the Pacific to the Atlantic and vice versa. This arrangement created certain transaction costs as goods were moved from ship to train and then back to ship. However, the costs were still less than those incurred during the six to eight weeks required to sail a vessel around the tip of South America.

With the distraction of the Civil War and the rebuilding that took place after it, support for the canal decreased, as other needs were more immediate (Mack 1944). However, in 1898, interest in a canal again took center stage during the U.S. engagement in the Spanish-American War, when the U.S. Atlantic fleet needed reinforcement from the Pacific fleet. To accomplish this, "the battleship Oregon took 68 days to sail from San Francisco through the Strait of Magellan to reach the Atlantic fleet" (*CQ Almanac* 1979: 381). The press had a heyday with the story, calling for the construction of a canal and claiming public support for the same. At the time, the French had already begun to build a waterway across the Panamanian isthmus. The company of Suez Canal builder Ferdinand de Lesseps began construction in 1898, but the project and company went bankrupt in 1899, before they could get very far along in construction (*CQ Almanac* 1979; Mack 1944).

President William McKinley next set up the Isthmian Canal Commission to study the bankrupt French project. Included in this study was pricing information should the United States want to purchase the land and project from France. Aware of the intense American desire to build such a canal, the French engaged in price gouging by elevating the asking price.

The U.S. commission cleverly recommended that an alternative canal site in Nicaragua would be more cost-effective. Having learned of this, the French suddenly lowered their asking price for the property and rights of the canal in Panama to forty million dollars. The U.S. commission then recommended buying the nascent project from the French instead of starting anew in Nicaragua (Mack 1944).

In 1902, Congress approved and the president signed the Spooner Act, which formalized the offer to the French, provided that Colombia (of which Panama was a part at that time) would agree to deed the required land for the Canal Zone. In early 1903, the U.S. secretary of state, John Hay, and the Colombian ambassador to the United States, Tomas Herran, signed a treaty that provided the land per the Spooner Act. In March, the U.S. Senate quickly consented to the treaty. However, officials higher up in the Colombian government ultimately rejected the pact in August (Mack 1944). CQ Almanac (1979: 381) reported, "Reluctant to lose the canal and desirous of independence from Colombia in any event, [the] Panamanians staged a successful revolution on November 3, 1903." The United States immediately recognized the new government and country three days later. Shortly thereafter, Secretary Hay negotiated a treaty with the Panamanian minister to the United States, Philippe Jean Bunau-Varilla. The treaty was quickly ratified by Panama and then consented to by the U.S. Senate the following February (Mack 1944).

The Hay–Bunau-Varilla Treaty, as it came to be called, gave the United States a ten-mile-wide strip of land for the canal in perpetuity. The United States was also given power and authority over the Canal Zone as if it were a territory. CQ Almanac (1979: 381) reported, "In return, the United States paid Panama $10 million, plus annual fees of $250,000 beginning in 1913. The treaty was revised in 1936 and 1955,[10] increasing annual U.S. payments to Panama to $1.93 million." The canal was finally completed in 1914, with direct costs of close to four hundred million dollars and indirect costs of many millions more (Mack 1944).

Issues of sovereignty quickly arose after the treaty's signing and especially after the completion of the canal. As might be the case for a foreign business, the Panamanians always saw the entire Panama Canal system as owned by the United States but still on Panamanian land. Panamanians also eventually were resentful that their main economic engine was owned by someone else and that the United States was behaving as if it were sovereign (Jackson and Storrs 1978). Many in the U.S. government interpreted the "perpetuity" aspect of the treaty to mean much more than that—to essentially give the United States a satellite over which it had full control (Mack 1944). The two nations persisted with the tense arrangement until conflict emerged about the flying of flags in the area. The United States had long flown its flag there. *CQ Almanac* (1979: 382) reported, "In 1959 Panama requested that her flag be flown alongside the American flag in the Canal Zone. Despite strong opposition in Congress, including a House resolution, approved by a vote of 381–12, protesting such action, President Dwight Eisenhower allowed the two flags to be flown together at certain sites." However, neither flag was to be flown on school grounds within the Canal Zone.

When a group of American students disobeyed that order and flew the American flag at their school on January 7, 1964, anti-American riots quickly broke out (Jackson and Storrs 1978). Four Americans and twenty-one Panamanians died in the violent exchange, and the Panamanians ended relations with the United States because of it (*CQ Almanac* 1979). Jackson and Storrs (1978: 2) explain, "[This] provided the impetus to reopening treaty negotiations. The Joint Declaration of Apr. 3, 1964, between representatives of the United States and Panama committed the parties to negotiations which would accommodate, in part, Panamanian claims." In June 1967, President Lyndon Johnson and Panamanian president Marco Aurelio Robles reported that three new pacts had been negotiated, the central one calling for a binational commission to run the Panama Canal. Congressional opposition was so considerable that the treaties were never submitted for consent by President Johnson. One year later, a militarist regime took over in Panama, placing General Omar Torrijos Herrera in charge. The general quickly rejected the draft treaties because they did not assuage Panamanian concerns adequately.

Canal Consideration in the 1970s

The core choice in the Panama Canal Treaties, whether or not to give control of the Panama Canal and the surrounding Canal Zone to the Panamanians, was a salient foreign policy issue at the presidential level at many points throughout the 1970s. President Richard Nixon picked up in 1970 where President Lyndon Johnson had left off, with bilateral talks on the future of the canal that included some additional benefits for Panama (Jackson and Storrs 1978). By this time, the Panamanians had long wished the United States would abandon its "occupation" of the Canal Zone. In 1974, President Nixon dispatched the secretary of state, Henry Kissinger, to work out an agreement of principles with the Panamanian government. Secretary Kissinger and Panamanian foreign minister Juan Tack signed an agreement of principles as the basis for formal negotiations. Once Watergate broke, the effort took a backseat, as Nixon resigned and Ford became president.

The Panama Canal issue next took on importance in the Republican primaries in the 1976 presidential election, in which former governor of California Ronald Reagan repeatedly hammered President Ford, who favored giving some authority to the Panamanians since the canal sits within their country. Reagan's repeated tagline was, "We bought it, we paid for it, we built it and we intend to keep it" (*CQ Almanac* 1978: 383). Reagan's stance on the canal resonated with Americans, who saw the canal as a source of pride and American ingenuity. For many decades, the canal had struck a patriotic chord with Americans. After all, American vision and engineering technology had made the travel of ships between the Pacific and Atlantic oceans possible. To Panama and other countries in the hemisphere, continued American occupation of the Canal Zone smacked of American imperialism. What would eventually transpire during the Carter administration and in the Senate is an illustrative tale of the politics present in treaty making.

Though growing public opposition to give up the Panama Canal emanated from the 1976 Republican primaries, President Jimmy Carter nonetheless moved quickly to negotiate two treaties with General Torrijos during Carter's first six months in office. President Carter and General Torrijos signed the treaties on September 7, 1977. The first treaty (occasionally referred to as the "basic treaty") was called the Panama Canal Treaty, and the second was called the Treaty concerning the Permanent Neutrality and Operation of the Panama Canal (also known as the Neutrality Treaty).

The first, or basic, treaty would confirm Panama's sovereignty over the Canal Zone; terminate the treaties of 1903, 1936, and 1955; and expire on December 31, 1999 (i.e., it would not be in perpetuity like the 1903 treaty). At this expiration point, Panama would have sole ownership of the Panama Canal and the Canal Zone. The United States would operate the canal basically as it had all along, until the year 2000. However, Panama would immediately assume jurisdiction over the Canal Zone, acquire land within the Canal Zone not needed for operation of the canal, and receive a larger share of canal tolls (Jackson and Storrs 1978; Moore 1977). With the second treaty, the Neutrality Treaty, both countries agreed to keep a permanent arrangement of neutrality pertaining to the canal. The Neutrality Treaty also would guarantee both the United States and the Republic of Panama the right to defend the permanent neutrality of the waterway.

Reaction to the announced treaties was quick and forceful. Opponents

were arguably louder, judging from press coverage and the flow of constituent mail to senators whose papers we examined in the Carl Albert
Center Congressional Archives in 2005. In addition, a *CBS News/New York
Times* poll taken shortly after the treaties were signed showed that 49 percent of Americans were against the treaties, while only 29 percent approved; 22 percent were undecided. The opponents thought it important
for U.S. sovereignty (which they assumed existed all along) to continue in
the Canal Zone, to assure "the defense and efficient operation of that vital
enterprise" (Jackson and Storrs 1978: 2).[11] The proposed treaties did not
promise to continue that sovereignty and indeed handed it, as well as
ownership of the canal, over to the Republic of Panama. With the canal in
Panama's hands, how could the United States be assured that its ships
could pass through? In discussing a further concern, American Legion national commander Robert Smith (1977: 3) argued, "Should the canal ever
be closed to U.S. ships, the Commerce Department estimates a \$932 mil-
lion jump in the price of U.S. exports, a \$583 million jump in the price of
imports. The impact would be chaotic." In making reference to the *CBS
News/New York Times* poll mentioned earlier, Senator Dewey Bartlett (R-
OK) posited, "The survey demonstrates that the Treaties are unpopular
because they simply do not guarantee the absolute right of the United
States to intervene to maintain the neutrality of the Panama Canal"
(Bartlett 1977a: 1).

Proponents—including the administration, through their statements—argued that the new treaties enjoyed Panamanian support, not
disdain, and that they provided the best option to secure the canal and
protect U.S. security and commercial interests (Carter 1977; *CQ Almanac*
1979; Jackson and Storrs 1978). Speaking to the angst that Panama felt toward the status quo at the time, President Carter's director of congressional liaison, Frank Moore, argued, "Under the 1903 Treaty, the United
States has total control of Canal operations. The United States also ad-
ministers the Canal Zone—an area of Panamanian territory five miles
wide on either side of the Canal. In this area Panama has sovereignty while
we have 'as-if-sovereign' rights permanently. This arrangement is deeply
resented in Panama and a liability in our relations with Latin America and
with many other nations of the world." He went on to say, "In negotiating
a new treaty, the United States has proceeded on the basis that its national
interest lies in assuring that the Canal continues to be efficiently operated,
secure, neutral, and open to all nations on a non-discriminatory basis.
Fundamental to this objective is the cooperation of Panama" (Moore
1977: 4–5).

In terms of consent to ratification, the two countries must follow very different processes. The United States has the Senate treaty consent process, which requires a two-thirds vote of those present and voting on final passage of the resolution consenting to ratification. President Carter submitted the treaty to the Senate on September 16, 1977. The Republic of Panama requires a plebiscite, or vote of the people, to confirm; a similar two-thirds threshold must be met. After already submitting the treaty to the Senate, Carter administration officials contemplated the Senate treaty consent process with the Senate powers that be. As hearings began in the SFRC in late September, administration officials promptly received feedback from Senate leaders about a central concern that could jeopardize the treaties when they were formally considered in the Senate (Jackson and Storrs 1978). Senators thought that the wording of key provisions in the Neutrality Treaty did not assure the United States the ability to defend the canal's neutrality or the expeditious passage of American ships through the Panama Canal during emergencies. On October 14, 1977, President Carter and General Torrijos formulated an additional "understanding" that explicitly allowed the United States to defend the canal if its neutrality was in question and that allowed U.S. ships to move to the front of the line of waiting ships (Jackson and Storrs 1978; U.S. Government Printing Office 1978).[12] Many people were concerned that these concessions by the general would negatively affect the Panamanian vote to be held nine days later, on October 23. The concern was that the people of Panama might see the changes as indication that the United States was again bullying the small Central American country. While the changes were criticized by some in Panama, they did not appear to have a substantial effect on public opinion. The plebiscite comfortably passed the two-thirds threshold. The general complimented the Panamanian people: "I had no doubt it was going to happen this way because I knew our people would not turn their backs on the country when the country demands their presence" (CQ Almanac 1979: 382).

An Unpredictable Senate Process

While the additional understanding struck by President Carter and General Torrijos made it possible to move forward with a realistic chance of passage, it certainly did not squelch the opposition. CQ Almanac (1978: 385) reported, "Majority Leader [Robert] Byrd (D-WV) said the statement improved chances for Senate ratification, but he cautioned that 'the great majority' of senators were still uncommitted." What would transpire over the next six months was a political battle on many different levels, between internationalists and isolationists, conservatives and liberals, and Republicans and Democrats, all using the unique rules of the Senate that allow considerable debate and amendment.

Hearings, which had begun prior to the new understanding between Carter and Torrijos, continued in the SFRC. In addition, other committees held hearings, including the Senate Armed Services Committee, the Senate Judiciary Committee's Separation of Powers Subcommittee, the House International Relations Committee, the House Armed Services Committee, and the House Merchant Marine and Fisheries Committee's Panama Canal Subcommittee (Jackson and Storrs 1978). President Carter sent the secretary of state, Cyrus Vance, and other present and past officials to make the case for ratification of the two treaties. These leaders touched on several themes. First, they argued that passage of the treaties would garner the United States respect from other nations and set a positive tone for inter-American relations for the foreseeable future. Second and conversely, they posited that blockage of the treaties would be devastating to international relations within the Western Hemisphere and would put the security of the canal in jeopardy. The proponents also argued that passage of the treaties would put the United States in a better position to defend the canal. Finally, administration officials stated that passage did not require additional money from U.S. taxpayers beyond what was already appropriated.

One of the more forceful comments made at the hearings came from former secretary of state Dean Rusk, who said, "If, God forbid, it should ever become necessary for a President and a Congress to take strong measures to keep the canal functioning and safe, they would be in a far stronger position to do so under the treaties of 1977. The Neutrality Pact alone gives the United States all that we need to maintain our essential interests, . . . passage and security of the canal itself" (U.S. Government Printing Office 1978). Other supporters at the hearings and beyond included former president Ford, former secretary of state Henry Kissinger, the AFL-CIO, and the Committee of Americans for the Canal Treaties. Also, while the opponents had former actor (and former California governor) Ronald Reagan in their court, proponents had John Wayne.

Wayne was a frequent visitor to Panama, had lived there for a few years, and was very close with the family of a previous Panamanian president. He had previously been against renegotiation of the earlier treaties (especially in the wake of the coup that put Torrijos in charge in the late 1960s). However, Wayne had studied the issue more closely and had time to ponder how things were going in Panama under Torrijos, and he ultimately changed his mind on the pacts. He sent a letter to U.S. senators on October 11, 1977, clarifying his support for the treaties because "as usual, our dear provocative press misquoted me" (Wayne 1977: 1). The letter contained an attachment of three single-spaced pages, in which he explained his take on the matter and his position of support for both treaties. Wayne had originally been flabbergasted when President Eisenhower allowed the Panamanian flag to be flown inside the Canal Zone. Wayne (1977: 2) wrote, "In checking to find the reason for President Eisenhower's actions, I found that although we had the rights to ownership and jurisdiction of the Canal that Panama had not surrendered sovereignty of same. I also found out that the United States in the Arias-Roosevelt Treaty of 1936, ratified by our Congress in 1939, recognized the sovereignty of Panama in the Canal Zone as it was originally stated in the 1903 agreement." In contrast to the earlier sound bites of Ronald Reagan ("We bought it, we paid for it, we built it and we intend to keep it"), Wayne finished his letter to the senators with eloquence.

> I have carefully studied the Treaty, and I support it based on my belief that America looks always to the future and that our people have demonstrated qualities of justice and reason for 200 years. That attitude has made our country a great Nation. The new Treaty modernizes an outmoded relation with a friendly and hospitable country. It also solves an international question with our other Latin American neighbors, and finally the Treaty protects and legitimates fundamental interests and desires of our Country. (Wayne 1977: 4)

Opponents, including Ronald Reagan, brought their points to the committee process as well. In a September 9 House International Relations Committee hearing (occurring prior to the new understanding struck by Carter and Torrijos), Reagan raised the point that Torrijos had ties to Cuba and Castro and that there was a chance that the Soviet Union and Cuba might increase their hold in Panama. The former California governor offered, "It should never surprise us that whenever the United States withdraws its presence or its strong interest from any areas, the Soviets are ready, willing, and often able to exploit the situation. Can we believe that the Panama Canal is any exception?" (*CQ Almanac* 1979: 383). Another point raised by opponents included the unfairness of the proposed financial arrangement with Panama. Senator Dewey Bartlett (1977b) argued that "the proposed Treaties would cost hundreds of millions of dollars in various forms of assistance to the Republic of Panama."

Opponents also argued that the neutrality language was too vague and did not therefore protect U.S. interests and that the security of the canal would potentially be in jeopardy if the pacts were signed. In addition to Reagan and opposition senators, other opponents at this juncture included the American Legion, the American Conservative Union (ACU), and the ACU's Emergency Coalition to Save the Panama Canal.

The ACU and the American Legion headed up opposition letter-writing campaigns. These campaigns were highly successful, as the constituent mail coming into senators' offices was disproportionately against the treaties. For example, internal memoranda from Senator Bartlett's office showed that correspondence coming into the office regarding the treaties was nine to one against the treaty.[13] In a newsletter to constituents in September, Bartlett (1977b) stated, "In the last three months alone, I have received more than 2,500 cards, letters and petitions from the people of Oklahoma expressing virtually unanimous opposition to any agreement which would surrender the United States' sovereign rights over the Panama Canal and Canal Zone."

One of the more interesting aspects of Senate consideration of the treaties was the frequent-flier miles logged for various field trips of senators and State Department staff to Panama and the Canal Zone "to undertake fact-finding missions" (Jackson and Storrs 1978: 7). The traveling was especially brisk during the winter months of 1977–78, when weather in Panama was decidedly nicer than the cold confines of Capitol Hill or the frigid folkways of Foggy Bottom. Jackson and Storrs (1978: 8) report, "The itinerary of the visits included meetings with General Torrijos and other Panamanian officials, discussions with the U.S. Ambassador and the head of the U.S. Southern Command, and an inspection of the Canal. Among those participating were Senate Majority Leader Byrd, Senate Minority Leader Baker and the entire Senate Foreign Relations Committee."

The Senate minority leader, Howard Baker (R-TN), remained undecided before traveling to Panama. He hence utilized the trip to ask a variety of questions related to his own concerns about the treaties. First, he asked about human rights. Telling Senator Baker and his delegation that "he would improve the human rights situation in Panama," General Torrijos "extended an invitation to the Organization of American States to conduct on-the-spot inspections, and stated that he would resign from office if he was deemed to be an obstacle to ratification of the treaties" (Jackson and Storrs 1978: 8). In a separate communication with the Senate majority leader, Robert Byrd, Torrijos said that some restrictions on political expression had already been rescinded and that censoring would soon stop. Also during his trip, Senator Baker talked with General Torrijos about amending the actual language of the treaty in the Senate, to reflect the October 14 understanding. The general said that would be satisfactory (Jackson and Storrs 1978).[14] On January 16, with those concerns allayed, Senator Baker, to whom many undecided Republican senators were looking, came out in support of both treaties, provided the Neutrality Treaty be amended as previously discussed. A subsequent trip by the entire SFRC further solidified General Torrijos's willingness to amend the Neutrality Treaty. Committee members also learned that such a revision would not require another vote of the Panamanian people.

The SFRC voted to report both treaties favorably on January 30, 1978 (Jackson and Storrs 1978), and the treaties were officially ordered as reported on February 3 (Library of Congress 2005). The committee vote was fourteen in favor to one opposed, with the recommendation that the full Senate amend portions of the Neutrality Treaty to reflect the new Carter-Torrijos understanding. These amendments were later offered jointly by the Senate majority and minority leaders (Byrd and Baker) as amendments 20 and 21 to the treaties.

The Truth Squad and President Carter's Lobbying Efforts

In the wake of the SFRC's overwhelming support in reporting the treaty, a group of twenty senators opposed to the treaty took clear form. They were lead by Senator Paul Laxalt (R-NV), a powerful conservative who would later be President Ronald Reagan's chief lieutenant in the Senate. The group of Senate treaty opponents began to be called the "Truth Squad" because they sought to expose the inadequacies, risks, and innuendo present in the treaty documents. The group met regularly for strategy sessions, often over breakfast in the early morning. They had two main goals. First, the Truth Squad sought to convert undecided senators to opposing votes on the treaties and thereby to defeat the treaties. Second, they organized to make systematic attempts to block the treaty on the floor with delay tactics, to include the raising of amendments and other motions. On the first dimension, the group went so far as to gather and share head counts. Toward this end, Senator Laxalt wrote in a memorandum to the group, "Five among the undecided were considered likely to go in our direction, while four others were considered likely to defect in the event the leadership needed them."[15]

On the second dimension, this organized group of opponents sought to kill the treaties on the floor through delay and the offering of killer amendments. The group went so far as to organize by individual title within each of the treaties, since they had heard that the floor managers would proceed with debate along those lines. One of Senator Bartlett's staffers wrote in a strategy memorandum, "[Senator Laxalt] wants to divide leadership of the anti-treaty forces along functional lines so that experts will be on the floor at all times. Laxalt's letter laid out 6 functional areas to be organized around, from sovereignty and legal matters to economic provisions." A division of labor was sought, with at least two experts on the floor continuously for the given topic. "Ideally," Laxalt wrote, "I would like to see two Senators assume full floor responsibility for each section. This would in no way inhibit anyone's right to speak out against any part of the Treaty. But, it would insure that we have at least two knowledgeable opposition spokesmen on the floor to rebut the proponents arguments at all times. I will be contacting you later with suggested floor times."[16]

The pro-treaty forces were well aware of the existence of the Truth Squad (if not their specific strategies or the "if-you-need-me" votes that could go the leadership's way), and they mobilized to go after undecided senators and retain tentative supporters who had concerns about parts of the treaties. In particular, as *CQ Almanac* (1978: 392) reported, President Carter pulled out all the stops: "President Carter threw virtually every high official of his administration and the nation's defense and foreign policy establishment into the fray in the final days before the vote on the Panama Canal neutrality treaty March 16, 1978. The President courted reluctant senators from the White House with a heavy schedule of phone calls and Oval Office visits." Walter Mondale, then vice president and a former senator, proved especially effective as he interacted with former colleagues. According to *CQ Almanac* (1978: 392), the administration had a policy that any senator could talk to any administration official about the treaty at any time, and "at least one senator, at his request, saw all four of the Joint Chiefs of Staff." The administration claimed that public opinion polls showed strong support for the treaties, once the understanding was in effect.[17]

Floor Debate and Final Passage

Floor debate on the Neutrality Treaty took twenty-two days, beginning the first week of February. This particular pact gave the United States and Panama the permanent right to defend the canal and assure that their ships would get quick passage through during emergencies (Jackson and Storrs 1978). During the lengthy period of floor consideration, dozens of amendments, reservations, and understandings were proposed. Many were proposed by members of the Truth Squad to change the treaties so much that they would be unacceptable to President Carter or General Torrijos. None of these killer amendments passed, though one (to change the order in which the treaties were considered, to take the basic treaty first) came within one vote of passing. Had that passed, many senators would have voted against the basic treaty to give over sovereignty if they did not know what the arrangement would be after 2000. Two amendments (including the Byrd-Baker amendment to revise the treaty per the understanding between Carter and Torrijos from the previous fall) passed, as did two minor reservations and five understandings (Jackson and Storrs 1978). After opponents failed to win a majority on any of their amendments, they surprisingly agreed to a final passage vote, to be taken March 16.

The Senate voted to consent to the ratification of the amended Neutrality Treaty by sixty-eight to thirty-two (with one more favorable vote than the sixty-seven required to muster the two-thirds majority). In a rare scene, all one hundred senators were present at their desks on the floor for the vote (*CQ Almanac* 1978: 391).[18] Immediately after the vote, the Senate began consideration of the main Panama Canal Treaty, or basic treaty. That treaty gave Panama full responsibility for running the canal as of December 31, 1999; until then, a joint U.S.-Panamanian commission would operate it. A controversial reservation added to the treaty at the demand of Panama just prior to the vote left the final outcome very much in doubt. In response to a reservation added to the Neutrality Treaty and passed by the Senate, Panama demanded that any action by the United States to keep the canal open (the content of the reservation) did not give the United States the right to intervene in Panama's internal affairs. Many senators saw this is as too strong a concession to the Panamanians. The final outcome on the basic treaty was, until the last second, assumed to be in doubt. The Senate leadership (Senators Byrd and Baker) was able to keep the coalition together, however, and after sixteen days of debate and many more attempts to kill the treaty by the Truth Squad, the Panama Canal treaty was supported by the Senate. The exact same vote of sixty-eight to thirty-two occurred on the resolution of ratification. All one hundred senators voted, and all senators voted the same way they did on the Neutrality Treaty.

President Carter got his treaties through the Senate by the thinnest of margins. The Panama Canal treaties are perhaps the best modern example of tense treaty politics. While significant and illustrative, we cannot conclude, however, that the fight over the treaties is at all representative of treaty politics more generally. Certain similarities exist, however, with the case of the U.S.-Soviet Consular Treaty. Most significant are the importance of ideology, presidential leadership, and the role of the SFRC. In their analysis of the two Panama treaty votes, McCormick and Black (1983) found ideology to be the most significant factor in explaining how senators voted. Conservatives were much more likely to oppose the treaties, whereas liberals were much more likely to support them. Their analysis suggests that ideology trumped presidential leadership, regionalism, and political party and that the effects of ideology were most pronounced for late-deciding senators. While ideology was certainly an important factor in the voting on the treaty, our discussion here points to the significance of a variety of salient factors prior to the floor votes. In short, our analysis emphasizes prefloor activity, particularly actions in committee and efforts on behalf of the treaty by the administration, both in the Senate and in negotiations with Panama.

The Genocide Convention

A handful of conservatives have blocked Senate approval of a United Nations treaty outlawing genocide. In what had the same effect as a filibuster, Sen. Jesse Helms, R-N.C., and other conservatives used procedural tactics and the threat of amendments to thwart action on the treaty.

    —CQ Weekly's John Felton on October 13, 1984, thirty-five years after the Senate first received the treaty for advice and consent from President Truman

We have waited long enough. As a nation which enshrines human dignity and freedom as a God-given right in its Constitution, we must correct our anomalous position on this basic rights issue.

    —Senate majority leader Bob Dole (R-KS) after the Senate consented to ratification of the Genocide Convention on February 19, 1986

The Senate has a long tradition of allowing individual senators to slow down or halt the legislative process through the use of holds and filibusters. These procedures may, for the most part, be used interchangeably on bills, treaties, presidential nominations, and budgets.[19] The tradition of minority rights in the Senate is often portrayed as guaranteeing a high level of deliberation compared to the quicker, majority-oriented House of Representatives. Yet no one would likely argue that Senator Helms (R-NC) and Senator Steven Symms (R-ID) were seeking an improved deliberative environment in the Senate through their blocking of the Genocide Convention, which was originally transmitted to the Senate by President Truman in 1949. After all, the treaty had been under consideration by the Senate for thirty-five years. It does not take much study and analysis to surmise that Senators Helms and Symms were not seeking more deliberation; they simply wanted to block the treaty from final consideration. Senate rules allow intense minorities to block the desire of a latent majority. Moreover, the supermajority requirement for Senate consent on treaties empowers the minority on treaty politics. In some respects, that tradition explains why it took so long for the Senate to give its consent to the Genocide Convention. After all, the Genocide Convention had widespread majority support along many of the years it was sitting idle in the United States Senate, especially over the final fifteen years.

Historically, conservatives in the U.S. Senate have routinely blocked human rights treaties (Kaufman 1990; Lowery 1993). The Genocide Convention is an interesting case, not only because it languished in the Senate for several decades despite widespread support, but also because it was the first major UN human rights treaty that the United States ratified since the 1950s[20] and because it preceded the ratification of three major human rights treaties during the late 1980s and 1990s.[21] Another interesting component of the ratification battle over the Genocide Convention is the success of the opposition, despite the fact that the U.S. negotiators had won at every turn when negotiating the original treaty and subsequent changes (LeBlanc 1991).

Background

The treaty, formally called the Convention on the Prevention and Punishment of the Crime of Genocide (Exec. O, 81st Cong. 1st sess. [1949]), was formulated as a response to Nazi atrocities carried out during World War II. From 1939 to 1945, the Nazi Holocaust included the extermination of six million Jews plus millions of Poles, Soviet POWs, and others. The countries that constituted the initial and fledgling membership of the United Nations wanted to establish a standard in international law to deter such despicable acts and to provide punishment of violators should such acts be carried out (LeBlanc 1991).

The agreement was initially approved by the United Nations on December 9, 1948, a pact to which the United States was a party. U.S. negotiators pushed hard for the convention. President Truman submitted the treaty to the Senate on June 16, 1949. The main thrust of the Genocide Convention was to make genocide a crime under international law. Genocide was defined broadly to include conspiracy to commit genocide, public incitement to commit genocide, and complicity in genocide. The treaty as initially constructed also required signatories to grant extradition to requesting countries and stipulated that disputes between parties would be settled in the World Court (known formally as the International Court of Justice). These last two provisions (complicity and extradition) were the treaty's most problematic aspects, according to opponents of the treaty's ratification.

Human rights pacts have had particular difficulty over the years in the U.S. Senate, and the Genocide Convention was no different (Kaufman 1990). The typical concern, voiced by conservative isolationists, is that entering into such pacts risks American sovereignty. The basic fear is that the U.S. government and/or the several states within it would be thrown in front of the International Court of Justice for crimes in "gray areas" that the United States or its agents do not define as problematic. Such concern was magnified during the Cold War years, with the hypothetical, if farfetched, scenario of the Soviet Union bringing forth such a case against the United States. It was even suggested by a legislative aide to U.S. senator Richard Lugar (R-IN) that U.S. ratification of the Genocide Convention might permit Native Americans to bring a case against the U.S. government in the World Court (*CQ Almanac* 1987). To the most vociferous opponents, human rights are not the domain of international agreements but, rather, a domestic concern. Human rights treaties are therefore an infringement on U.S. sovereignty (Kaufman 1990).

These concerns underlaid opposition and hence help us understand why the treaty took so long to get through the Senate. The initial Truman campaign to obtain Senate consent to the Genocide Convention did not so much as garner a report from the Senate Committee on Foreign Relations. The committee is required to give their assent for the Senate chamber to take up the resolution of ratification. The treaty bogged down in the committee during the Eighty-first Congress, owing primarily to sovereignty issues. Senators on the committee did not want to relinquish sovereignty and be called in front of an international court. Some also feared that racial discrimination and lynchings occurring at that time in certain southern U.S. states might qualify as genocide (LeBlanc 1991).[22]

Another key locus of opposition in 1949 was the American Bar Association (ABA), as George A. Finch (1949: 732) described:

The [Genocide] Convention was the subject of thorough consideration by the American Bar Association at its 72nd Annual Meeting in St. Louis, September 5–9, 1949. It came before the Association through two channels, the Association's Special Committee on Peace and Law Through United Nations and the Association's Section of International and Comparative Law. Both the Special Committee and the Section agreed that the Convention should not be ratified by the United States as submitted.

In addition to the concerns already raised, the debate before the full ABA concluded that the Genocide Convention should only apply to mass killings that happen with approval by some authority (Finch 1949). As written, ABA members were concerned that under the terms of the convention, the United States could be found complicit on even isolated crimes defined broadly under the genocide umbrella. With such significant reservations within and outside the Senate, it is not surprising that the SFRC did not report on the treaty during the Eighty-first Congress.

There was no push for the Genocide Convention in the Eighty-second Congress, and after President Truman, President Dwight D. Eisenhower, who took the oath of office in 1953 and served until January 1961, went on record in opposition to the treaty (*CQ Almanac* 1954). Since presidents hold the final say on whether a treaty consented to by the Senate is ultimately ratified, the Senate did not have an incentive to move the treaty forward during this time. In addition, the aforementioned concerns persisted, and opposition from the ABA was significant enough to bury the treaty. The Genocide Convention was also tied into the debate over the Bricker Amendment (which we discussed in chapter 1), which certainly did not help its cause in the Senate (Kaufman 1990).

Although Presidents Kennedy and Johnson favored adoption, the next president after Truman to significantly push for adoption of the Genocide Convention was President Richard Nixon, in 1969–70. President Nixon made multiple public pleas for the pact (U.S. Government Printing Office 1971), and in February 1970, he sent the Senate a renewal of request for consent to the treaty's ratification (Exec. Doc. B, 91-2). The treaty finally made progress in the Senate. The SFRC held hearings and formally reported the treaty to the full Senate late in the Ninety-first Congress, on December 8, 1970 (Exec. Rpt. 91-25). While the committee signed off, the full Senate would not take it up before sine die adjournment of the Ninety-first Congress. There was much discussion in early 1971 about having the committee report the resolution of ratification once again. At this time, several senators mobilized to oppose the treaty, and it went nowhere. Senator Sam Ervin (D-NC) was the most visible opponent. Known as an expert on constitutional matters, Senator Ervin circulated a Dear Colleague letter to all other senators on March 16, 1971, in which he called into question the legality of the treaty on constitutional grounds. His attached list of fifteen objections ranged from larger legal issues to specific issues with wording and definition.[23] Emphasizing legal technicalities was a favored tactic of opponents of the convention (Kaufman 1990: 196–97; LeBlanc 1991: 243; Lowery 1993: 202).

The SFRC again took up the issue in 1976, reporting the treaty with understandings in April (Exec. Rpt. 94-23), but the full Senate did not act. Despite efforts by President Carter to revive the treaty in the Senate, which included a speech before the UN General Assembly on March 17, 1977, little Senate action occurred during his administration. Though the SFRC did hold ratification hearings the following May (Congressional Information Service [1977] no. 77-S381-41), it did not report the treaty to the full Senate. So, despite having a Democratic majority in control of the Senate and the support of Republican and Democratic presidents, conservatives within the minority party effectively blocked final Senate action on the treaty for several years. In 1981, the SFRC again held ratification hearings, but no report was issued (Congressional Information Service [1981] no. 82-S381-11).[24]

In an interesting twist of fate, the Genocide Convention was revived by President Reagan in a Senate controlled by Republicans. The next significant push for the convention occurred late in the first term of the Reagan administration. An important prelude to this push in the early 1980s was the prior switching of positions by the American Bar Association. On international matters, the ABA had long been a bastion for conservative isolationists. For example, during the 1950s, the ABA had supported the Bricker Amendment, which would have curtailed the use of executive agreements (Tananbaum 1988). The ABA forged the initial 1949 opposition discussed earlier and sustained that position for over twenty-five years. In 1976, the ABA reappraised the situation and reversed course by formally supporting the Genocide Convention. Hence one important source of early opposition was not present when President Reagan endorsed adoption of the treaty in a speech to Jewish groups while campaigning for reelection in 1984 (Kaufman 1990; LeBlanc 1991). However, another source of opposition was nonetheless waiting in the wings.

Senators Helms and Symms Block the
Genocide Convention

With a supportive conservative Republican president, a prestigious and powerful attorneys' group on board, and widespread support among senators in both parties, the Genocide Convention appeared ready to move through the Republican-controlled Senate in late 1984. President Reagan announced his support of the treaty on September 5. On September 19, the SFRC approved the treaty by a vote of seventeen to zero, in effect reporting it to the full Senate (Exec. Rpt. 98-50). Senator Jesse Helms (R-NC), who was then caught in a tough reelection battle in North Carolina and was taking heat on his position on the Genocide Convention, voted "present" in the committee vote.

Once under consideration by the full Senate, Senator Helms and Senator Steven Symms (R-ID) sought to block the treaty through procedural tactics. Although not saying outright that the Senate should defeat the pact, the senators' delay tactics had the same effect, as time was running out in the Ninety-eighth Congress. When the Senate began floor consideration of the Genocide Convention on October 10, Senator Helms was present on the floor and asked a series of questions about proper floor consideration of treaties. The presiding officer, Senator Dave Durenburger (R-MN), "revealed that the Senate was required to take at least two days to give final approval to the treaty and an associated resolution of ratification unless Senate rules were waived by unanimous consent" (*CQ Almanac* 1984: 2626).[25]

Senator Helms stopped short of opposing the treaty outright, but he made it clear through questioning of the presiding officer that he would rise to oppose any unanimous consent agreement that allowed the Senate to proceed more quickly than the required two days. With time running out in the session before one-third of the senators had to return to their states to face election, Helms's maneuver had the same effect as defeating the treaty through filibuster. Senator Symms, who had been even more outspoken in his opposition to the pact than Helms, had threatened to filibuster final consideration.[26] With the waiving of the two-day requirement not seeming possible given Senator Helms's floor remarks and with the likelihood that Symms would filibuster should they take up the resolution of ratification, Senate floor leaders relented, as time was running short in the session. Instead of taking up the resolution of ratification, senators quickly considered and overwhelmingly passed (by a vote of eighty-seven to two) a resolution supportive of the Genocide Convention's ideas, pledging to move quickly on the pact during 1985 (LeBlanc 1991).

Breakthroughs on Several Fronts

Senators Helms and Symms underestimated the wherewithal of many Republican colleagues, including Senate majority leader Bob Dole and Senator William Proxmire (D-WI), the latter of whom brought remarks on the treaty to the Senate floor every day from January 11, 1967, up to the final passage in 1986. To give readers a sense of how long this treaty languished in the Senate, Proxmire took up the cause of daily floor remarks about the Genocide Convention after the treaty had already been in the Senate for eighteen years. He then made a daily pilgrimage from his Senate office to the U.S. Capitol, where he rose to make remarks on the treaty in the Senate chamber every day the Senate was in session for over nineteen years.

The other protagonists were President Reagan, Senate majority leader Bob Dole, and Senator Lugar, who chaired the SFRC. President Reagan continued to support the Genocide Convention in 1985. As Lawrence Leblanc (1991: 241) explains, Reagan's support for the treaty was pivotal: "[It] dramatically changed the conditions under which the debate over ratification would henceforth be conducted. After his endorsement, only the most extreme fringe elements could continue to oppose ratification." Senator Lugar convinced key Republicans to support the pact. However, to attract enough Republican support, the SFRC incorporated two key reservations. One of the reservations added language clarifying that extradition would be allowed only when the alleged crime in question was illegal in both the country requesting extradition and the United States. The other reservation, which critics argue gutted the treaty, declared that the United States could refuse jurisdiction of the World Court if doing so would be in the national interest (LeBlanc 1991).[27]

The Reagan administration had opposed the latter reservation in 1984 but realized that it was needed to finally pass the pact through the SFRC, where Senators Helms and Symms had in effect achieved a logjam in early 1985. Finally, on July 18, 1985, the SFRC issued its final favorable report on the Genocide Convention (Exec. Rpt. 99-2). On February 19, 1986, the final floor vote on the resolution of ratification was eighty-three to eleven. Senators Helms and Symms voted against final passage. Symms had again threatened to filibuster, but he removed the threat when Senate majority leader Bob Dole made it clear that he would move forward on cloture to stop the filibuster. A final attempt to defeat the pact was attempted by Symms when he introduced a killer amendment. That amendment failed by a vote of thirty-one to sixty-two. After almost thirty-seven years of consideration, the U.S. Senate had finally given its consent to the Genocide

Convention. After implementation legislation finally brought U.S. law in line with the provisions of the Senate-passed pact in 1988 (Orentlicher 2007; Public Law 100-606), the Genocide Convention was ultimately ratified by President George H. W. Bush when he deposited the instruments of ratification with the United Nations on February 23, 1989.

The long and sordid tale of the Genocide Convention highlights the potency of arcane Senate rules in delaying and blocking Senate action on an important international agreement. The United States championed human rights internationally, even to the point of taking the lead on most human rights pacts, but was unable to ratify the very agreements it had negotiated. This is baffling until one considers how dedicated ideologues can use the Senate procedures to bury a treaty. Despite the support and lobbying efforts of Democratic and Republican presidents and despite several favorable reports from the SFRC during the 1970s and 1980s, the Genocide Convention languished year after year in the Senate. Proponents of the treaty had to eviscerate it with reservations and understandings to attract conservative supporters. As a result, ratification amounted to a symbolic accomplishment. In addition to the salience of ideology, the case of the Genocide Convention highlights the significance of the topic of a treaty. Simply put, different types of treaties are likely to engender greater opposition from conservatives, which can lead to differing politics in the Senate. Treaties that codify international norms (e.g., human rights and environmental treaties) have the potential of altering domestic law—an affront to sovereignty in the eyes of isolationists—and are thus likely to attract determined opposition.

The Comprehensive Nuclear Test Ban Treaty

I was honored to be the first of 146 leaders to sign the Comprehensive Test Ban Treaty, our commitment to end all nuclear tests for all time—the longest-sought, hardest-fought prize in the history of arms control. It will help to prevent the nuclear powers from developing more advanced and more dangerous weapons. It will limit the possibilities for other states to acquire such devices . . . Our common goal should be to enter the CTBT into force as soon as possible, and I ask for all of you to support that goal.

—President Bill Clinton in an address to the Fifty-second Session of the UN General Assembly, September 22, 1997

Many who had questions about the treaty worked hard to
postpone the vote because they knew a defeat would be
damaging to America's interest and to our role in leading the
world away from nonproliferation. But for others, we all know that
foreign policy, national security policy has become just like every
domestic issue—politics, pure and simple.

> —President Bill Clinton on October 13, 1999, in response to the
> defeat of the Comprehensive Nuclear Test Ban Treaty on the
> Senate floor

What today's treaty rejection does say . . . is that our
constitutional democracy, with its shared powers and checks and
balances, is alive and well.

> —Senator Jon Kyl (R-AZ) after the floor defeat of the Comprehensive
> Nuclear Test Ban Treaty

The quotes from President Clinton and Senator Kyl that serve as epigraphs to this section do not sound like remarks that you would hear from a president and senator if the Senate process on treaty advice and consent were pro forma. The most stunning presidential floor defeat on a treaty in modern times is the poster child for the political nature of Senate treaty consideration and the increasing role of partisanship in the upper chamber (Evans and Olezsek 2003). In terms of background on relations between Democratic president Bill Clinton and the Senate, the president was able to move some international agreements (and their implementation legislation) through the Democratically-controlled Senate in 1993–94. Thereafter, Senator Helms, who chaired the SFRC when the Senate went to Republican rule, roughed up Clinton's foreign policy proposals across the board (Evans and Olezsek 2003). This roughening-up included the very salient floor vote defeat of the Comprehensive Nuclear Test Ban Treaty (CTBT). One observer labeled the CTBT failure "the president's worst foreign policy defeat in Congress" (Deibel 2002: 142).

Background

Since President Eisenhower, the banning of nuclear testing had been a goal of U.S. arms control strategy. In his 1960 State of the Union address, Eisenhower remarked on the need for a test ban when he stated, "Another avenue may be through the reopening . . . of negotiations looking to a controlled ban on the testing of nuclear weapons." With the fear of a possible World War III prompted by the Cold War rivalry of the United States and the Soviet Union, such a goal long had public and political support. During thirteen famous days in 1962, the Cuban Missile Crisis during the administration of President John F. Kennedy heightened such concerns, as the United States and the Soviet Union nearly went to war in a context in which nuclear technology was expected to see quick employment. Lawrence Evans and Walter Olezsek (2003: 100) report, "The next year the Kennedy Administration signed the Limited Test Ban Treaty, which prohibited nuclear explosions in space, in the atmosphere, and under water." Kennedy argued, "The conclusion of such a treaty [to end nuclear tests] . . . would check the spiraling arms race in one of its most dangerous areas. . . . It would increase our security—it would decrease the prospects of war."[28] The presidents since Kennedy have been proponents of controlling nuclear arms, and each has brokered a significant international agreement on nuclear weapons. When the Soviet Union imploded at the end of the Cold War, the focus of the disarmament movement shifted toward a comprehensive focus on nonproliferation. Banning nuclear tests is a key step in the nonproliferation regime.

Negotiation and ratification of the CTBT was a top foreign policy priority of President Clinton and his administration. Supporters of the pact argued that it offered the best method of stopping the global nuclear arms race. President Clinton explained the basic logic of the pact when he stated, "The test ban treaty will restrict the development of nuclear weapons worldwide at a time when America has an overwhelming military and technological advantage. It will give us the tools to strengthen our security, including the global network of sensors to detect nuclear tests, the opportunity to demand on-site inspections, and the means to mobilize the world against potential violators" (U.S. Government Printing Office 1999). After lengthy negotiations at the United Nations, which resulted in a near unanimous vote of support there, President Clinton signed the treaty on September 24, 1996. He transmitted the treaty to the Senate one year later, on September 23, 1997. Before and after submittal to the Senate, President Clinton went to great lengths to publicly lobby for the pact. To the president, the need for the CTBT seemed obvious. He declared, "This agreement is critical to protecting the American people from the dangers of nuclear war. It is, therefore, well worth fighting for" (U.S. Government Printing Office 1999). The president would be in for quite a fight in the Senate.

The Senate CTBT Process (or Lack Thereof)
Once President Clinton submitted the treaty to the Senate in 1997, it did not take long for Senator Helms to get involved. Right away, as chairman

of the SFRC and hence in control of scheduling committee hearings, Senator Helms used delay tactics familiar to those he used on the Genocide Convention during the 1980s and on the Chemical Weapons Convention just a few years earlier (Evans and Olezsek 2003). Helms refused to even hold hearings unless President Clinton forwarded two items that Helms wanted to defeat: the recent Kyoto Protocol on global warming and changes to the Anti-Ballistic Missile Treaty, originally forged in 1972.

As had been the case during the Genocide Convention process, Helms was opposed to the pact. This time, however, he was more vocal about it, and as SFRC chairman, he controlled the committee agenda. Senator Helms and many of his fellow partisans felt that the CTBT would be impossible to implement. Helms also thought passing it would weaken the defensive capabilities of the United States, because it would give countries outside the coalition undue benefit over those that signed and followed the pact. Helms also continued to stake out a consistently isolationist position on foreign agreements (Evans and Oleszek 2003).

With SFRC chairman Senator Helms setting the foreign policy agenda in the Senate, the CTBT appeared permanently blocked. However, in the early fall of 1999, Senate Democrats became more vocal in their demands that the CTBT be formally acted on. Led by Senator Byron Dorgan (D-ND), Democrats pressed publicly for the Senate leadership to take up the treaty: "On July 20, all 45 Democratic senators released a public letter to Jesse Helms (R-NC), the chairman of the Foreign Relations Committee, urging him to hold hearings on the treaty and report it out for a vote. But he rejected the appeal out of hand. Confronted in the fall with Helms' determination to hold the treaty hostage, Dorgan decided to do some hostage-taking of his own" (Deibel 2002: 151). Should the Senate majority leader, Trent Lott (R-MS), not agree to consider the treaty, Dorgan, backed up by his Democratic colleagues, threatened to hold Republican priorities and budget proposals hostage by delaying GOP legislation as it made its way to the floor (Evans and Olezsek 2003).

This campaign prompted action from Senator Lott. However, the action he instituted was hardly what CTBT supporters would have wanted. Sensing he had the votes to defeat the measure soundly on the floor,[29] Senator Lott surprised the Democrats by proposing, in a unanimous consent agreement (UCA), for very quick scheduling of a floor vote, after the pact was suddenly fast-tracked through Senator Helms's SFRC with only minimal discussion at the hearings. Democrats were in a lose-lose situation. If they opposed the UCA, they would appear to be unsupportive of the treaty. If they did not oppose the UCA, the treaty was doomed to failure.

Ultimately, the Democrats agreed to the UCA. So, after being blocked for two years in committee, the CTBT was now moving too quickly, in a manner that assured defeat.

President Clinton and Senate minority leader Tom Daschle (D-SD) could see that defeat was imminent, and they had very little time to reverse course and save the treaty for a later day (Evans and Oleszek 2003). Allowing the treaty to fail in a recorded vote was not without its political risks for Republicans, however, as a clear majority of the American public supported its ratification (Deibel 2002). Realizing this, Senator Daschle gathered a small group of moderate Republican supporters and approached Senator Lott with a request to essentially table the vote. *CQ Almanac* (1999: 2866) reported, "Lott said he would withdraw the treaty from the Senate schedule only if the administration promised not to push it for the remainder of Clinton's term. The White House would not agree with this demand."

Next, a group of sixty-two senators, led by Senator John Warner (R-VA) and Senator Daniel Patrick Moynihan (D-NY), sent a letter to Senator Lott requesting that the vote be postponed. Twenty-four Republicans signed the letter. A separate letter from three very conservative Republicans who wanted the treaty defeated outright—Senator Tim Hutchinson (R-AR), Senator Robert Smith (R-NH), and Senator James Inhofe (R-OK)—argued that the vote should not be delayed. Evans and Oleszek (2003) adeptly point out that Lott was in a procedural bind at this point, because, per Senate rules, the UCA to consider the CTBT had to be implemented as originally passed, unless the Senate passed another UCA to delay or drop consideration. Regardless of the sixty-two senators wanting the vote delayed, Senator Hutchinson (or Smith or Inhofe) could simply rise in opposition to the new UCA, thereby defeating the measure. "The bottom line," explain Evans and Oleszek (2003: 106), was that "all 100 senators needed to agree to postpone the vote." The status quo of fast-track consideration was obtained, and Senator Lott went ahead with floor consideration and the vote.

After twenty-two hours of debate, the Senate voted down the resolution of ratification for the CTBT by a vote of forty-eight to fifty-one. The ayes did not achieve even a majority, let alone the two-thirds supermajority required for treaty consent. Internationalist Republican senators Lugar (R-IN) and Domenici (R-NM), who had supported Clinton on prior items, voted against it. President Clinton was livid: "Never before has a serious treaty involving nuclear weapons been handled in such a reckless and ultimately partisan way" (U.S. Government Printing Office 1999). Senator Byrd (D-WV) complained that the Senate used procedural tactics "that 'effectively abdicated its duty' to advise and consent" on a major nuclear proliferation treaty. Senator Lott countered, "It was not about politics; it was about the substance of the treaty, and that's all it was" (quoted in Deibel 2002: 159).

President Clinton underestimated the wherewithal of opponents to the treaty and did not establish an effective lobbying plan as he had on the Chemical Weapons Convention (Evans and Oleszek 2003). Unlike a previous treaty victory for Clinton on a pact that President George H. W. Bush had originally negotiated (the Chemical Weapons Convention), this treaty started and finished with Clinton. Hence the president misread the political context, assuming he would get the same treatment on the CTBT that he received on the Chemical Weapons Convention earlier (Evans and Oleszek 2003). Clinton and his Senate allies may have misread the vigor at which conservative senators and their supporters opposed the treaty, in part because it was Clinton's brainchild. In the words of one Republican aide, "They [grassroots activists and right-wing media] wanted us in the end zone, spiking the ball on something that belonged to Bill Clinton" (quoted in Deibel 2002: 160).

Epilogue: The George W. Bush Administration

In 2001, the Bush administration explored ways to permanently get around the unapproved Comprehensive Nuclear Test Ban Treaty. In effect, they wanted to throw the CTBT away. Thom Shanker and David Sanger (2001) reported, "But State Department lawyers told the White House that a president cannot withdraw a treaty from the Senate once it has been presented for approval [on the floor]. So, administration officials said, President Bush has resolved to let the Comprehensive Test Ban Treaty languish in the Senate, where its supporters concede they do not have the votes to revive it." The fact that Bush could not quickly dispose of the CTBT invites us to examine the incentives that exist for presidents (in this case, Clinton) to go the treaty route instead of employing the executive agreement. If treaties are utilized, the final outcome and earlier steps of the process are not removable by subsequent presidents. While executive agreements are easier to forge, it only takes a subsequent president to come along and reverse course with a new executive agreement. Subsequent presidents cannot unilaterally reverse course of prior presidents when treaties have been processed and/or ratified, outside of reinterpreting a treaty (where the international and domestic law is murky) or terminating a duly ratified treaty. While plausible, such outcomes are rare and politically charged, as we discussed in chapter 1.

As of May 2007, 177 nations have signed the CTBT, including the United States. Of those nations, 138, including Russia and every member of NATO except for the United States, have ratified the treaty (Medalia 2007). Of the forty-four nations that must ratify the agreement in order for it to enter into force,[30] only nine, including the United States, have not done so, and three of those nine (India, Pakistan, and North Korea) have yet to sign the accord. The other nonratifying signatories include China, Egypt, Indonesia, Iran, and Israel.[31] Jonathan Medalia (2007) has reported, "In 2002, the administration said it continues to oppose the CTBT, continues to adhere to the test moratorium, has not ruled out resumed testing, and has no plans to test." The United States, once the champion of nuclear nonproliferation and lead proponent in pushing the treaty at the United Nations, is grouped with states suspect of nuclear proliferation, such as Pakistan, Iran, North Korea, and China. As recently as November 2007, the United States was the lone vote against a UN General Assembly resolution calling for speedy ratification of the treaty by signatories in order to facilitate its entry into force. China, Pakistan, and Iran voted in favor of the resolution, which passed 166 in favor to 1 against.[32]

Prospects for ratification of the treaty are dim, considering the high degree of partisan polarization that persists in the U.S. Senate. Thus the CTBT is unlikely to enter into force any time soon. Even if a pro-CTBT administration were to be elected, along with a Democratic Senate, the tools afforded ideologically inclined senators will remain, and achieving supermajority support for the CTBT may prove a Herculean effort. It is possible, as occurred with Reagan's pivotal support of the Genocide Convention, that a Republican president could revive the CTBT in the U.S. Senate, as conservatives may be less inclined to thwart one of their own. In the meantime, however, proponents of the treaty argue that U.S. international leadership in the nonproliferation regime is significantly compromised.

Conclusion

The four fascinating cases presented in this chapter illuminate the rich political context involved in Senate advice and consent on important treaties. Treaty advice and consent in the Senate does not appear to be entirely pro forma. U.S. senators assert themselves early and often in the process, taking advantage of Senate procedures that empower individual senators, particularly in blocking or delaying action on treaties. Moreover, the prefloor process in the Senate Foreign Relations Committee is important to understand. Finally, some treaties languish for years, even decades, before receiving Senate floor consideration and consent, and this delay is consequential for American diplomacy. When negotiating their more controversial treaties, presidents ought to take into consideration likely opposition in the Senate, given the tools available to any likely opponent and the required supermajority for Senate consent.

While we do not argue that these cases together constitute a random sample, we believe that they are four good choices for examination. They include a diplomatic treaty (the U.S.-Soviet Consular Treaty), a territory treaty (the Panama Canal Treaty), a human rights treaty (the Genocide Convention), and a post–Cold War arms control treaty (the Comprehensive Nuclear Test Ban Treaty). These treaties also include two multilateral treaties and two bilateral treaties, and they also feature temporal variety, with one treaty from the 1960s, one from the 1940s–80s, one from the 1970s, and one from the 1990s. The cases of the U.S.-Soviet Consular Treaty and the Panama Canal Treaty feature unified partisan control of the Senate and presidency, the case of the CTBT shows divided government, and the Genocide Convention experienced all kinds of different partisan control arrangements over a thirty-seven-year period. Finally, the homogeneity of Senate parties varies across the cases, with diverse intraparty views early in the period (in the case of the U.S.-Soviet Consular Treaty) and high partisan polarization later (in the case of the CTBT).

In conclusion, the varying processes featured in these four cases of treaty consideration in the U.S. Senate suggest a multifaceted approach to systematic analysis of Senate advice and consent on treaties. This approach should include analysis of outcomes as well as duration of Senate consideration. We next turn to a chapter employing such an approach, to build more systematically on the case studies developed here.

5 | Delayed Diplomacy: Gridlock in the U.S. Senate

On January 13, 1993, President George H. W. Bush signed a multilateral treaty designed to eliminate all forms of chemical weapons within a twenty-year period. The Chemical Weapons Convention (CWC), signed by more than 120 nations, including Russia and China, was hailed as a truly significant international pact that outlawed the use of chemical weapons in warfare and eliminated a horrific weapon from the stockpiles of twenty-two nations (Palmer 1994: 2586; Towell 1997a: 550). Initial prospects for speedy approval in the Senate were positive. The treaty had been negotiated by the Reagan and Bush administrations and was submitted to the Senate for advice and consent by President Clinton on November 23, 1993 (Treaty Doc. 103-21). The treaty had substantial bipartisan support. Why, then, did the treaty languish in the Senate until April 24, 1997?

The reasons for delayed action on the part of the Senate are numerous. President Clinton did not submit the treaty right away, because his focus was on another significant arms control treaty, the Strategic Arms Reduction Talks (START II), which he transmitted to the Senate on inauguration day (Treaty Doc. 103-1). His advisors recommended focusing on that treaty first (Hersman 2000: 86).[1] Given the crowded foreign policy agenda during late 1993 and early 1994 (Evans and Oleszek 2003: 92), the Senate Foreign Relations Committee did not take up the issue until it held brief hearings in March and April 1994 (Hersman 2000: 87). With elections looming and Senate focus fixed on other foreign policy issues, Chairman Claiborne Pell (D-RI) and the SFRC failed to report out a resolution of ratification in 1994. The results of the 1994 congressional elections nearly doomed the CWC, as Republicans gained control of the Senate and Senator Jesse Helms (R-NC) became the chair of the SFRC.

Helms, the most conservative member of the Senate,[2] was known as an obstructionist when it came to arms control treaties and other internationalist foreign policies, and his behavior on the CWC followed suit. He wanted a significant State Department reorganization, but the administration and Democrats opposed his legislation. Determined to get his legislation to the floor, he held hostage numerous foreign policy measures in committee, including the CWC and START II (Hersman 2000: 88–90). Eventually, a compromise was struck, and the SFRC issued its report on the CWC to the full Senate on April 25, 1996 (Evans and Oleszek 2003: 94).

While the treaty had cleared a major hurdle in committee, the administration was faced with significant uncertainty on the floor, as getting the two-thirds majority constitutionally mandated would require substantial support on the part of Republicans. Many of the Senate's most ardent conservatives remained opposed to the treaty. Despite his having worked to schedule floor debate for early September 1996, former Senate majority leader and 1996 Republican presidential nominee Robert Dole (R-KS) came out against the treaty in a letter to Republican Senate majority leader Trent Lott (R-MS) on September 12, 1996. Treaty opponents seized on this new opportunity to block the treaty, and the number of Republicans publicly voicing concerns for the treaty increased enough that the president, realizing the votes for consent were not there, requested that the Senate table the treaty and send it back to committee (Evans and Oleszek 2003: 95; Hersman 2000: 92–93; Towell 1997b).

There the treaty sat until April 17, 1997, when a unanimous consent agreement was worked out between Helms, Lott, and the Senate minority leader, Tom Daschle (D-SD). The agreement discharged the CWC from committee and placed it on the executive calendar. To overcome the gridlock that had blocked the CWC, Senate Democrats threatened stalemate of their own on dozens of unrelated issues, including national missile defense, a Republican priority. Moreover, President Clinton and other high-level administration officials undertook a "full-court press" on the CWC in early 1997 (Evans and Oleszek 2003: 96). Clinton took seriously Republican reservations on the treaty and worked toward a bipartisan compromise. He also turned up the political heat on the opposition, calling for the Senate to ratify the CWC in his 1997 State of the Union address on February 4 and repeatedly bringing up the treaty in his public statements.[3] Time was now critical. The president cited April 29 as the deadline for ratification, as that was the date the treaty would enter into force. If the United States failed to ratify the CWC by that date, it would be shut out of administering the treaty. Finally, the president got his vote on the CWC on April 24, just five days prior to the deadline. The Senate voted seventy-four to twenty-six to approve the convention, with twenty-nine Republicans joining all forty-five Democrats to approve the treaty (Evans and Oleszek 2003: 95–100; Towell 1997b).

The travails of the CWC and other significant treaties we studied in chapter 4 indicate that delay in the ratification of such treaties can derail a president's foreign policy and presents serious problems for the exercise of American diplomacy. The case study evidence suggests that the politics of treaties are not unlike the legislative politics of other major foreign policies in that gridlock can be explained, in part, by an overfull agenda, partisan politics, and ideological divides between the parties in the Senate and between the Senate and president (Binder 1999; Edwards, Barrett, and Peake 1997; Peake 2002). Moreover, the case evidence highlights the significance of having the support of the chair of the SFRC. However, we are hesitant to generalize from these case studies, and we here seek a more comprehensive explanation for treaty gridlock, as expressed in both the duration and success of the treaty consent process. In this chapter, we focus on process and, more specifically, on explaining treaty consideration dynamics.

Why Treaty Delay?

As we have argued, the legislative politics of treaties deserve further scholarly scrutiny. Successful American diplomacy relies on the president and Congress working jointly in making and ratifying international agreements. The shared treaty power, however, predictably complicates diplomatic matters. It serves to build domestic consensus and sends important signals to diplomatic partners, yet Glennon notes, "The hand that signs is not the hand that delivers; what looks like a good bargain to diplomats at the negotiating table may look altogether different to legislators . . . Thus the domestic value of pluralistic governmental decision making competes with the international values of reciprocal expectations." To the degree that the treaty process in the Senate is gridlocked, the president and Senate are less able to achieve American diplomatic goals jointly and "to enlarge the area of confidence between governments" so significant for the preservation of international order (Glennon 1990: 123).

In terms of temporal dynamics, the duration of the treaty ratification

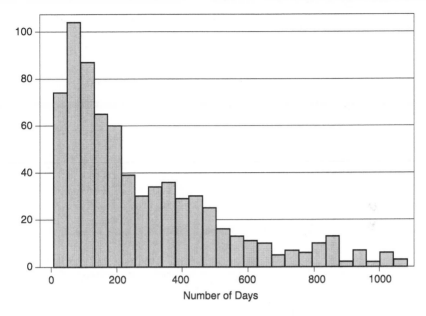

FIG. 2.   Histogram of days to Senate consent (for treaties taking less than 3 years to receive Senate consent. $N = 724$.)

process can vary from approval within a few weeks to substantial delay measurable in years. Figure 2 graphs the time to Senate consent from initial transmittal for the 724 treaties (submitted by the president from 1949 to 2000) that received consent within three years (or 1,095 days). The remaining 126 treaties either were never given Senate consent ($N = 63$) or languished longer than three years ($N = 63$).[4] Fully 206 (28 percent) of the treaties given consent within three years took between one and three years to gain Senate consent. The graph clearly shows that while a majority of treaties are processed through the Senate within a year of transmittal, many take significantly longer. Treaties languishing longer than the three years are also not uncommon. Of those treaties that languished longer than three years, 71 percent failed to receive Senate consent. Of the treaties that were not dealt with by the transmittal Senate or the subsequent Senate, 50 percent failed to ever receive consent. Consent delay, then, is a clear indicator of treaty gridlock.

The data suggest that numerous treaties languish in the Senate for substantial periods of time, which can frustrate presidential leadership in foreign policy and significantly hinder U.S. diplomacy. This time is on top of any delay that might arise between the time the president enters into the agreement (by signing the treaty documents) and the time he transmits the document to the Senate for advice and consent.[5] Ratification delay may come after years of frustrating negotiations. For example, President Kennedy submitted the Limited Test Ban Treaty of 1963 after five years of difficult negotiations with the Soviets, spanning two administrations (Loeb 1991).

It is important to analyze the duration of treaty consideration for a variety of reasons. First, delay of treaty consideration creates an environment for opponents to step up their efforts to alter or defeat the treaty. Opponents can hold the treaty hostage and secure administration support for their own priorities, as Republicans did with the CWC in 1996. Second, whether or not a treaty ultimately succeeds, a long treaty consideration process has an agenda-setting impact. Presidents and their White House staff members, SFRC members, and senators all have finite time and resources to pursue policy issues. In other words, they have a scarcity of time to get everything done (Hall 1996). The longer a particular treaty stays on the president's and the Senate's agendas, the less attention these actors have available to direct to other critical foreign policy issues (Peake 2001). Presidents are often faced with deciding which major treaties to push and expend their political capital on in an effort to achieve Senate consent. The Clinton administration, for example, pushed seven major treaties during its first two years. Two of the major arms control treaties, the CWC and START II, competed for space on the president's and Senate's agendas, which were crowded with national missile defense and a major State Department reorganization (Hersman 2000: 88–94).

Third, from the standpoint of the president, stagnating treaties have the potential to display the chief executive as ineffective in dealing with the Senate on foreign policy matters. When that occurs, there may be significant consequences. Perhaps the president's standing with the press and public will decrease. Within the Senate, there could be even greater political costs for the president in treaty delay. To the extent a president intensely desires the Senate's consent on a treaty, the Senate or specific senators critical to the consent process will be in a better position to negotiate for the president's support on other items, such as legislation and budgets, in exchange for consent or movement on the treaty. As already shown, this scenario occurred in 1996 when, in exchange for committee approval of the CWC, President Clinton conceded to demands from SFRC chair Jesse Helms to agree to a bureaucratic reorganization bill the senator favored. The treaty had languished in the Senate for nearly three years. In pushing for the Panama Canal Treaties prior to SALT II, President Carter expended a great deal of political capital on the unpopular treaties—resources he could have used in pursuing SALT II or other foreign policy priorities (Caldwell 1991b: 297; Moffett 1985).

Extensive delay on a treaty might also contribute to alterations of the document while it traverses the Senate, which may require renegotiation by the president with treaty partners. Conversely, a quick consent process does not raise such political stakes. Presidents routinely signal to the Senate their preferences concerning which treaties the Senate should act on, so presidents are cognizant of the delay that arises in the process. The State Department typically sends a yearly communication to the SFRC indicating the president's priorities for treaties before the Senate. The list is called the priority list and is vetted both at the White House and in the State Department. The committee is usually responsive to priority lists; however, presidents have sometimes failed to transmit the list to the committee and have not always indicated their priorities clearly. For example, in 2001, the Bush administration moved the Convention on the Political Rights of Women up on the priority list; as a result, SFRC chair Joe Biden held hearings on the treaty, yet members of the administration argued against Senate consideration.[6]

Lastly and perhaps most straightforward, the president, other treaty signatories, and treaty supporters in the Senate all support a treaty's passage presumably because the document contains important and meaningful changes in policy. Otherwise, why would a president transmit the treaty to the Senate for consent in the first place? To the extent that the treaty is delayed in the Senate, those policy changes are not being acted on or implemented. Until Senate consent is achieved and presidential ratification occurs, the undesirable policy status quo continues. From a standpoint of diplomacy, this is problematic for presidents and American foreign policy more broadly. If the Senate ignores a pending treaty or if Senate consent is uncertain or delayed, other heads of state may balk in signing significant international agreements with presidents. The lengthier the delay, the more likely it is that treaty partners may question the president's ability to attain legislative support for the treaty and fulfill international obligations. Work by Martin (2000: 70–71) suggests that presidents are less able to make credible international commitments when the likelihood of legislative cooperation decreases.

Delay in the consent process may send the wrong signals to treaty partners, as they may surmise that the president is not working hard enough on behalf of the treaty, that it lacks Senate support, or that the opposition in the Senate plans to attach killer amendments to the treaty, changing it to the point that it is unacceptable to the signatories. Killer amendments were nearly attached to the Intermediate-Range Nuclear Forces Treaty in 1987 by Senators Jesse Helms and Larry Pressler (R-SD). The amendments would have killed the treaty because the Soviets were unlikely to have accepted them. The full Senate defeated these efforts, however, after Senator Byrd (D-WV) threatened to invoke cloture, in effect shutting down debate on the treaty. Such a move would have led to the first cloture vote on a treaty since the debate over the Treaty of Versailles (Hastedt 2006; Nolan 1991: 382–83). Put simply, a protracted treaty consent process, especially on significant treaties, can have a "corrosive effect on American prestige" (Krepon and Caldwell 1991: 4).[7]

In summary, the duration of Senate treaty consideration has significant implications for the president, the Senate, and American foreign policy.[8] No prior study has looked carefully at the treaty advice and consent process from a duration standpoint. In this chapter, we systematically examine treaty politics through consideration of two questions: First, how long does it take to secure consent to a president's treaties? Second and more specifically, why do some treaties face substantial delay while others sail through the Senate?

In pursuing why delay occurs, it is helpful to consider an analogous Senate process that has received comparatively more scholarly attention: the advice and consent role of the Senate in confirming executive and judicial nominations. Several scholars have examined the dynamics of the confirmation process, highlighting the delay that can occur when nominations languish in the Senate (Binder and Maltzman 2002; Bond, Fleisher, and Krutz 2006; DeRouen, Peake, and Ward 2005; McCarty and Razaghian 1999; Shipan and Shannon 2003). In this chapter, we apply similar logic to the dynamics of senatorial advice and consent on treaties. Because treaties require the support of two-thirds of the Senate, the hurdles are more serious in the treaty consent process than in the nomination process, which only requires a majority. In the treaty consent process, substantial opposition may materialize in committee, as the committee must account for the supermajority requirement for Senate floor consent on a treaty.[9] Even so, treaty failures on the floor of the Senate are so rare that the interesting dynamic becomes the time it takes for the Senate to conduct its advice and consent. McCarty and Razaghian (1999) make a similar argument in narrowing their focus on the delay of Senate consent on nominations, as failed votes on nominations are extremely rare.

Also of interest is the role that the SFRC plays in the treaty process. The

SFRC has a great deal of influence over the treaty process, whereby it can attach reservations or understandings to treaties, perhaps delay the ratification process as the committee deliberates the merits of treaties, or even ignore a treaty altogether. In chapters 2 and 3, we demonstrated the significance of the SFRC on presidential decisions on the form of their international agreements. Despite its importance, the extant systematic literature on treaty politics fails to consider the SFRC as an independent institutional actor (e.g., Auerswald 2006). The SFRC is the primary hurdle that treaties must surmount. Additionally, ratification delay is most likely to occur at the committee stage of the process, as the Senate floor typically moves rapidly on treaties once they are reported out of committee.[10] We therefore focus much of our attention here on the chair of the SFRC.

In this chapter, we model the duration of the treaty consent process from the point that the president transmits a treaty to the Senate to the time when the SFRC reports the treaty to the full Senate, then from the point when the SFRC reports the treaty to the time when the full Senate gives its consent. We also present a model of treaty consent failure. The results suggest that our current understanding of the treaty consent process is overly simplified. We find that while the standard partisan theories of legislative politics contribute little to our understanding of the delay that occurs in the treaty consent process, hypotheses derived from pivotal politics theory and committee politics prove fruitful. As the preferences of pivotal institutional players in the process diverge, successfully moving a treaty through the consent process becomes more difficult. Domestic politics contribute significantly to delayed diplomacy in the United States.

Scholarship on Treaty Politics in the Senate

Despite the constitutional and international significance of treaties, very little systematic study has focused on the politics of treaty consent.[11] Most of the research consists of case studies of a single important treaty (e.g. Caldwell 1991a; Jorden 1984; Moffett 1985) or focus on a subset of important treaties (e.g., DeLaet and Scott 2006; Kaufman 1990; Krepon and Caldwell 1991). The case evidence we presented in chapter 4 suggests that the consent process is, at times, rife with politics; yet we know little in terms of generalizations regarding the process, as few comprehensive analyses have sought to explore it.

Several early studies of treaty consent were written subsequent to the failed Treaty of Versailles (e.g., Fleming 1930; Holt 1933). According to

Holt (1933), for significant portions of U.S. history, partisan and sectional politics played an important role in the length of the treaty approval process. Presidents had to fight for approval of their important international agreements, and more often than not, they failed. Teddy Roosevelt once complained, "The individual Senators evidently consider the prerogatives of the Senate as far more important than the welfare of the country" (quoted in Holt 1933: 178). Holt's analysis of the Treaty of Versailles clearly shows that the battle in the Senate was primarily based on partisanship. As shown in chapter 1, politics clearly played a role in Senate consideration of major treaties in the late nineteenth and early twentieth centuries, as few treaties were given consent without significant presidential efforts (see also Lindsay 1994: 15–17).

While the early history is replete with treaty failures, conventional interpretations point to the paucity of modern presidential failures on treaties, as only three treaties have been rejected on the floor in the modern era (see, e.g., O'Brien 2003). Focusing on floor failures fails to account for treaties defeated by filibuster or other arcane Senate procedures, those withdrawn from consideration by the president for political reasons (e.g., SALT II in 1980), and other obvious Senate consent failures. In addition, focusing on floor votes and other final outcomes (e.g., attachment of reservations) does not take into consideration the considerable delay that can result during the process. It is clear that previous scholarship overestimates the quiescence of the Senate during the modern era. Lindsay (1994: 78–80) shows that historically (from 1789 to 1992), 10 percent of all treaties submitted to the Senate did not result in consent.[12] Our data show that 7.4 percent of treaties submitted since 1949 failed to receive Senate consent, a percentage similar to that in the greater historical period examined by Lindsay. In one of the only systematic analyses of treaty consideration in the literature, Auerswald and Maltzman (2003) demonstrate that the Senate alters treaty documents by attaching reservations roughly 20 percent of the time and that various political factors explain why some treaties get a reservation while most do not. In summary, while the conventional wisdom in the literature suggests a compliant Senate, a few works point to politics as a key explanation of treaty outcomes and delay.

Explaining Delay in the Advice and Consent Process

In this section, we consider the factors that are expected to help determine how long the Senate takes to process a treaty. Drawing from recent theoretical advancements in legislative studies, our model of treaty consent delay focuses on traditional political factors and on the pivotal role of important members of the Senate. This approach allows us to test rigorously if and how politics matter in the treaty duration process. Our model also incorporates treaty characteristics and the broader historical context as control factors.

Partisanship and Pivotal Politics in the Treaty Process

Political parties provide the mechanisms by which the Senate is organized, policies are developed, winning coalitions are built, and relations with the executive are fostered (Schattschneider 1942). Given the importance of political parties in facilitating interbranch cooperation, cooperation is reduced substantially and legislative gridlock is more common when government is divided between the parties (Binder 1999; Edwards, Barrett, and Peake 1997), even in foreign policy (Lohmann and O'Halloran 1994; Milner 1997; Peake 2002). When the Senate and presidency are controlled by the same party, the president has a political ally controlling the agenda of the SFRC; but during divided government, a president must deal with a committee chair with a different agenda (Taylor 1998). Studies that show the demise of the "two presidencies" and an increase in partisanship in foreign policy suggest that gridlock caused by party differences carry over into foreign policy (Fleisher et al. 2000; McCormick and Wittkopf 1990). As a result, conventional political understanding would suggest that when the president has more copartisans in the Senate, his policies (including treaties) are less likely to face gridlock.

However, there is a debate in the legislative politics literature over the contribution of divided government to legislative gridlock (e.g., Brady and Volden 1998; Mayhew 1991). When institutional preferences are accounted for, the significance of divided government decreases (Binder 1999). Auerswald and Maltzman's (2003) analysis suggests that this may also be the case in the treaty process. They found no significantly greater probability for reservations in the context of divided control of the presidency and Senate. Moreover, we demonstrated in chapters 2 and 3 that the strength of a president's party in the Senate has little impact on presidential decision making regarding the form of international agreements.

Whether the government is divided or unified, the preferences of key institutional players are pivotal in the legislative process, as argued by Keith Krehbiel in *Pivotal Politics* (1998). This is especially evident given the supermajority required for treaty consent. Scholars since Krehbiel have focused their attention on the preferences of these pivotal institutional players, finding that the distribution of individual preferences among institutions is critical to understanding legislative gridlock (Binder 1999; Coleman 1999). Additionally, the preference distributions of the congressional leadership are significant (Chiou and Rothenberg 2003). As congressional leaders play a particularly important role in agenda setting, especially at the committee level, and as these roles are structured by political party (Cox and McCubbins 1993), we expect that partisan and preference distribution arguments may help explain delay in the treaty consent process.[13]

In the politics of treaty approval, the pivotal institutional players are clear: they are the president, the SFRC chair, and the treaty pivot (the senator located at the critical two-thirds position within the chamber).[14] The important factor then becomes how these different individuals important to the process relate to one another ideologically. The SFRC chair is an important gatekeeper on treaties, as all treaties must receive the committee's approval prior to moving to the floor. There is strong evidence in the historical and political science literature that conservatives are likely to hold suspicions regarding presidential treaty making on a wide range of treaties (see DeLaet and Scott 2006; Kaufman 1990). Liberal senators, however, proved critical in their support of numerous significant treaties in the modern era (Krepon and Caldwell 1991) and have promoted internationalist foreign policies more generally (L. Johnson 1984; R. Johnson 2006). We expect, then, that highly conservative SFRC chairs (e.g., Senator Helms) are likely to contribute to gridlock on treaties, whereas more liberal SFRC chairs (e.g., Senator Fulbright), favoring internationalist foreign policies, are likely to support treaty making. In explaining how long it takes the SFRC to complete its work on a treaty, we expect the SFRC chair's ideological preferences to be especially important.

Moreover, we expect that significant preference differences between the president and the treaty pivot will contribute to treaty gridlock in the Senate. The SFRC chair must account for the treaty pivot in giving committee approval to a treaty, as the floor could veto the treaty. That this happens rarely (seven times in our data set) suggests that chairs are cognizant of what it takes to receive floor approval. Generally, once the treaty has been reported, the committee chair is an advocate for its adoption, so the focus is on persuading the treaty pivot to go along with the treaty.[15] The most significant ideological spatial relationship, then, is between the president and the senator located at the treaty pivot. If the treaty pivot is an ideologue, however, getting floor support for the president's treaty should prove more difficult, as that individual's preferences must be satisfied and are likely far from the president's own preferences.

Presidential Resources

Since treaties are presidential policies, the resources presidents are able to muster in support of a treaty might impact the speed of Senate action on the treaty. Presidents often speak on behalf of treaties prior to transmitting them to the Senate and during Senate consideration. Presidential efforts on behalf of a treaty send signals to the Senate of its importance to the president and, more broadly, to U.S. foreign policy. In turn, these signals may encourage the Senate to move on a treaty. Research has shown that presidential speeches provide signals to other policy makers in the system regarding the significance of a policy to the president's agenda (Barrett 2005; Eshbaugh-Soha 2006). It is possible, however, that presidents may signal their special interest in a treaty for the very reason that it may be controversial and receive more scrutiny in the process. Of the 850 treaties in the time period under discussion here, presidents spoke on behalf of 78 prior to transmitting them to the Senate; they spoke on behalf of 74 after transmittal. Combined, presidents signal their support publicly on behalf of only 12 percent of treaties.[16] Most treaties, therefore, may not receive clear public support by the president beyond the standard transmittal document. Anecdotal evidence suggests that public lobbying by the president can have substantial effects on the senatorial consent debate, as was the case for President Kennedy when he made a nuclear test ban treaty a priority of his administration and spoke at length about it publicly (Loeb 1991).

A broader set of presidential resources may also prove important. The president's public prestige, central to the political resources of an administration (Neustadt 1960), may play a role in structuring the treaty approval process. Popular presidents may receive greater leeway from the Senate when seeking consent for their treaties. Moreover, given the salience of national security issues on the president's approval ratings, public prestige equals credibility, and senators are less likely to oppose a highly credible president on national security issues. Krepon and Caldwell (1991: 462) conclude in their book on seven key arms control treaties that "highly popular presidents . . . have been ideally suited to mollify senatorial and public concerns about arms control treaties." They cite popularity as key reasons for Kennedy's success on the Limited Test Ban Treaty and Reagan's success on the Intermediate-Range Nuclear Forces Treaty, but they downplay its insignificance for Nixon during the debate over the Anti-Ballistic Missile Treaty.[17]

Treaty Characteristics

Not all treaties are of equal significance, and the differences may affect how long the Senate takes to process treaties. Significant treaties might prove more problematic during the approval process than more mundane treaties. For instance, important treaties receive greater attention through the hearings process, perhaps drawing more attention from opponents, delaying Senate consent. If presidents dominate the process, as conventional understanding suggests, it makes sense for the Senate to avoid blocking or delaying the more significant treaties, as senators will be predisposed to support the president on his major international agreements. We suspect, however, that senators take their role of advice and consent more seriously on important treaties and are less likely to treat them in a perfunctory manner.[18] Following similar logic, new treaties might also attract greater attention in the Senate, contributing to delay. Substantial percentages (46 percent) of the treaties submitted for advice during the time period under discussion here are new treaties. The remainder includes treaties that alter previously ratified agreements or are extensions of previous treaties. As treaties that alter previously ratified treaties have been vetted in the Senate before, it is likely that new treaties take longer to approve.

The number of parties to a treaty may play a role in structuring Senate behavior. Bilateral treaties are more likely to draw reservations (Auerswald and Maltzman 2003), for example, because senators realize it is easier to negotiate understandings with one other country than with several when a treaty is multilateral. Alternatively, adding parties to a treaty may draw more opposition or at least make senatorial consideration more complicated, contributing to delay. Furthermore, many multilateral treaties are UN treaties that may attract the opposition of conservatives uncomfortable with sovereignty issues related to U.S. participation in international organizations. Thus we expect multilateral treaties to take longer in the approval process.

Finally, the topic of a treaty may influence Senate behavior in the treaty consent process. Auerswald and Maltzman (2003) found that treaties involving "high politics" (sovereignty and security issues) were more likely to draw reservations than treaties involving "low politics" (everything else). Therefore, the type of treaty should be controlled for in any model predicting approval success and delay. Senators may take greater interest in high politics, engendering greater debate and more hearings on related treaties. However, senators may be less inclined to put on hold treaties with obvious foreign policy significance, as is more often the case with high politics. Treaties related to economics (e.g., fisheries agreements) and international norms (e.g., human rights agreements) may engender greater domestic opposition given their clear linkages to specific political groups within the United States (see Kaufman 1990). The opposite relationship could emerge. It is clear that the treaty's domain may play an important role.

Historical Context

Historical era may play a role in the treaty approval process. A substantial change in the context of world politics may alter senatorial incentives to challenge presidential leadership on international agreements (DeLaet and Scott 2006). Some scholars argue that the "Cold War consensus" broke down following the Vietnam War (Mann 1990). Others claim that noticeable change only resulted with the end of the Cold War era (Lindsay 1994; Melanson 2000). Senatorial incentives to challenge presidential leadership in foreign policy increased with the end of the Cold War, as a unifying security threat to American hegemony evaporated (Wittkopf and McCormick 1998). For example, the Senate has more readily attached reservations to significant security agreements since the end of the Cold War (Auerswald 2006).

Methods and Data

We test the aforementioned theoretical expectations by examining the population of treaties submitted by the president to the Senate from 1949 to 2000—a total of 850 treaties.[19] First, we analyze the duration (in days) from presidential transmission of the treaty to the SFRC's first report of the treaty, both for all 850 transmitted treaties and separately for two hundred treaties we identified as most significant.[20] The lion's share of treaty gridlock (in terms of both delay and failure) occurs at the committee stage, as most treaties are quickly dealt with on the floor once they are reported. However, some treaties languish on the Senate floor or fail to reach the floor altogether. To account for the next stage of the process, we examine the duration (in days) from the original SFRC report to the Senate's full consent.

Finally, because we are interested in final outcomes, we examine a model of treaty failure, defining a consent failure as the inability to process a treaty within the transmittal Senate or the subsequent Senate.[21] We collected much of our data from documents using the Congressional Information Service, available via LexisNexis, supplemented with hard-copy versions of the *Congressional Record*. The dates of transmittal, SFRC report, and ratification are the instrumental data for the duration analyses, as the dependent variables are the number of days from transmittal to the SFRC report and from the SFRC report to full Senate consent. To analyze the duration of the treaty process during the two stages, we employ "hazard" analysis, as duration data violate several assumptions of ordinary least squares (see Bennett and Stam 1996; Box-Steffensmeier and Jones 1997).[22] We employ "rare events" logit analysis (see Tomz, King, and Zeng 1999) to explore the determinants of treaty failure in the consent process. The dependent variable is coded 1 if the treaty failed to receive consent in a timely fashion and 0 otherwise. We use rare events logit because the failure category of our dependent variable occurs in only 15 percent of our cases. Rare events logit provides more appropriate coefficient estimates given the dependent variable's distribution.

Independent Variables

Our independent variables account for treaty characteristics, the broader policy-making context, presidential resources, and the partisan/ideological context relative to the pivotal players in the treaty process. The independent variables of greatest interest in our analyses represent the partisan and ideological context that may influence the ratification process. To account for the partisan context in the Senate, we include a variable measuring the number of presidential partisans in the Senate.[23]

Given the supermajority requirement for treaty consent and the significance of the SFRC in the process, we have already argued that these pivotal institutional players in the Senate are likely to greatly influence the disposition of treaties before the Senate. For treaties, the pivotal member of the Senate is not the median member (in terms of ideology) but the member located at the treaty pivot.[24] We include as a measure the absolute difference between common-space ideology scores (CS-NOMINATE) for the treaty pivot and the president at the time of treaty transmittal. We hypothesize that as the relative difference score increases, treaty duration and the likelihood of gridlock will increase, as reconciling the policy preferences among these important players grows in difficulty. To account for the preferences of the SFRC chair separately, we include the chair's CS-NOMINATE ideology score in the model.[25]

Presidential resources and efforts on behalf of a treaty may also play a role in the process. We account for the political resources of the president by controlling for his average yearly public approval during the year of treaty transmittal.[26] We use the *Public Papers of the Presidents* (various editions) to account for presidential signals on behalf of a treaty. Specifically, we count the number of lines devoted to each treaty in the *Papers* where the president spoke publicly on behalf of the treaty prior to transmitting it to the Senate.[27]

We use Auerswald and Maltzman's (2003) treaty classification, using dummy variables to classify treaties in terms of their primary topic: security, sovereignty, economic issues, legal issues, and norms.[28] Additionally, we control for whether or not the treaty is multilateral, with all treaties with three or more party nations coded 1 and with bilateral treaties coded 0. As we did in chapters 2 and 3, we use Axelrod's (2000) compilation of historically significant treaties in *American Treaties and Alliances* to determine whether or not a treaty is important.[29] Important treaties are given a code of 1; all others receive a code of 0. Finally, new treaties are given a code of 1, while other treaties are coded 0. To control for historical era, we code treaties transmitted from 1949 to 1989 as Cold War treaties, which receive a code of 1. The size of the Senate's treaty agenda is likely to have a positive impact on the duration of the process—a more crowded agenda is likely to contribute to delay and gridlock. We include an agenda variable, which is the raw count of important treaties transmitted during a Senate.[30]

Statistical Method

Making sense of hazard models can be tricky, as interpretation of coefficients is not as straightforward as ordinary least squares regression. It is important to first clarify how the analysis works conceptually. In a hazard model, the coefficients demonstrate the impact of the variables on the underlying hazard rate. An increase in the hazard rate means that the variable has the effect of speeding up a treaty decision (fewer days), while a decrease in the hazard rate means that the variable slows down a decision (more days), thus increasing gridlock. Hazard rates reflect the probability of the examined process ending. In our case, ending the process is reflected in the successful reporting out of a treaty by the SFRC or consent by the full Senate.[31] To assess the substantive effects of our independent variables on the duration of the treaty approval process, we estimate a baseline predicted median value and compare the marginal effects of changes in the significant independent variables on duration. We report the estimated impacts in percentages in the tables that follow.

The Politics of Treaty Gridlock

The findings suggest that the preferences of pivotal institutional players and treaty characteristics are important in the treaty approval process and help explain treaty gridlock. In particular, as the policy preferences (ideologies) of the president and the treaty pivot diverge, gridlock increases. Moreover, conservative SFRC chairs slow the process of Senate consent considerably. Presidential resources (i.e., approval) impact treaty gridlock marginally, but in different ways depending on the stage of the process. The duration analyses confirm our expectations that domestic politics matter in the process, contributing significantly to treaty gridlock in the Senate. Our findings are robust across the different stages of the process and when we narrow our examination to those treaties considered historically significant.

Treaty Gridlock in Committee

As highlighted earlier, most of the delay in the treaty approval process occurs within the SFRC. What factors determine the length of time a treaty takes to clear the SFRC? In table 5, we report results from a hazard model estimating the duration of the treaty approval process in the SFRC for all of the treaties submitted by presidents from 1949 to 2000 and for the subset of important treaties transmitted during this period. As we report in table 5, an important contributor to treaty delay at the committee level is the committee chair. As hypothesized, conservative committee chairs are more likely to drag out the treaty process.[32] In model 1 (for all treaties), having a conservative SFRC chair (one standard deviation above the mean ideology score) adds about 14 percent more time to the committee stage of the process. For important treaties (model 2), the marginal effect is much greater, increasing to 39 percent, or about 3.5 months.[33]

We also hypothesized that as the ideological preferences of the president and the treaty pivot diverged, delay would noticeably increase. The results reported in table 5 clearly support this hypothesis during the committee stage. Partisan polarization greatly increases the ideological distance between the president, who is generally around the median of his party, and the pivot, who is typically, but not always, a member of the opposite party. Substantively, the median duration in committee is increased by 26 percent (or about two months) when the differences in ideology between the president and treaty pivot are significantly high. For the subset of important treaties, the marginal effect is even greater—the substantive impact represents an increase of nearly five months. The standard parti-

TABLE 5. Hazard Model for Treaty Delay in SFRC Report, 1949–2000

dependent variable	All treaties (Model 1)			Important treaties (Model 2)		
	Hazard ratio	|z|	Impact on duration	Hazard ratio	|z|	Impact on duration
Treaty characteristics						
Important treaty	1.20	1.45*	−20%	—	—	—
Multilateral	0.85	1.13		0.67	−1.69**	+39%
New treaty	0.70	−3.40**	+41%	0.97	−0.15	
Security	0.99	−0.05		0.71	−1.10	
Sovereignty	1.00	−0.72		0.73	−1.77**	+40%
Economic	0.92	0.12		0.64	−1.84**	+58%
Norms	0.70	−2.12**	+49%	0.44	−2.77**	+116%
Policy context						
Cold War	0.81	1.30*	−22%	0.81	−0.61	
Size of treaty agenda	0.98	−0.80		0.95	−1.42*	+19%
Presidential resources						
Presidential approval	1.01	1.67**	−10%	1.01	1.67**	−15%
Presidential statements	1.001	1.86**	−4%	1.000	1.05	
Political context						
Number of presidential partisans	0.99	−1.53*	+13%	0.97	−2.34**	+32%
SFRC chair ideology	0.72	−1.92**	+14%	0.37	−2.95**	+39%
Distance from president to pivotal senator	0.29	−2.22**	+26%	0.11	−3.38**	+54%
Gamma	−0.001	8.58**		−0.001	−5.51**	

Number of subjects = 850   Number of subjects = 200
Number of failures (reports) = 804   Numbers of failures (reports) = 190
Total time at risk = 692,813 days   Total time at risk = 167,959 days
Log-likelihood = −1,474.5   Log-likelihood = −351.0
Wald chi^2 (14) = 60.44**   Wald chi^2 (13) = 110.4**
Baseline median duration = 229   Baseline median duration = 264

Note: The dependent variable was the time (in days) from the point of treaty transmittal to when the SFRC first reported on the treaty. The standard errors are Hubert-White (robust) standard errors, clustered by Senate. Hazard ratios below 1.0 indicate an increase in duration, whereas hazard ratios above 1.0 indicate a decrease in duration. Impact on duration indicates the percentage effect on the baseline estimate of the median duration to committee report when the independent variable of interest is moved from its mean value (or 0 if a dummy variable) one standard deviation above its mean (or 1 if a dummy), with all other variables held at their mean values. Legal treaties are the reference category for treaty type. The analysis was conducted in Stata 9. Impacts were computed using the "mfx compute" command therein.
*$p < .1$ **$p < .05$ (one-tailed)

san measure, however, does not perform as expected. In fact, the results suggest that when other factors are taken into account, the more partisans the president has in the Senate, the more delay treaties will face. We do not put too much stock in this counterintuitive finding, except to conclude that straightforward party measures do not explain treaty delay in line with received wisdom, once ideology is taken into account.[34]

Public approval ratings appear to have important effects on the duration a treaty sits in committee. When the president is especially popular (one standard deviation above the mean value, or 65 percent) the estimated duration a treaty remains in committee is decreased by 15 percent (or forty days) for the important treaties and 10 percent (or twenty-three days) for all treaties. Presidents appear unable to speed up the committee process through the use of rhetoric prior to transmittal of the treaty, however, as their statements have only minimal (though statistically significant) effects in just the one model.

Our committee analysis provides only modest and mixed support for the importance of the policy context as represented by the variables of agenda size and the Cold War. During the Cold War period, treaties were dealt with more quickly by the SFRC. The marginal effect of the Cold War, among all treaties, is to decrease duration by 22 percent. As hypothesized, since the end of the Cold War, the SFRC has been slower to act on treaties before it; but this relationship does not hold when we narrow our focus to the important treaties. For the significant treaties, however, the size of the treaty agenda matters. A fuller treaty agenda increases delay by an estimated 19 percent among the important treaties.

Treaty characteristics impact duration of the process in committee as expected. Among all treaties considered by the SFRC, important treaties are handled slightly faster, while new treaties are processed by the SFRC much more slowly than treaties that alter previously ratified agreements. We also find that treaties related to international norms (e.g., human rights treaties) generally take longer, no matter the set of treaties we examine. Norms treaties are an especially big target when they are deemed historically significant, as the duration of the committee process is more than doubled for norms treaties when compared to the reference category of legal treaties. Among important treaties, sovereignty and economic treaties face more committee gridlock than legal treaties. Interestingly, important security treaties do not register as significant. This may be the case because opposition to these agreements (particularly those dealing with arms control) during the earlier years of our study emerged from the Senate Armed Services Committee rather than the SFRC (Krepon and Caldwell 1991; R. Johnson 2006).

To isolate substantive effects, table 6 shows predicted durations for two categories of treaties (legal and norms) given specified values of statistically significant independent variables of interest: SFRC chair ideology, president/pivot difference, and presidential approval. If the control variables for Cold War, new treaty, important treaty, and multilateral treaty are held at 1, with all others at their median (or 0 in the case of dummy variables), the estimated duration is 262 days for a legal treaty and 401 for a norms treaty. If all the same conditions apply with the exception that the chair's ideology difference is set 1 standard deviation above the mean, the predicted duration increases substantially to 321 and 499 days, respectively. By additionally setting the president/pivot difference to one standard deviation above its mean, the predicted durations are 377 and 594 days. Hence the combined effects of a conservative chair and significant preference differences between the president and treaty pivot are substantial. Looking last at the impact of presidential approval, we see that under the same conditions ripe for treaty gridlock, a popular president can expect to reduce the delay by a little over a month for legal treaties and over

TABLE 6.   Predicted Durations Given Specified Values of Independent Variables, from Transmittal to Committee Report, All Treaties

	Legal Treaty	Norms Treaty
Predicted median duration to committee report when *new, important, multilateral,* or *Cold War* equals 1; others are at median (or 0)	262 days	401 days
Predicted median duration to committee report when *new, important, multilateral,* or *Cold War* equals 1; *SFRC chair ideology* is set one standard deviation above its mean; others are at median (or 0)	321 days	499 days
Predicted median duration to committee report when *new, important, multilateral,* or *Cold War* equals 1; *SFRC chair ideology* and *president/pivot difference* are set one standard deviation above their means, others are at median (or 0)	377 days	594 days
Predicted median duration to committee report when *new, important, multilateral,* or *Cold War* equals 1; *SFRC chair ideology, president/pivot difference,* and *presidential approval* are set one standard deviation above their means; others are at median (or zero)	340 days	431 days

five months for norms treaties. Therefore, while popular presidents appear better able to get their treaties more rapidly through the committee, the impact is nowhere near as great as the ideological dispositions of pivotal Senate actors in the process.

Treaty Gridlock on the Floor

While most of the delay in the treaty approval process occurs in committee, some treaties languish even with the committee's approval. Once a treaty has moved through the committee, it is still a work in progress, and reservations may be added during floor deliberations, possibly contributing to delay. At this late stage of the treaty consent process, the preferences of the floor, particularly the senator located at the treaty pivot, are likely to matter most. Presumably, the major proponent of the treaty (the president) and the SFRC chair have worked through any differences on the treaty. Moreover, given the paucity of treaty failures in the modern era, Senate leaders are unlikely to bring to the floor a treaty that does not have the supermajority required.[35] Additionally, the SFRC chair's ideology is likely less significant at this stage of the process, since he or she has already given his or her blessing to the treaty by reporting it to the full chamber. Given this logic, we focus our attention at this stage of the process on the preference of the Senate pivot vis-à-vis the president. In table 7, we report the results of a survival model where the days from SFRC report to full Senate approval is the dependent variable.[36] Recall that the median duration at this stage in the data set is only eight days. Therefore, the duration increases we discuss here are rather minimal but do have some bearing on the amount of time a treaty is before the full Senate and therefore on the extensiveness of the debate there.

Generally, our expectations are supported in the floor model reported in table 7, though the preference difference variable is not as robust for all treaties as in the analysis presented in table 5. As the floor pivot's preferences differ from the president's, treaty delay on the floor is increased—ranging from a 23 percent marginal impact when considering all treaties to an impact of 30 percent (or an additional five days) when considering the important treaties. The apparent effects of presidential signals on the floor stage differ substantially from those effects reported during the committee stage. Presidential statements on behalf of a treaty prior to its transmittal to the Senate increases delay on the floor, and this increase is especially apparent among the important treaties, having a marginal effect of doubling (+109 percent) the time a treaty spends on the floor. The indication that the treaty is a significant part of the president's agenda might

Survival Model for Treaty Delay from Committee to Senate Floor, 1949–2000

dependent variable	All treaties (Model 1)			Important treaties (Model 2)		
	Coefficient	|z|	Impact on duration	Coefficient	|z|	Impact on duration
eaty characteristics						
Important treaty	0.27	2.14**	+29%	—		—
Multilateral	−0.004	−0.02		1.25	0.69	
New treaty	−0.08	−0.63		0.95	−0.13	
Security	−0.12	−0.32		1.44	0.91	
Sovereignty	0.14	0.51		2.42	2.35**	+105%
Economic	−0.06	−0.35		1.82	2.89**	+69%
Norms	0.13	0.69		2.68	3.09**	+107%
licy context						
Cold War	0.51	1.71**	+47%	1.60	1.22	
Size of treaty agenda	0.05	1.14		1.04	0.97	
esidential resources						
Presidential approval	−0.002	−0.16		1.004	0.39	
Presidential statements	0.003	3.11**	+31%	1.003	2.84**	+109%
litical context						
Number of presidential partisans	0.002	0.14		1.02	1.01	
SFRC chair ideology	−0.01	−0.05		1.45	0.55	
Distance from president to pivotal senator	1.26	1.31*	+23%	4.49	1.85**	+30%
atural log of gamma	−0.14	−2.27**		−0.01	0.10	

Number of subjects = 804 Number of subjects = 190
Number of failures (consent) = 787 Number of failures (consent) = 181
Total time at risk = 187,819 days Total time at risk = 99,118 days
Log-likelihood = −1,500.4 Log-likelihood = −384.6
Wald chi^2 (14) = 31.03** Wald chi^2 (13) = 177.6**
Baseline median duration = 10.2 Baseline median duration = 15.1

Note: The dependent variable was the time (in days) from the point of the SFRC report to when the full Senate .ve its consent. The standard errors are Hubert-White (robust) standard errors, clustered by Senate. In survival odels (using a log-logistic distribution), positive coefficients indicate an increase in the time ratio for survival, 1ich means a reduced probability that the process will end at a given point in time (when the full Senate votes to ›nsent). A positive relationship indicates positive impact on duration (the opposite of the hazard model reported table 5). *Impact on duration* indicates effect on the baseline estimate of the median duration to full Senate con- nt when the independent variable of interest is moved from its mean value (or 0 if a dummy variable) to one andard deviation above its mean (or 1 if a dummy), with all other variables held at their mean values. Legal eaties are the reference category for treaty type. The analysis was conducted in Stata 9. Impacts were computed .ing "mfx compute" command therein.

*$p < .1$ **$p < .05$ (one-tailed)

embolden the opposition to delay on the floor, perhaps through debate and amendment procedures. Treaty characteristics become significant when we examine the important treaties—sovereignty, economic, and norms treaties all take, on average, roughly twice as long to process on the floor as the significant legal treaties within the data set. More generally, important treaties take slightly longer on the floor, as do Cold War treaties.

To further delineate substantive effects, we computed predicted durations between committee report and Senate consent for two categories of important treaties (legal and norms) given specified values of statistically significant independent variables of interest: president/pivot difference and presidential statements. If the control variables for new treaty, multilateral treaty, and Cold War are held at 1, with all others at their median (or 0 in the case of dummy variables), the baseline changes to 8.3 days for a legal treaty and 22.5 days for a norms treaty. If the same conditions apply with the exception that the president/pivot difference is set one standard deviation above the mean, the predicted durations increase marginally to 9.9 days and 26.7 days, respectively. Looking last at the impact of presidential statements, we see that under the same conditions, when we increase the presidential statements variable one standard deviation above the mean, the predicted duration increases significantly to 23.4 days and 63.5 days, respectively. Therefore, while presidents have some ability to shorten the length of the process from transmittal to committee report by making a pitch for a treaty prior to transmittal (see table 5), such tactics actually can lengthen the process between committee report and Senate floor consent.

Overall Success in the Treaty Consent Process

We can gain a more complete understanding of the treaty approval process by examining the overall success of the entire process. We do so in table 8, in which we report rare events logit models where the dependent variable is treaty consent failure. Failure is here defined as the Senate not giving its consent during the transmittal Senate or the subsequent Senate.

By and large, our hypotheses related to pivotal institutional players receive support in the model predicting consent failure, whereas hypotheses more closely related to partisan theories receive no support. For example, treaties submitted when the president has a greater number of partisans in the Senate are marginally more likely to fail than treaties submitted when the average numbers of presidential partisans are in the Senate, which is the opposite of the result predicted by partisan theories (probability is .17

Rare Events Logit for Treaty Approval Failure, 1949–2000

dependent variable	All treaties (Model 1)			Important treaties (Model 2)		
	Coefficent	|z|	Impact	Coefficient	|z|	Impact
eaty Characteristics						
Important treaty	0.03	0.10		—	—	
Multilateral	0.25	1.07		0.23	0.60	
New treaty	0.63	2.70**	.18	−0.10	−0.22	
Security	0.20	0.40		0.93	1.30*	.30
Sovereignty	0.40	1.01		0.83	1.07	
Economic	0.30	0.90		1.31	1.79**	.39
Norms	1.01	2.76**	.28	1.95	2.85**	.45
licy Context						
Cold War	0.51	1.54*	.15	−0.37	−0.65	
Month transmitted	−0.01	−0.88		−0.04	−1.37*	.14
Size of treaty agenda	0.06	1.61*	.16	0.11	1.47*	.17
residential Resources						
Presidential approval	−0.02	−1.69**	.11	−0.02	−1.21	
Presidential statements	0.0002	0.28		−0.00004	−0.04	
litical Context						
Number of presidential partisans	0.03	1.83**	.17	0.10	3.03**	.33
SFRC chair ideology	0.50	1.19		1.66	2.54**	.25
Distance from president to pivotal senator	1.48	1.73**	.17	3.15	1.83**	.26
onstant	−4.70	−2.97**		−8.38	−2.88**	

$N = 850$
% in modal category = 85
Baseline predicted $Pr(1) = .13$
Log-likelihood = −331.7
LR chi^2 (15) = 50.6**
Pseudo $R^2 = .07$
PRE statistic = .06

$N = 200$
% in modal category = 79
Baseline predicted $Pr(1) = .17$
Log-likelihood = −81.9
LR chi^2 (14) = 41.8**
Pseudo $R^2 = .17$
PRE statistic = .43

Note: The dependent variable was coded 1 if a treaty transmitted by the president failed to gain Senate consent ithin the transmittal or subsequent Senate. The standard errors are Hubert-White (robust) standard errors. Le- l treaties are the reference category for treaty type. The impacts were calculated with all variables set at mean and ith variable of interest set at one standard deviation above mean for continuous variables and at 1 for dichoto- ous variables. The impacts were calculated using ReLogit (Tomz, King, and Zeng 1999) and represent the esti- ated probability of failure given the stated change in the variable of interest.
*$p < .1$ **$p < .05$ (one-tailed)

vs. the baseline of .13). The ideological difference between the president and the treaty pivot matters in a direction that confirms the pivotal hypothesis, though the substantive relationship is likewise small. The substantive impact of these variables increases substantially when we limit our sample to the important treaties, however.

The SFRC chair's ideology, while statistically insignificant when we analyze all treaties, is an important indicator of treaty failure when we narrow our focus to the important treaties. This provides further empirical evidence that the preferences of the chair matter significantly in the process for the consequential treaties. An ideologically extreme SFRC chair (e.g., Senator Jesse Helms) contributes to treaty gridlock and delayed diplomacy. In table 9, we provide simulated estimates from the rare events logit model reported in table 8. We report the simulated effects of selected SFRC chairs during our historical period on various types of important treaties. When we hold all the variables, other than treaty type, at their mean values, the significance of an ideologically conservative chair becomes especially clear.

Senator Helms, being the most conservative chair in modern history, is estimated to have substantively significant effect on treaty gridlock. The effect is especially apparent on norms and security treaties and when compared to his more liberal counterparts, such as Senators Fulbright and Pell. For example, the estimated probability of failure for a security treaty under Helms is .39, as compared to a probability of just .12 for Fulbright. According to our model estimates, Helms deserves his reputation as a significant obstacle to consequential internationalist policies (Hersman 2000: 88–89) on the part of recent presidents (both Republican and Democratic), as Fulbright deserves his reputation for helping modern presidents pursue internationalist policies (R. Johnson 2006). It was with the support of Fulbright that many of the first and most important arms control agreements sailed through the Senate (e.g., the Limited Test Ban

TABLE 9. Predicted Probability of Failure given Specified SFRC Committee Chairs' Ideologies on Important Treaties, with Other Variables Held at Mean Values

	Ideology score	Legal treaty	Norms treaty	Security treaty
Sen. Fulbright (86th–93rd Senates)	−.226	.06	.28	.12
Sen. Percy (97th–98th Senates)	.006	.08	.36	.17
Sen. Lugar (99th Senate)	.290	.12	.48	.25
Sen. Pell (100th–103rd Senates)	−.384	.04	.24	.10
Sen. Helms (104th–106th Senates)	.656	.19	.63	.39

Treaty in 1963, given consent in a mere forty-seven days, and the Anti-Ballistic Missile Treaty in 1972, which took only fifty-one days; see Loeb 1991; Platt 1991).

Pivots or Party?

In summary, our analysis of the politics of treaties in the Senate suggests that the ideological preferences of pivotal institutional players explain much of the gridlock that sometimes plagues the treaty process. We do not, however, want to leave the reader with the impression that party is of little consequence in the treaty process, as proponents of pivotal politics often argue is the case in legislative politics more generally. The clearest counters to this argument are the facts that political party determines the chair of the SFRC and that, during divided government, the chair and president are opposing partisans, which should greatly complicate policy making.

We ran separate models from those presented in tables 5, 7, and 8, excluding from the models our president/pivot difference and presidential partisans variables and including a measure for divided government and party polarization in the Senate. In every instance, divided government was either insignificant or significant in the opposite direction than expected—it sped up the process or contributed to treaty success. Polarization, however, is significant in the expected direction—suggesting that when the two parties are ideologically polarized, treaty gridlock increases substantially.[37] That polarized parties also contribute to the ideological polarization of the pivotal players in the process is not surprising. The alternative analyses suggest that while divided government alone does not appear to delay diplomacy in the Senate, ideological (preference) polarization clearly does. Given the two-thirds requirement, a bipartisan coalition is almost always required to approve a treaty. As a result, partisan ideological polarization, rather than divided government, is the clearest partisan contributor to treaty gridlock.

Conclusion

Treaty ratification is pro forma and uninteresting because presidents use executive agreements to negotiate the lion's share of the most controversial international pacts during tough governing circumstances. As a result, presidents dominate the treaty ratification process in the Senate. That intertwined logic underlies the conventional wisdom of presidential-congressional relations on international agreements. Our findings in this chapter and in earlier chapters provide a significant challenge to the conventional wisdom. In this chapter, we find strong support for a more politics-laden ratification process than others have suggested. A much larger proportion of treaties falter in the prefloor process as a result of politics than anyone realized, and the dynamics of treaty gridlock appear driven in part by the political preferences of key institutional players.

In addition to further testing our theoretical framework, the tenor of our political explanations of treaty outcomes and duration speak to broader debates on presidential-congressional relations. Our results are consistent with the systematic empirical results reported in chapters 2 and 3 on the use of executive agreements vis-à-vis treaties. We find little support for strictly partisan explanations of treaty outcomes and duration, while we find strong support for explanations centered on the preferences of key institutional players. The results provide further support for our initial framework that partisan explanations are insufficient in explaining the domestic politics of international agreements. The policy preferences of key institutional players (in particular, the SFRC chair and the floor pivot) determine treaty outcomes. Despite this nonfinding for partisan theories, treaty consent in the Senate presents a significant hurdle for presidents completing international agreements, as the delay is often substantial. The supermajority requirement for ratification contributes to treaty gridlock, both at the committee stage and at the floor stage, as our most robust finding was that the preference of the SFRC chair and the relative preferences of the president and the treaty pivot matter greatly. The logic that presidents base their decisions on international agreements partly on the ideologies of key institutional players in the Senate is further strengthened by our results.

The supermajority requirement of the treaty consent process makes pivotal politics more critical than otherwise might be the case. Scholarship that supports the party government model primarily uses data on House behavior (e.g., Aldrich and Rohde 2000). Given the majoritarian nature of that institution and the strength of the party leadership, it is not surprising that party matters more in the House. However, the strength of party leaders is not as great in the Senate, given the Senate's supermajoritarian nature. Our most robust finding is that the policy preferences of the chair and the floor pivot matter greatly. This suggests that the foreign relations committee considers floor preferences when processing treaties. Yet, because of the two-thirds requirement on treaties, the committee must account for minority views as well. Even so, our findings on the significance of chair conservatism in contributing to treaty gridlock on the important treaties indicate that the chair can be a significant hurdle no matter the distribution of floor preferences or supermajoritarian institutions. Given that most of the delay occurs within the SFRC, this is an important generalizable finding that comports with evidence from case studies.

We should keep in mind, however, that our findings are limited, given our focus on the treaty process, not the legislative process more generally. It could be that because we deal with important foreign policies, the partisan model explains less in terms of domestic politics. After all, scholars have long held that bipartisanship is the norm in foreign policy and that members of Congress typically show deference to the executive (P. Peterson 1994; Wildavsky 1966). However, the fact that party appears (aside from ideological predispositions) unimportant in the politics of treaty consent in the Senate does not mean that the process is not highly political and costly for presidents. Our findings clearly show an important influence of politics in structuring presidential-senatorial relations in foreign policy. Gridlock is quite apparent in the treaty ratification process. Thus, even in the treaty process, where the Senate considers the nation's most solemn international commitments, politics do not stop at the water's edge. Instead, the politics are of a different type—not the more familiar partisan politics.

To this point, our analysis of the domestic politics of international agreements has focused on the U.S. Senate. However, given the significance of America's international agreements—from committing the United States to significant alliances to altering the foundations of international trade—it is likely that the House of Representatives takes a keen interest in America's international commitments. In the next and final empirical chapter, we explore the role played by the House in the domestic politics of international agreements.

6 | The Forgotten House? The Role of the House of Representatives in International Agreements

To this point in our analysis of the domestic politics of international agreements, we have focused our attention on the U.S. Senate. Our logic in focusing on the Senate is understandable, given its constitutional obligations in the treaty process. After all, when presidents choose to complete their international agreements as executive agreements rather than as treaties, they are skirting the Senate and perhaps trespassing on senatorial prerogatives. Presidential decisions on international agreements do not just impact the Senate, however. The House of Representatives plays an important role in the politics of international agreements—a role heretofore largely ignored by scholars.

When presidents complete executive agreements, they often do so with the knowledge that the agreement requires the support of both the Senate and the House. Hence, by choosing to avoid the Senate and the long drawn-out treaty consent process, presidents often directly involve the House. The so-called congressional-executive agreements, or statutory agreements (L. Johnson 1984), sometimes require the assent of both the House and Senate by joint resolution or other method of congressional approval. The rise of executive agreements has solidified the role of the House in the politics of international agreements, especially in the realm of foreign trade (Ackerman and Golove 1995).[1] Moreover, ratified treaties are not always self-executing and sometimes require implementing legislation, hence moving the postratification politics to the House of Representatives.

In this chapter, we explore the extent to which the House interjects itself into the realm of international agreements. We systematically examine and compare House and Senate interest in international agreements by focusing on trends in House and Senate hearings from 1973 to 2004. We demonstrate that over time, House committees are more actively engaged in the realm of international agreements than committees in the Senate. This engagement is especially prevalent in the oversight and investigatory arenas and is not limited to emphasizing executive agreements (where the House has a legal role) over treaties (where it typically does not). The data suggest that when treaties require implementation legislation, House committees hold more hearings than do Senate committees.[2] The Senate tends to focus on its constitutional responsibilities in the treaty advice and consent process, with less attention devoted to oversight and investigatory hearings. Furthermore, the House is more deeply involved than the Senate on international agreements involving economics, and these economic agreements account for much of the House-Senate difference.

Our results suggest that the rise in executive agreements affords the House greater opportunities to affect the direction of international commitments and American foreign policy than otherwise would occur if treaties were the dominant form of international agreements. The findings lend further support to our central contention that the Congress has been a willing partner in the rise of executive agreements. Executive agreements have clearly allowed the House to play a significant role in American diplomacy, a role that would not exist if all agreements were done as treaties. Additionally, our framework emphasizes the significance of legislative delegation to the executive in treaty making. In order for delegation to work effectively in a system of shared powers, Congress must exercise its role of oversight and investigation. In this chapter, we find a very active House engaged in oversight and investigatory activity, as measured by hearings, lending further support for our theoretical framework. The data suggest that the House plays an important role in monitoring executive activity related to the treaty-making power.

First, we discuss bicameral responsibilities vis-à-vis international agreements. We outline the constitutional argument behind House involvement in international agreements and relate the discussion to our findings in earlier chapters. Second, we briefly survey the legislation on international agreements that have led to the direct involvement of the House in the agreement process. Third, we present hearings data (from 1973 to 2004) to compare the extent to which the House is involved in the process relative to the Senate. We examine hearings by the type of hearing and by the international agreement domain. Finally, we conclude by placing our results in the context of our broader arguments on the domestic politics of international agreements.

International Agreements, Bicameralism, and the Constitution

As we showed in chapter 2, since 1949, 94 percent of international agreements have been completed as executive agreements. However, when only the major international agreements are considered, this number is cut in half. Further analysis suggests that the modern Senate has acquiesced to this important institutional evolution—that of the executive agreement—in order to provide for efficiency and to further U.S. international commitments. To do otherwise would bog the Senate down with numerous inconsequential international agreements in the form of treaties (hundreds each session) and would make the treaty consent process perfunctory. Hence, the rise in the modern executive agreement can be explained rather simply as a mechanism for institutional and policy efficiency. Indeed, our results from chapters 2 and 3 indicate that the logic of strategic evasion on the part of the president falls flat when executive agreement usage is analyzed systematically.

Left unconsidered to this point, however, is the important role that the House of Representatives now plays in the modern executive agreement process. The congressional-executive agreement, or statutory agreement, has become the primary vehicle for the completion of international agreements by American presidents. Loch Johnson (1984) estimates that over 90 percent of executive agreements are pursuant to a statutory grant of power to the president or require ex post congressional approval (through joint resolution) before the agreement enters into force. The rarer executive agreement that relies entirely on the executive's plenary powers in foreign policy is referred to as a sole executive agreement or presidential agreement (Klarevas 2003: 394). Modern trade agreements, which require bicameral approval, are probably the best example of significant international agreements that are completed outside of the formal treaty process under the form of the congressional-executive agreement.

The political branches have recognized areas of policy where a congressional-executive agreement is most appropriate and areas where a formal treaty is most appropriate. As shown by Spiro (2001), when an international agreement deals with a power of Congress (e.g., the foreign commerce power), the congressional-executive agreement is considered, in practice, most appropriate. A treaty here would endanger the prerogatives of the House. Several times, when this method was challenged legally, the House defended its turf based on arguments of House responsibilities in economic policy under the commerce clause in Article I of the U.S.

Constitution (see Ackerman and Golove 1995). However, when an international agreement deals with powers outside of Article I, a treaty is most appropriate; hence extradition agreements are typically done by treaty. These practices have led to the development of an "ad hoc typology," where some types of agreements are routinely submitted as treaties and others are routinely treated as congressional-executive agreements (Spiro 2001: 993). Similar types of executive agreements are used to complete international agreements on fisheries and atomic energy (Fisher 1991).[3]

While this ad hoc typology is apparent, it is not iron clad. Arms control agreements, for example, typically are done by treaty according to this understanding. However, as we have shown in earlier chapters, presidents have floated the idea of completing significant arms control agreements as executive agreements rather than as treaties (e.g., Carter with SALT II and George W. Bush with the Moscow Treaty), and President Nixon completed the original SALT agreement as an executive agreement, which then involved the House directly, as the agreement required bicameral legislative consent. The Anti-Ballistic Missile Treaty, which Nixon signed in conjunction with SALT, was submitted to the Senate as a treaty for advice and consent.

It is fairly clear, then, that the rise of the modern executive agreement has afforded the House opportunities to have a direct say in the international agreement process. As we discussed in chapter 1, this important institutional tool was partly a response to the mid-twentieth-century perception that the Senate's monopoly on the treaty power endangered foreign policy goals supported by a majority of Americans. In 1945, for example, the House approved a constitutional amendment that would have required that treaties receive the consent of a majority in both chambers, but unsurprisingly, the Senate never took up the amendment. Undeterred, opponents of the Senate treaty monopoly looked for alternative means to complete major international agreements and found it in the modern executive agreement (Ackerman and Golove 1995).

The House, however, is not completely shut out of the treaty process in many cases. While many treaties are self-executing, should a treaty require implementing legislation or obligate the United States to spend sums of money, the House of Representatives plays a significant role after ratification (Vasquez 1995).[4] Through normal legislative channels, Congress must appropriate the funds necessary for carrying forth the treaty's provisions. Furthermore, if the treaty involves commercial interests (e.g., a fishing treaty or one proscribing trade in certain products) or the disposition of territory (e.g., the treaty purchasing Alaska from Russia in 1867), legislation is required (Fisher 1998: 186–87). This is partly why significant international agreements involving commerce often take the form of executive agreements, as majority bicameral support is required anyway (in the form of implementing legislation) in order to carry out a treaty. Completing a commercial agreement as a treaty would raise the legislative stakes: a supermajority would be required for approval in the Senate, then House approval would be required to implement the treaty.[5] Moreover, to be fully implemented, treaties often require appropriations—a fundamental power of the House (Corwin 1984: 243; O'Brien 2003: 71).

It becomes clear, then, that the House has historically played an important role in the politics of international agreements. Outside of specific treatments of trade politics (e.g., Biglaiser, Jackson, and Peake 2004), we know little regarding the extent to which the House becomes involved in the process. In this chapter, through a systematic analysis of committee hearings, we describe and compare the extent to which the House and Senate are interested in the international agreement process. First, however, we briefly survey the legislation routinely used to directly involve the House in that process.

Congressional Approval Requirements as a Constraint

More often than not, when scholars write of presidents behaving unilaterally through the use of executive agreements (e.g., Crenson and Ginsberg 2007), they discount the role Congress plays in constraining presidential actions. We have seen that presidents are cognizant of domestic politics when deciding how to complete their international agreements—whether as treaties or executive agreements—and that their behavior does not support the evasion hypothesis. Instead, our analysis indicates that presidents are mindful of congressional constraints when completing their international agreements. Presidents tend to work within the boundaries set by the system of separate institutions sharing power. When the Congress demands inclusion, presidents often respond by changing their behavior. When presidents fail to respond in this manner, Congress acts to constrain the president. In the 1950s, it used the threat of constitutional amendment, with the Bricker Amendment. During the 1970s, it used the Case-Zablocki Act and its several amendments.[6] These instances mark dramatic and historical confrontations between the branches on international agreements. At other times, Congress or, more specifically, the Senate has acted to limit presidential behavior on treaties—especially in regard to specific, controversial treaties.

On several fronts, Congress has sought to constrain presidential behavior on executive agreements. The primary focus of these various constraints has been twofold. First, Congress established procedures that keep it informed of executive actions on treaties and executive agreements. The procedures are governed by the Case-Zablocki Act of 1972. Second, Congress has acted to "ensure most of the important international agreements have the status of treaties or are authorized by the entire Congress" (U.S. Senate Committee on Foreign Relations 2001: 233). An important step in ensuring congressional authorization is consultation between the State Department and the relevant congressional committees on the legal form important international agreements shall take once they are finalized. Two procedures have emerged to facilitate consultation between the State Department and Congress. First is the formal C175 procedure, which we reviewed in chapter 3, whereby staffers in the Legal Office at the State Department must consult with their counterparts in Congress when controversy could arise in how an agreement is finalized. Second, after negotiations between the State Department and the foreign relations committees of both the House and Senate during the 1970s, an informal procedure emerged whereby the State Department would periodically send confidential lists of important international agreements to Congress in order to consult on their form (U.S. Senate Committee on Foreign Relations 2001: 233–34).[7]

Formal and informal requirements for the executive to inform and consult with Congress on executive agreements are not enough to constitute serious constraints on the president's treaty-making power, however. A more significant means by which Congress can constrain presidential behavior is to insert itself directly into the process, even when presidents choose the executive agreement method to complete their international agreements. While studies focusing on executive agreements mention that many require the assent of both chambers of Congress before they can go into effect (e.g., Martin 2005), such requirements often are not addressed empirically or theoretically as constraints on presidential behavior. The fact is presidents are constrained anytime their actions require legislation. Congressional-executive agreements, including most of the significant executive agreements identified in our study, require such action in some form. Congress often delegates to the executive the authority to enter into executive agreements (e.g., in areas of commerce) but retains the right to reject the agreements after their negotiation. In recent decades, important enactments have constrained presidential behavior on executive agreements. The best example of this is the Trade Act of 1974 (Public Law 93-618), which delegates international commerce powers to the president but retains the right for Congress to approve (and therefore reject) significant agreements.

Several significant enactments since 1954 have required presidents to submit their executive agreements to the Congress for approval.[8] The Atomic Energy Act of 1954 (Public Law 83-703) governs executive agreements in the area of nuclear cooperation. Presidents must transmit the civil nuclear cooperation agreements thirty days prior to the agreement entering into force; this waiting period is increased to sixty days when the nuclear materials could have military purposes. Then the Congress must either approve the agreement by joint resolution or disapprove the agreement by joint resolution. Presumably, if the legislature disapproves through legislation, the president can veto, thus requiring a two-thirds majority in each chamber in order to legislatively disapprove nuclear cooperation agreements. A similar process governs trade agreements. Congress requires that trade agreements, governed by the Trade Act of 1974 and the Omnibus Trade and Competitiveness Act of 1988 (Public Law 100-418), be submitted to the Congress for joint resolution of approval prior to their entry into force. Failing congressional approval, the agreements cannot enter into force. Fisheries agreements must be submitted sixty days prior to their entry into force (Fishery Conservation and Management Act of 1976, Public Law 94-265). Within that sixty-day period, Congress is then able to pass a joint resolution disapproving of the agreement. Should Congress not act on the agreement, it goes into effect.[9]

While congressional rejection of congressional-executive agreements is a rarity, the requirement that presidents seek legislative approval places significant constraints on presidents in terms of agreement making. This is especially the case with trade agreements. For example, to secure congressional approval of NAFTA, President Clinton expended significant political resources in delivering the votes of House Democrats amid the opposition of Democratic House leaders. Moreover, getting Democratic support required that Clinton renegotiate parts of the agreement (see Livingston and Wink 1997; Uslaner 1998). A major policy initiative of the George W. Bush administration was to secure numerous bilateral and multilateral trade agreements with the nations of Latin America to create a free trade area in the Western Hemisphere. President Bush barely succeeded in securing passage of the Central American Free Trade Agreement in 2005. Normally pro-trade, even Republicans balked at supporting Bush's trade agreements. Twenty-seven House Republicans voted against CAFTA, and the legislative victory was secured, by one vote, only after significant arm-twisting on the part of the White House and Republican House leaders (Peake, Jackson, and Biglaiser 2007: 94–95).[10]

President Bush negotiated several bilateral trade agreements with Latin American nations, some of which languished in the Democratic-controlled 110th Congress. Trade agreements with Peru, Panama, and Colombia met with significant Democratic resistance during 2007 and 2008, forcing the administration to renegotiate parts of the deals in order to secure congressional approval (Irwin 2007). For example, President Bush, at the behest of House Speaker Nancy Pelosi (D-CA), negotiated additional side agreements with Peru, which cleared the agreement for House approval in November 2007. The Senate gave its approval in early December, providing Bush a rare trade victory during 2007 (Weisman 2007). Continued victory was not to be, as the trade agreement with Colombia was scuttled by House Democrats in April 2008, when they voted to table the agreement. Speaker Pelosi refused to reconsider the agreement unless the president compromised on other economic policies, prompting Bush to respond, "She's effectively killed it," while suggesting that the pact's failure would weaken regional security and damage U.S.-Colombian relations (Myers 2008; see also Hulse 2008). Requirements for congressional approval, therefore, can have significant effects on international agreements by placing formal constraints on presidential actions.

House and Senate Involvement in International Agreements

The degree of House and Senate interest in international agreements, as expressed through committee hearings, allows us to assess and compare the involvement of both chambers in the politics of international agreements. Hearings are commonly used to gauge the degree to which an issue has attained the legislative agenda or the attention of the Congress (Baumgartner and Jones 1993; Deering 2003; Edwards and Wood 1999; Flemming, Wood, and Bohte 1999). By holding hearings on international agreements, the committees in Congress can accomplish a number of important legislative and administrative goals. Hearings are basic to the legislative process, and it is during hearings that much of the hard work of legislating occurs (Hall 1996). Nonlegislative hearings allow legislators to express opinions on a range of issues and investigate the need for legislative solutions to pressing political problems, serving informational needs of legislators (Diermeier and Feddersen 2000) and providing opportunities for policy entrepreneurship on the part of committee chairs (Talbert, Jones, and Baumgartner 1995). More important, hearings allow for legislative oversight of the executive branch and the implementation of international agreements, an important responsibility of the congressional foreign policy committees (Aberbach 1990; Kaiser 1977). Oversight is critical to theories of legislative delegation, as it provides a primary constraint on executive behavior (McCubbins and Schwartz 1984) and is an indicator of the discretion granted to the executive through delegation (Epstein and O'Halloran 1999).

We collected hearings data on international agreements for the years 1973 to 2004 (93rd through 108th Congresses)[11] using electronic searches on the LexisNexis congressional database.[12] The hearings were separated by chamber and coded for the type of hearing, whether the agreement discussed at the hearing was a treaty or executive agreement, the topic or domain of the international agreement (using the same categories as in chapter 5),[13] and the committee that held the hearing. We code for five mutually exclusive types of hearings. They include (1) legislative hearings (where specific pending legislation is discussed, but not treaty implementation bills), (2) treaty ratification hearings (where pending treaties are discussed), (3) treaty implementation hearings (where a bill to implement a ratified treaty is discussed), (4) oversight hearings (where oversight of the implementation of existing international agreements is discussed), and (5) investigative hearings. The investigative category includes those hearings that deal with an issue/problem in the international agreement realm, considering possible legislative vehicles (but not a specific bill), calling for executive action, discussing draft agreements and ongoing negotiations, and so on.[14] Finally, we include a sixth type of hearing, process hearings, which are not mutually exclusive of the others (they also fit into one of the other categories). This category includes discussion of the treaty/agreement process (e.g., changes in the Case-Zablocki Act, which covers the reporting of executive agreements to Congress, fast-track procedures for the consideration of trade agreements, etc.).

There were only fourteen joint hearings over the time period, which we exclude from the analysis. We coded nearly fifteen hundred hearings over the twenty-year period. Aggregate data, by Congress, are split by chamber and presented in tables 10 and 11.

In table 10, we present the hearings data for the House. In table 11, we

TABLE 10. House Hearings on International Agreements, by Hearing Type

Years	Congress	Hearings	Legislative hearings	Ratify hearings	Treaty implement	Oversight	Investigatory	Process	Executive agreements	Treaties
1973–74	93	36	8	3	6	4	15	1	17	19
1975–76	94	56	15	0	4	17	20	1	31	25
1977–78	95	60	9	2	14	10	25	2	20	40
1979–80	96	58	17	0	12	10	19	1	28	30
1981–82	97	44	13	1	3	16	11	0	22	22
1983–84	98	56	12	0	7	22	15	0	30	26
1985–86	99	56	14	2	3	17	20	0	26	30
1987–88	100	74	13	1	5	22	33	1	37	37
1989–90	101	61	10	4	7	16	24	0	33	28
1991–92	102	75	12	0	5	22	36	3	52	23
1993–94	103	77	9	3	6	16	43	1	58	19
1995–96	104	46	8	0	5	18	15	2	26	20
1997–98	105	58	15	0	4	22	17	6	23	35
1999–00	106	38	9	1	2	14	12	0	13	25
2001–02	107	23	3	0	1	6	13	1	15	8
2003–04	108	31	10	1	1	9	10	0	15	16
Total		849	177	18	85	241	328	19	446	403
Average		53	11.1	1.1	5.3	15.1	20.4	1.2	27.9	25.2
Percentage of total			20.8	2.1	10	28.4	38.6	2.2	52.5	47.5

Note: Process hearings are not an exclusive category, in that they are also included as oversight or legislative hearings, for example, so the total rows on hearing type do not add to the total number of hearings.

TABLE 11. Senate Hearings on International Agreements, by Hearing Type

Years	Congress	Hearings	Legislative hearings	Ratify hearings	Treaty implement	Oversight	Investigatory	Process	Executive agreements	Treaties
1973–74	93	38	12	14	4	3	5	2	14	24
1975–76	94	43	13	17	0	5	8	4	16	27
1977–78	95	64	13	26	6	7	12	6	17	47
1979–80	96	75	13	34	4	7	17	4	19	56
1981–82	97	58	8	27	2	12	9	1	13	45
1983–84	98	45	7	19	2	9	8	1	10	35
1985–86	99	31	9	4	4	3	11	0	8	23
1987–88	100	45	4	16	3	8	14	3	19	26
1989–90	101	40	7	9	3	11	10	0	16	24
1991–92	102	56	5	21	1	9	20	5	23	33
1993–94	103	50	5	12	2	11	20	2	27	23
1995–96	104	28	3	8	0	12	5	0	10	18
1997–98	105	42	7	7	2	14	12	3	11	31
1999–00	106	29	3	6	1	7	12	3	11	18
2001–02	107	24	3	3	1	9	8	1	12	12
2003–04	108	23	3	8	0	3	9	0	12	11
Total		691	115	231	35	130	180	35	238	453
Average		43.2	7.2	14.4	2.2	8.1	11.3	2.2	14.9	28.3
Percentage of Total			16.6	33.4	5.1	18.8	26	5.1	34.4	65.6

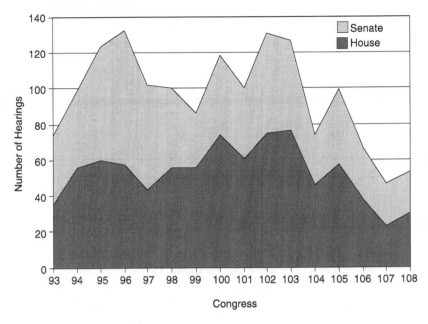

FIG. 3.   Total hearings on international agreements, by chamber. (*Note:* House average, 53.1; Senate average, 43.2. Difference of means test: $F = 3.4$, $p = .07$.)

present the Senate data. Clear differences exist between the chambers' levels of interest in international agreements over the time period. The House is much involved in the vetting of international agreements, as it has held an average of 53 hearings per two-year Congress over the time period, while the Senate average is 43.2. Whereas the Senate has held a much greater average number of treaty hearings compared to hearings on executive agreements (28.3 vs. 14.9), the House holds, on average, a similar number of hearings on both forms of international agreement (25.2 vs. 27.9). From our cursory examination, we are able to verify that the House is indeed interested in international agreements, and its interest is across both forms of agreement. We graph the raw totals of hearings across time for the House and Senate in figure 3. The graph clearly shows that over the last two decades (during the 98th through 108th Congresses), the House has held more hearings on international agreements than has the Senate; however, the difference is only marginally significant statistically.[15]

House interest in treaties, in terms of raw numbers of hearings, comes close to matching Senate interest. House interest in executive agreements,

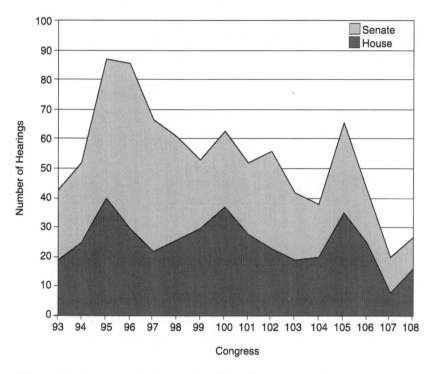

FIG. 4. Hearings on treaties, by chamber. (*Note:* House average, 25.2; Senate average, 28.3. Difference of means test: $F = 0.7, p. = 41.$)

however, far exceeds Senate interest. We graph side by side the trends in House and Senate hearings on treaties and executive agreements in figures 4 and 5, respectively. The Senate, as expected (given its constitutional responsibilities on formal treaties), tends to have greater interest in treaties than executive agreements, as expressed through hearings, though the difference is not significant. The differences on treaties were greatest during the Ninety-sixth through the Ninety-eighth Congresses (1979–84), but the House matches Senate interest during other Congresses. The differences in attention to executive agreements, as shown in figure 5, are significant and clearly favor the House. On average, the House has double the number of hearings on executive agreements than the Senate, and the difference is statistically significant. Given these data, it is clear that the House, as a result of the widespread use of executive agreements, is much involved on international agreements. House involvement, we suspect, would not be nearly as great if it were not for the prevalence of executive

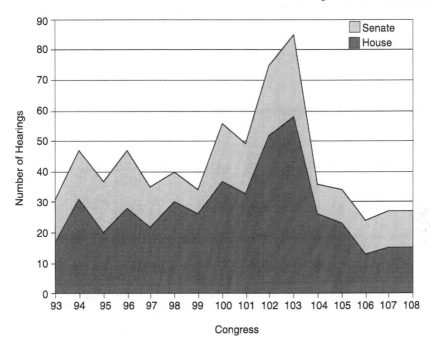

FIG. 5.   Hearings on executive agreements, by chamber. (*Note:* House average, 27.9; Senate average, 14.8. Difference of means test: $F = 14.4$, $p = .001$.)

agreements vis-à-vis treaties. The degree of interest by the House in formal treaties, however, is greater than expected and therefore interesting.

Variation by Hearing Type

How does each of the chambers get involved in the international agreement process? Clear constitutional responsibilities exist for Senate involvement in the ratification of formal treaties. It is unsurprising that much of what the Senate does in the international agreement realm revolves around providing advice and consent on treaties. One-third of the hearings in the Senate were ratification hearings, the modal category (see table 11). Rarely, however, is the ratification of a current treaty a topic of House hearings (see table 10). The Senate averages 14.4 treaty ratification hearings to only 1.1 in the House.[16]

Hearings provide the opportunity for the legislature to use nonlegislative means to constrain the president on international agreements, most notably through oversight. Oversight generally takes the form of commit-

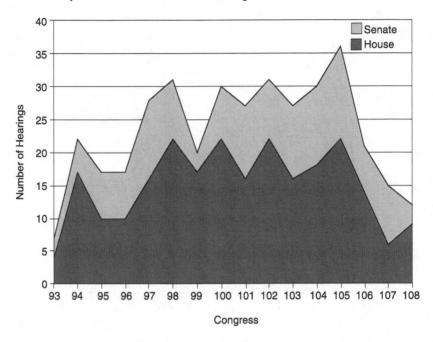

FIG. 6. Oversight hearings on international agreements (executive agreements and treaties), by chamber. (*Note:* House average, 15.1; Senate average, 8.1. Difference of means test: $F = 16.9$, $p = .000$.)

tee hearings and required reports regarding executive implementation of already approved agreements (U.S. Senate Committee on Foreign Relations 2001: 243). Talbert, Jones, and Baumgartner (1995) suggest that nonlegislative hearings allow for committee chairs to expand on jurisdictional claims. If this is the case, our data suggest that House committee chairs have used nonlegislative hearings to interject their chamber into the politics of international agreements. When nonlegislative hearings are considered, the House appears especially involved. As measured by oversight and investigative hearings, nonlegislative hearings account for two-thirds of all House hearings (28 percent oversight and 39 percent investigative). In terms of the raw number of oversight and investigatory hearings, House interest is nearly double that of Senate interest across time.

We graph the measures of oversight and investigative hearings in figures 6 and 7, respectively. The figures show that, consistently across time, the House has played a leading role in nonlegislative hearings on in-

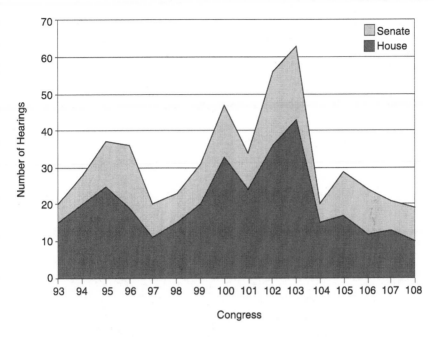

FIG. 7. Investigative hearings on international agreements (executive agreements and treaties), by chamber. (*Note:* House average, 20.5; Senate average, 11.3. Difference of means test: $F = 12.2$, $p = .002$.)

ternational agreements. Interestingly, the House is particularly active in oversight hearings when the majority party differs from that of the president. During periods of divided partisan control of the House and presidency, the House averages 17.3 oversight hearings, whereas the average is only 10.2 when control is unified. The difference is statistically significant ($F = 7.2$, $p = .02$). No significant difference exists between measures accounting for unified and divided control of the Senate and White House, however, suggesting that the oversight hearings in the House may be more politically charged. That the House tends to play a more active role in oversight of treaty making during divided government, when Congress is least likely to grant discretion to the executive, is unsurprising and fits with theories of delegation (Epstein and O'Halloran 1999).

Legislative hearings dealing with international agreements are less common than nonlegislative hearings. However, if the legislative category is combined with treaty implementation hearings (which also involve legislation), we find that 31 percent of House hearings on international agreements involve legislation. In the Senate, the share is smaller, at 22 percent. The House averages 16.5 hearings on bills (legislative plus implementation hearings), whereas the Senate average is only 9.4, a statistically significant difference ($F = 9.5$, $p = .01$). When Congress considers legislation (outside of instruments of ratification for treaties) through hearings, our data suggest that the House takes a leading role.

These data tell us two things that are significant. First, House interest in international agreements pervades the entire process (outside of advice and consent on treaties), from investigating the need for new international agreements, through legislating on existing international agreements, to oversight of executive implementation. The Senate, by comparison, is primarily focused on investigating the need for new international agreements and on its role in advice and consent on treaties. This suggests that once a treaty is ratified, Senate interest in formal treaties wanes, as a majority (51 percent) of all Senate hearings on treaties are of the ratification variety. The House, however, becomes especially involved once a treaty has been ratified, as it must in many cases pass legislation to implement the treaty. The House averages 5.3 treaty implementation hearings, which is more than double the Senate average of 2.2 ($F = 10.02$, $p = .00$). Clearly, the Senate appears to take less of an interest in treaties once it has given its advice and consent. We cannot say for certain that this carries over into oversight of formal treaties, but the data suggest that this is probably the case.[17]

Variation by Agreement Topic

Examining the data more closely, we find that 1991–94 represented a particularly active period for House investigative hearings. The issue that drew so much attention in the House was the negotiation and discussion of NAFTA, negotiated by President George H. W. Bush and pushed through Congress by President Clinton. Trade agreements, which are typically congressional-executive agreements, drew widespread attention in the House over the time period,[18] but this was especially the case beginning with NAFTA. NAFTA also marks a sea change in the politics of trade agreements within the House. Research has demonstrated that the political implications of NAFTA have proven problematic for presidents in securing important trade agreements since the mid-1990s and have led to periods of time where Presidents Clinton and George W. Bush were unable to secure passage of fast-track trade authority (Bardwell 2000; Biglaiser, Jackson, and Peake 2004; Conley 1999; Peake, Jackson, and

Biglaiser 2007). It is important, therefore, to consider the topics of agreements when making comparisons.

We examine the distribution of hearings across chambers based on the topics (or domain) of the international agreement. We provide these data in table 12. The data verify our suspicion that the commerce power and the House's constitutional claim there have deeply involved the House in international agreements, as much of the House interest centers around economically oriented agreements. In the House, economic agreements are the modal category in all but one of the Congresses we examine and never fall below ten hearings in a given Congress.[19] The House averages 25.3 economic agreement hearings per Congress, which is significantly higher than any of the other categories. The Senate averages 16.8 economic agreement hearings per Congress, which is higher than any of the other categories.

In the Senate, while economic agreements are the most common topic, other topics also draw significant attention across time. Economic agreements are the modal category in the Senate in all but two of the Congresses—during the 104th and 105th Congresses, Senate hearings on security agreements (in particular, the Chemical Weapons Convention, various changes to NATO, and the Comprehensive Nuclear Test Ban Treaty) overtook economic agreement hearings. When we compare the topic averages across chambers, we find the level of interest in security, sovereignty, and legal agreements to be roughly equivalent. The House has also expressed greater interest in norms-related agreements than has the Senate (with an average of 9.9 agreements vs. 7.3, respectively).

With these data, we cannot conclude that the Senate has taken the lead on issues denoted as "high politics" and typically considered the realm of formal treaties (i.e., security agreements). Moreover, it becomes clear that even with the increased House interest due to many agreements involving economics, the House also plays a significant role in other areas involving traditional high politics (security and diplomacy). To illustrate, if all economic hearings are excluded from the set of hearings, the House total for hearings would stand at 444, and the Senate total would stand at 422.

We also find that interest in the House is much more spread out between the committees than is interest in the Senate. In the House, about one-third of all hearings on international agreements (31 percent) are held by the House Foreign Affairs (International Relations) Committee, which averaged nearly seventeen hearings per Congress.[20] In comparison, the Senate Foreign Relations Committee held about half of the Senate

TABLE 12. House and Senate Hearings on International Agreements, by Agreement Domain

Congress	House security	Senate security	House sovereignty	Senate sovereignty	House economic	Senate economic	House norms	Senate norms	House legal	Senate legal
93	8	7	2	5	17	15	6	6	2	5
94	9	5	7	5	30	20	4	6	6	7
95	7	6	9	14	24	23	14	11	5	9
96	10	29	11	7	23	30	12	6	2	3
97	7	14	3	12	22	20	7	10	5	4
98	14	11	2	5	26	16	10	6	5	7
99	14	6	4	0	27	12	6	7	5	7
100	19	17	4	0	33	19	13	7	5	5
101	17	10	2	3	19	15	17	10	7	5
102	11	13	1	1	50	23	11	11	2	7
103	8	7	3	1	54	22	12	8	1	2
104	10	16	3	0	21	9	9	4	3	1
105	7	15	1	2	22	8	21	9	7	8
106	7	7	1	1	10	11	10	6	10	6
107	3	7	1	0	14	11	1	5	4	1
108	5	3	2	0	13	15	6	4	4	1
Total	156	173	56	56	405	269	159	115	73	78
Average	9.8	10.8	3.5	3.5	25.3	16.8	9.9	7.3	4.6	4.9
Percentage of Total	18.3	25.0	6.6	8.1	47.7	38.9	18.7	16.6	8.6	11.3

Note: *Percentage of total* indicates the percentage of domain hearings over the total number of hearings for the chamber.

hearings on international agreements (49 percent), averaging twenty-one hearings per Congress. The Senate foreign relations panel emphasized its role of advice and consent on treaties, however.[21] All but a handful of ratification hearings occurred in the SFRC.[22]

Conclusion

Most studies of Congress and the treaty process have focused on the Senate, given its Constitutional role in advice and consent. Our central argument in this chapter is that the House, which we characterize as "forgotten" with respect to the domestic politics of international agreements, may indeed be a more active participant in the process through congressional hearings and requirements for legislative approval of major executive agreements. Our empirical evidence shows a very active House. Indeed, in many respects, the House is more active than the Senate and may be regarded as the leader. The propensity of the House to hold committee hearings on international agreements is wide-ranging and suggests an assertive legislative institution that is unwilling to sit quietly while the Senate and president complete the nation's diplomatic business. Contrary to received wisdom, the House plays a crucial role in the domestic politics of international agreements.

Our analysis of House and Senate hearings on international agreements verifies many of our original suspicions regarding the lack of attention given to the House when scholars discuss the domestic politics of international agreements. The House of Representatives is profoundly important in understanding the domestic politics of international agreements. The framers of the U.S. Constitution designed a bicameral legislature, and despite making the formal treaty process the realm of just one chamber (the Senate), the institutional evolution that the rise in executive agreements represents has afforded the House much more direct influence in the process than perhaps was originally intended. This becomes clear when one considers the significance, in some cases, of bicameral approval for many types of congressional-executive agreements, most notably in the arena of foreign trade. When we examine congressional hearings across time, we also find significant participation on the part of the House, especially in terms of nonlegislative hearings. Our analysis demonstrates that the process has evolved to the point where the House is a full participant in the international agreement process. To be sure, the Senate still holds the constitutional responsibility of advice and consent on treaties, but the House has been vigorous in its oversight of both treaties and executive agreements and has encouraged the use of congressional-executive agreements.[23]

More important, our results in this chapter contribute to our understanding of the domestic politics of international agreements and supplement the results of earlier chapters. We have found that executive agreements have supplanted treaties, in most cases, because of institutional concerns for efficiency in American diplomacy. To put it simply, using formal Article II treaties for most international agreements is unrealistic, and executive agreements provide benefits for both the White House and the Senate. Presidents have not completely abandoned the treaty vehicle, however, and appear to use it more often when completing the most significant agreements—thus not evading the Senate and keeping the executive agreement tool intact. Our analysis here demonstrates that the preponderance of executive agreements also clearly benefits the House of Representatives, having made the House a central player in the domestic politics of international agreements. This is apparent given the large number of significant executive agreements that require House approval and the clear interest the House shows through its use of committee hearings, particularly oversight and investigative hearings. Finally, given its interest in oversight and investigation on international agreements, the increased participation on the part of the House has served to constrain executive behavior on international agreements.

Conclusion: Evaluating the Change

I am certainly not an advocate for frequent and untried changes
in laws and constitutions. I think moderate imperfections had
better be borne with; because, when once known, we
accommodate ourselves to them, and find practical means of
correcting their ill effects. But I know also, that laws and
institutions must go hand in hand with the progress of the human
mind. As that becomes more developed, more enlightened, as
new discoveries are made, new truths disclosed, and manners
and opinions change with the change of circumstances,
institutions must advance also, and keep pace with the times. We
might as well require a man to wear still the same coat which
fitted him when a boy, as civilized society to remain ever under
the regimen of their barbarous ancestors.

—Thomas Jefferson one year after leaving the presidency, in a letter
to Samuel Kercheval, July 12, 1810[1]

Establishing formal relations with other countries is and always has been
at the core of foreign policy making. Thomas Jefferson, who served as
America's ambassador to France under the Articles of Confederation,
would no doubt agree with this notion. Even in the more isolationist mi-
lieu of the late eighteenth century, the founders of the United States were
aware of this fact. When gathered in Philadelphia in 1787, they therefore
pondered, debated, and otherwise racked their brains over the proper
sphere of authority for carrying out the crucial task of international
agreements. As they did with many other institutional features designed in
the U.S. Constitution, the founders concluded in the treaty clause that this
vital power was to be shared between the executive and legislative
branches. Presidents would initiate the process of treaty making, the advice and consent of two-thirds of the Senate would be required, and the
final step of ratification was to be carried out by the president (Article II,
Section 2).

Since World War II, American presidents have, it would seem, routinely trampled on this framework of shared power, specifically the treaty consent process in the Senate. The statistics are clear and staggering. Over the past sixty years (1947–2006), the United States has completed over seventeen thousand international agreements. In only 6 percent of the cases have presidents taken their treaties to the Senate as outlined by the Constitution. The remaining international agreements were completed as executive agreements, which do not require supermajority approval by the Senate. Executive agreements are not a modern invention, but their extensive use to replace the treaty process is a central element of the modern presidency, as the sea change began with President Franklin Roosevelt. Prior to Roosevelt, executive agreement usage was comparatively rare. From 1789 to 1933, when Roosevelt took office, the United States had completed 1,775 international agreements, 706 (40 percent) of which were treaties submitted to the Senate. Rather than treaties, presidents since Roosevelt have used executive agreements to complete the overwhelming majority of their international agreements and, in effect, to avoid the cumbersome and politicized process inherent in the U.S. Senate.[2]

In deciding whether to take their international agreements to the Senate, are presidents in effect trampling the checks and balances required by the Constitution? Do they base their decisions on domestic political circumstances and thus make the treaty approval process perfunctory because they only send treaties to the Senate for advice and consent when they are assured of passage? Or, when pondering their decisions, are presidents avoiding taking the bulk of international agreements to the Senate based on a rationale that considers matters of efficiency and diplomatic expediency? In short, is the modern use of executive agreements endemic of the imperial presidency? Does the innovation represent a unilateral effort on the part of presidents to circumvent constitutional requirements? Or is their use more a reflection on the constitutional construction that occurs when institutional actors in a system of shared powers must innovate in order to address a complex international policy environment?

Presidential decisions on international agreements have important domestic political ramifications, and as scholars of international relations posit, domestic politics can have profound effects on American diplomacy. To be sure, if presidents are imperial and unilateral in their conduct of American diplomacy through their use of international agreements—a major component of foreign policy—this surely is cause for alarm. The constitutional process has been usurped. Presidents can unilaterally commit the United States to major international relationships that outlast their administrations, as executive agreements are considered equivalent to treaties in terms of international law.

Even Alexander Hamilton, who, among the framers of the U.S. Constitution, was the strongest proponent of executive power, might be alarmed to see such a scenario, given his expectation that the legislature would play an important role in the treaty power (see Federalist Nos. 69 and 75). Democratic institutions are threatened, and checks and balances are thwarted. Or, to borrow from the title of a recent book, "presidential power" is "unchecked and unbalanced" (Crenson and Ginsberg 2007). To be sure, as documented in a number of recent studies, modern presidents have accumulated a vast array of formal powers, in both the domestic and international spheres. This array of powers is much greater than originally imagined by the architects of the constitutional balance. Modern presidents have routinely issued executive orders, proclamations, national security directives, and signing statements. They have initiated wars and, yes, completed executive agreements.

The theoretical framework presented in our introduction and the evidence presented throughout the remainder of the book rejects this alarmist line of reasoning, at least as it relates to the treaty power. While it is altogether clear that modern presidents have been given a great deal of discretion in how they execute their treaty-making powers, it does not follow that the rise of executive agreements represents a power grab on the part of the executive branch or an abdication of power on the part of Congress.[3] The empirical evidence presented throughout this book indicates that presidents are cognizant of congressional checks on their diplomatic powers and that they work within the boundaries set by a system of separate institutions sharing power. Rather than a usurpation of the balance of power, the modern executive agreement is a rational adaptation by modern presidents, in conjunction with Congress, to the complex foreign policy environment unforeseen by the framers of the Constitution. The quote from Jefferson at the opening of this conclusion suggests threshold effects. Below the threshold, moderate challenges can be dealt with pragmatically through practice and without wholesale change. However, more fundamental challenges require alterations in formal structures to keep pace with "the progress of the human mind."

The growth of the international system in the twentieth century was just such a fundamental challenge. Brought on by human minds, it required constitutional construction by the president and Congress. How could the framers have envisioned the dizzying number of formal relationships the United States would undertake with other nation-states and international organizations? Yet the language in Article II was clear and left little room for international agreements other than treaties. Despite this constitutional problem, out of political practice emerged a new legal doctrine on American treaties. Executive agreements signed by the president and entered into force without input by the legislature had essentially the same legal meaning as treaties that were subjected to the Senate process. The modern executive agreement, including all of its varieties, can be viewed, then, as a significant adaptation on the part of the political branches, which has since been validated by various Supreme Court cases. The behavior we document in this book suggests that they represent an institutional bargain grounded in requirements for efficiency that are demanded by modern realities.

We begin this conclusion by highlighting the answers to our core research questions, which on balance provide a wide sweep of support for our theoretical argument. In so doing, we incorporate two current items on the international agreement agenda of President George W. Bush: the Law of the Sea Treaty and the recent twenty-billion-dollar arms pact with Saudi Arabia and its neighbors. We then contemplate what our theoretical argument and these answers mean for theories of presidential power and presidential-congressional relations and for models of institutional change. We finish this conclusion and this book with a discussion of the key normative implications of our findings.

The ensuing discussions of the theoretical and normative implications of our work lead to three main arguments. First, theoretical conceptions of presidential power, which have understandably leaned quite heavily in the direction of unilateral presidential action during the George W. Bush years, need to be retrofitted to bring the concept of shared power back more centrally into the intellectual fold. While unilateral action can indeed be prevalent, it often stems from and is bounded by shared power. Second, scholars of institutional change, who, in recent decades, have fixated on microlevel, strategic explanations of institutional evolution, need to model in macrolevel environmental constraints (including the changing international scene and the constitutional separation of powers), which can induce efficiency and institutional concerns, rather than zero-sum politics. Assuming that institutional changes bubble up merely from the game of politics leads us to drastically underspecified models and inhibits greatly our understanding of the tenor and consequences of institutional change.

Finally, in exploring the tenor and consequences of this particular institutional change, we argue, in light of the findings, that the rise of executive agreements was a positive development from the standpoint of democratic theory and constitutional construction. While we remain somewhat critical of the founders' brief treaty clause, we believe that presidents and Congresses have successfully adapted by constructing a new constitutional framework, which retains the Article II process within it. Indeed, the brevity of the Constitution, combined with the changing requirements of international affairs, set the stage for successful adaptation of the presidential-congressional system.

Laying Out the Evidence

In this book, we sought answers to two empirical questions. First, why have we witnessed the rise in the use of the executive agreements by modern presidents? To answer this question, we had to probe why modern presidents alternatively use executive agreements and treaties, even though there are no apparent legal constraints, and why the Congress would allow this without halting critical interbranch processes. Second, when presidents do decide to take their international agreements to the Senate as Article II treaties, what does the process entail, and what sort of politics are they likely to find? Are the politics uninteresting, as presidents work their will on a most compliant Senate—as suggested by conventional wisdom? Or do treaty politics sometimes witness the same kind of bitter politics that arise when a system of shared powers handles consequential issues?

To address these questions, we first asked practitioners their views of the politics of international agreements. From Foggy Bottom to Capitol Hill, high-level staffers explained to us how the international agreement process was much less political than political scientists had previously argued and how the Senate worked to guard its treaty prerogatives. One long-serving staffer in the State Department smiled in a professorial way and then proceeded to lecture us about the apolitical nature of the process. Legal staff working for the Senate Foreign Relations Committee explained how executive agreements were not "all that political" and how, at times, the battles that did arise over international agreements tended to be of the institutional variety. Both sets of interviewees indicated the cumbersome nature of the treaty process and how, at times, it can become severely gridlocked. We thought this interesting. Political scientists over the years have grown concerned about the accumulating powers of the presidency, repeatedly citing executive agreements as evidence. Yet here were people in the executive and the legislative branches, with numerous decades of experience between them, representing both sides of the equation, telling us that conventional wisdom in political science is plainly wrong.

As is typical of political scientists, we sought to test these differing explanations of the politics of international agreements by using multiple methods, including systematic analysis of quantitative data. For the most part, what we found verifies what practitioners explained to us. The historical trend is clear: presidents have routinely substituted executive agreements for the cumbersome treaty. But when we began this study, it was less clear why they have done so.

Skeptics of the practice view executive agreements as being part and parcel to an imperial presidency that relies on a vast array of formal unilateral powers. Executive agreements afford presidents the opportunity to circumvent the constitutional process and upset checks and balances. Presidents, because they are free to act unilaterally and therefore are unconstrained domestically, routinely evade the Senate. Presidential use of executive agreements is deeply seated in political expediency. Hence the modern executive agreement presents a dangerous tool that modern presidents can use to promote undemocratic outcomes, curtail the constitutional process, upset the institutional balance of power and expand presidential power. Our results present a sobering check on these conclusions.

Most legal scholars take a more nuanced view of the use of executive agreements. Their writings point to unwritten traditions and changing political practices that in effect have altered the meaning of the Constitution (see Ackerman and Golove 1995; Spiro 2001). Our theoretical framework likewise allows for constitutional construction. As originally posited by Whittington (1999), constitutional ambiguities and changes in the political situation push political actors to construct their own constitutional understanding. To be sure, the political branches created this modern practice, and the courts determined their legality through several decisions during the 1930s and 1940s, as we reviewed in chapter 1. Legal scholars correctly point out that most executive agreements are actually congressional-executive agreements, which means that Congress remains involved in the process and, in many cases, can override the president's action. Placed in this context, the rise of executive agreements does not appear as disturbing as the alarmists indicate.

The Alternative Use of Executive Agreements and Treaties

Our empirical analyses in chapters 2 and 3 support a complimentary argument to constitutional construction. While politics play a role in the presidential use of executive agreements, the increased use of executive agreements vis-à-vis treaties to complete international agreements primarily reflects concerns for efficiency by the presidency and the U.S. Senate in completing diplomatic action. The politics that emerge suggests that presidents are cognizant of the ideological preferences of pivotal institutional players, particularly the chair of the Senate Foreign Relations Committee. In chapter 2, we analyzed two time series of executive agreement use vis-à-vis treaties from 1949 to 1998, finding little support for the evasion argument. Rather, when complexities arise in the international system, presidents increase their use of executive agreements (as well as the subset of important executive agreements) relative to treaties. As with presidential use of other unilateral powers (i.e., executive orders; see Mayer 2001), presidents behave as if they are constrained politically when using executive agreements. For example, they more often use treaties as a proportion of all agreements at the very time when governing circumstances (i.e., divided government) indicate that treaty support should be more difficult to achieve. Presidential behavior on executive agreements, we conclude, is contingent on leeway granted by the Senate to the executive.

In chapter 3, we gained a better handle on presidential decisions about the form agreements will take. We narrowed our analysis of the data to examine the set of individual cases where presidents had to decide whether to go with an executive agreement or treaty. Theory and the case evidence clearly indicate that decisions presidents make on the form their international agreements take have significant domestic and international political consequences. While the legal scholarship is clear that the two forms of international agreement are by and large legally interchangeable, theory is equally clear that they are not politically interchangeable. We also investigated the agreement classification process and learned that the decision process is primarily institutionalized within the State Department through the C175 procedure. Moreover, the decision process accounts for tradition and congressional views. When precedence is unclear, bureaucrats in the State Department consider Senate views. In the words of one State Department staffer, "you have to watch that line," as "that's where the discussion will go up and down" between State and the Senate.[4] Most important, we demonstrate that the White House is far removed from most decisions made on executive agreements. Hence a large percentage of the vast numeric divide between executive agreements and treaties can be explained simply as a function of an institutionalized bureaucratic process where State Department staff works closely with their counterparts in the Congress.[5]

The institutionalization of the process is an important point, as it becomes clear that the White House is only likely to play an important role on significant international agreements. In such agreements, one would expect strategic political behavior on the part of the president. Moreover, it is the important agreements that concern the skeptics. Focusing our empirical lens on those agreements, our analysis of presidential decisions further verifies the explanatory power of the efficiency perspective and, when combined with our aggregate results from chapter 2, supports our theory that executive agreements represent an important institutional bargain. Presidential behavior on agreement classification indicates that presidents understand the significance of their decisions as signals to international agreement partners and the Senate. The logic of this behavior suggests that presidents act to preserve the policy mechanism of the executive agreement. For example, presidents are less likely to use executive agreements when the opposing party dominates the Senate, because doing so may spark the ire of a Senate majority enough to threaten this important policy mechanism. In fact, our findings on the significant and salient agreements indicate that presidents are less likely to use treaties when their party dominates the Senate, a condition that, at first glance, is favorable for treaty approval.

Placed in broader perspective, the use of executive agreements as an efficiency mechanism fits well with the adaptive qualities of the presidency and the boundary-maintaining attributes of the constitutional system, as identified by other scholars examining unilateral powers (Mayer 2001: 218). Presidents are emboldened in their executive agreement use when they are likely to find support for their foreign policies in the Senate, much like they are emboldened when using other unilateral powers (e.g., executive orders) during unified government (Mayer 2001: 102). Howell (2003: 187) suggests that when considering unilateral action, presidents consider what they "can get away with." Our analysis adds to this consideration. Given the international nature of executive agreements, presidents also consider international factors, as their decisions send signals of commitment to agreement partners (see Martin 2000).

If presidential behavior on international agreements threatens the constitutional balance of power, why has Congress stood idly by to watch the usurpation of their foreign policy powers? The historical reality suggests that when enough members of Congress determine that the use of executive agreements threatens the balance of power, they act to curtail their abuse. This is the lesson of the Bricker revolt in the 1950s and the Case-Zablocki Act and its several amendments in the 1970s, which we reviewed in chapter 1. In these instances, presidents pushed the boundaries of executive power, only to be reeled back in. In specific cases, senators have communicated their desires for certain agreements to be completed as treaties, and presidents generally accommodate Senate views. More instructive, however, is the logic that executive agreements provide clear benefits to Congress.

Treaty Politics

Rather than painting the Congress as weak and ineffectual, our theory suggests that both the Senate and the House clearly benefit from the use of executive agreements. The benefits to the Senate are actually quite obvious. If all international agreements were transmitted to the Senate for approval, as clearly intended by the framers of the Constitution, then the Senate would be inundated with inconsequential agreements, and the treaty consent process would become perfunctory. The Senate Foreign Relations Committee would struggle to complete action on the hundreds of international agreements completed during each two-year Congress. Either the process would come to a halt, and thus American diplomacy and world leadership would be seriously threatened, or the Senate would completely yield its advice and consent role in order to get its work done. One SFRC staffer explained, "To do all executive agreements as treaties would increase our workload substantially."[6] The agenda costs would be staggering, as the committee is responsible for numerous ambassadorial nominations in addition to its normal legislative jurisdiction. A State Department legislative liaison stated, "They're just glad treaties are few and far between."[7] Our theory and analysis suggest that so long as presidents do not abuse the process on consequential agreements, the Senate is a willing partner.

Our study of treaty politics in chapters 4 and 5 clearly indicates that, when aroused, the Senate can mount a significant challenge to presidential leadership on treaties. Even with overwhelming support for a treaty in the Senate and among the public, Senate minorities have important institutional tools that allow them to block a treaty's movement through the process. In our analysis, we discovered that numerous consequential treaties are submitted to the Senate for consent each Congress and that many of these languish for years. Thus significant delays occur in finalizing American diplomacy. Our findings suggest that the pivotal player in the treaty process is the SFRC chair. Highly conservative committee chairs more readily blocked treaties and caused significant gridlock in the treaty process. For example, Senator Jesse Helms (R-NC), who loomed large in our case studies on the Genocide Convention, the Comprehensive Test Ban Treaty, and the Chemical Weapons Convention, was especially effective at delaying Senate action on treaties during his tenure as committee chair. His nickname of "Senator No" was well deserved. The inefficiencies of the Senate process are clearly borne out in our study. Despite these realities and their apparent freedom to use executive agreements instead, presidents still send important agreements to the Senate as treaties.

The delayed diplomacy we modeled in chapter 5 is consequential for several reasons. To the degree that the treaty process in the Senate is gridlocked, the president and Senate are less able to achieve American diplomatic goals jointly and "to enlarge the area of confidence between governments" so significant for the preservation of international order (Glennon 1990: 123). Senate disdain for certain types of treaties, particularly those dealing with international norms (e.g., human rights treaties), can jeopardize American leadership in the world. Refusal to consent to the Comprehensive Test Ban Treaty, as we documented in chapter 4, is a clear cause for embarrassment for American proponents of the nonproliferation regime. In major multilateral treaties, nonsignatories lose out because they do not have a seat at the table when it comes to implementing the treaty, as would have occurred to the United States had it not ratified the Chemical Weapons Convention.

"LOST" at Sea

The more recent story of the UN Convention on the Law of the Sea (Treaty Doc. 103-39), or the Law of the Sea Treaty, referred to as "LOST" by opponents, is instructive. The treaty is clearly significant, in that it "gives each nation control over its own coastal waters—an 'exclusive economic zone' extending 200 miles offshore—and then sets up rules governing navigation, fishing and protection of the marine environment in the rest of the oceans," and it "establishes an International Seabed Authority to govern mining on the ocean floor" (*New York Times* 2004). The treaty was originally drafted by the United Nations in 1982. President Reagan refused to sign it due to concerns over mining rights on the ocean floor. After the mining issues had been renegotiated, President Clinton signed the agreement on July 29, 1994, and transmitted the treaty to the Senate the following October, where it sat. Once Republicans gained majority control of the Senate in 1995, no action occurred on the treaty, despite a broad coalition in support of the agreement, including the oil industry, the U.S. Navy, and environmental groups. Helms, the SFRC chair, and other conservatives were inalterably opposed to the treaty. Finally, in 2004, with the more internationalist senator Richard Lugar (R-IN) as chair, the treaty finally saw movement. The committee reported the treaty (Exec. Rpt. 108-10), but a small minority of conservatives was able to block floor consideration, and at the end of that year, the treaty was automatically referred back to the committee in accordance with Senate Rule XXX.

In 2007, the treaty was revived. President Bush was convinced that the treaty was worth ratifying and implementing. To do so serves American economic and military interests, according to proponents, as the recession of Arctic waters due to global warming has opened up sea-lanes and possible access to mineral reserves. Ratifying the treaty "would allow the United States to play a leadership role on a whole range of global ocean issues, including overfishing and pollution," and time is of the essence: "Unless the United States ratifies the treaty, it will not have a seat at the table when it comes time to sort out competing claims" (*New York Times* 2007). With time running out before the treaty enters into force, the new committee chair, Senator Joseph Biden (D-DE), held hearings in September and October of 2007, and the panel gave its approval and reported the treaty to the full Senate on December 19, 2007 (Exec. Rpt. 110-9). As of this writing, the treaty sits on the Senate's executive calendar, awaiting action by the full Senate.

The House and International Agreements

Most studies of treaties ignore the role of the U.S. House of Representatives. Alarmists criticizing the apparent trampling of the Senate's treaty prerogative hardly mention the House and its involvement on executive agreements. In this study, we have characterized the House as "forgotten" and have investigated the degree to which the chamber directly involves itself in international agreements. As we described in chapter 6, the House receives clear benefits by the rise of executive agreements, a fact that contributes to our overall theoretical argument that the rise of executive agreements is attributable to an institutional bargain on the part of the presidency and Congress. The House is directly involved in executive agreements, from investigating the need for further agreements to passing legislation to implement completed agreements. Moreover, surprisingly, the House is involved in treaty politics outside of the standard ratification process, by participating in investigatory and oversight hearings and handling most of the implementation legislation.

When presidents complete executive agreements, they often do so with the knowledge that the agreement requires the support of both the Senate and the House. Hence, by choosing to avoid the Senate and the long drawn-out treaty consent process, presidents directly involve the House. Numerous mechanisms exist for House influence on international agreements. Treaties must receive funding, and some require implementation legislation. Moreover, congressional-executive agreements can directly involve both chambers of the legislature. This is especially apparent when one considers recent trade agreements, where presidents have had to work hard to secure congressional approval, particularly in the House. Our empirical evidence, then, shows a House very active on treaties and executive agreements.

On many consequential agreements, a bicameral approval process is required. It is difficult to reconcile the need for congressional approval on trade agreements with the notion that these very same executive agreements are somehow unilateral actions by the president. First, they are a clearly delegated power. Second, a majority in one chamber can block the implementation of the agreement, thus scuttling it. Finally, because of the second point, presidents lobby Congress for their approval. Perhaps attaining majority approval in both chambers for a commercial agreement is easier than attaining the two-thirds majority required for formal treaties. After all, the margins of victory in the Senate on NAFTA (approved by a vote of sixty-one to thirty-eight) and CAFTA (approved by a vote of fifty-four to forty-five) fell well short of the two-thirds requirement.

Congressional-executive agreements are not only used in the area of trade, however. Presidents must seek bicameral approval (or, in some cases, avoid a resolution of disapproval from Congress) for their nuclear cooperation agreements, fishing agreements, and arms transfers. This approval is required in addition to the Congress passing relevant appropriations, should they be necessary. On January 14, 2008, the Bush administration announced the completion of a major arms deal with Saudi Arabia and neighboring Gulf States friendly to the United States, including twenty billion dollars' worth of weaponry. Congress had thirty days to pass a resolution opposing or altering the deal but chose not to (Abramowitz 2008). Administration officials spent several months communicating with Congress as it negotiated the deal with the Arab states. The efforts to keep Congress informed of the deal belie the unilateral logic. David Cloud (2007) reported, "The Saudis had requested that Congress be told about the planned sale, the officials said, in an effort to avoid the kind of bruising fight on Capitol Hill that occurred in the 1980s over proposed arms sales to the kingdom."

Implications for Theories of Presidential Power

Taken together, the results of our analyses support our theoretical explanation of the rise of executive agreements. Like all institutional systems, the presidency and Congress must adapt to their environment as well as to the healthy interbranch battle of forces that the founders induced in our constitutional system. What does our study portend for theories of interbranch relations? The framework and evidence contained in this book suggest the need for a more balanced theoretical approach to understanding presidential power. In particular, theories of presidential power, which have leaned toward unilateral persuasion in recent years, need to swing back somewhat to incorporate the principle of shared power.

The theoretical emphasis in the literature on presidential power has ebbed and flowed. In the 1980s and 1990s, in moving away from assumptions of an imperial presidency, scholars tended to follow Neustadt's (1960) approach to power relationships, based on the limits of presidential power and the related persuasion in which successful presidents must engage. Major works by George Edwards (1989), Jon Bond and Richard Fleisher (1990), Mark Peterson (1990), and Charles Jones (1994) were designed to test theories about the president seeking to influence and succeed in the Congress. Edwards (1989) found presidential influence on individual member votes in Congress to be "at the margins." Hence successful presidents were reliant on leveraging their strategic position. Bond and Fleisher (1990) found that the hand that presidents were dealt in terms of the makeup of the congressional membership explained best the legislative success presidents had in Congress. In examining the fate of the president's agenda in Congress, Peterson (1990) found that many of the major initiatives passed into law from the executive's program bore the imprint of Congress as well. Peterson couched this finding in his "tandem institutions" perspective, in which he argued that the branches need one another to govern as a system. Jones (1994) rigorously studied a small random sample of David Mayhew's (1991) landmark enactments and found that each branch originated many of the bills and that the preponderant legislative outcome was one of shared power.

The new millennium brought a potent challenge to the Neustadt approach to power relationships. Works by Kenneth Mayer (2001) and William Howell (2003), which we have described at many points in this book, argued that looking for presidential power through persuasion missed many of the opportunities the executive has to act unilaterally without required consent of the legislative branch. These works hit the scene as President George W. Bush was empowered in the wake of the September 11, 2001, terrorist attacks, and they quickly became in vogue.

Even though many concur that President Bush's power has weakened during his second term as compared to the period immediately following September 11, 2001, the unilateral perspective continues to be forwarded in a noncritical, overly simplistic manner. Although Mayer and Howell did not intend their frameworks to be construed in such an absolute manner, some scholars have described the unilateral perspective as the president in charge, with the Congress largely irrelevant (e.g., Crenson and Ginsberg 2007). Outside the academy, alarmists continue to sound an even shriller note.

Based on the results of this study and a careful reading of the unilateral perspective, we believe that the principle of shared power needs to be more explicitly brought back into the fold. While unilateral action can indeed be prevalent, it often stems from and is bounded by shared power. Toward that end, our results are theoretically consistent with other recent comprehensive analyses of the modern use of presidential powers, particularly those that examine executive orders. For example, in his very careful analysis of executive orders, Kenneth Mayer (2001: 220) concludes that their use is unlikely to contribute to the imperial presidency, because "the use of executive orders is conditioned on presidents' overall political situation." In a similar vein, in his book cataloging executive orders, Adam Warber (2006: 129) concludes that they do not represent an increasing expansion of power on the part of presidents, because significant checks exist on their use. In the international relations field, Lisa Martin (2000) makes a contribution that shows the importance of an interbranch perspective on powers that might at first sight look unilateral. She makes the argument that legislatures are helpful for democracies in making credible commitments. Using "exchange theory," she claims that the making of foreign policy is more effective (in terms of commitments) when the executive and legislature work in conjunction to achieve mutually beneficial goals. Our perspective and results are intellectually consistent with such an approach. In summary, scholars should therefore cast a broader theoretical net in examining presidential power and presidential-congressional relations.

Implications for Theories of Institutional Change

In addition to impacting theories of presidential power, our framework and evidence also have implications for conceptions of institutional change. Modern treaty practice is representative of an evolutionary change in how the political institutions handle a complex international environment and policy given the constraints of the Constitution. A burgeoning line of scholarship, mostly in the legislative studies subfield, examines similar types of formal and informal institutional change. Two main perspectives of institutional change have been advanced.

Traditionally, organizational theorists sought to explain institutional changes as adaptation to a changing environment. Joseph Cooper and Cheryl Young (1989) argue that the nineteenth-century House of Representatives changed rules regarding members' bill introductions in reaction to the growing size and complexity of the governmental agenda. Recent studies of institutional change tend to leave out the organizational perspective and envision institutional evolution instead as the result of endogenous battles between rational, self-interested actors. Institutional alterations bubble up from the game of politics. For example, Sarah Binder (1997) argued that short-term partisan goals—not broader societal trends, as recommended by Joseph Cooper (1977)—determine the rise and fall of minority rights in the U.S. House.

With regard to the rise of executive agreements, the system has evolved to be flexible (perhaps much more so than under the original design) to the international environment and the interbranch balance of forces. Hence we find a role for both perspectives. Our theory and evidence therefore suggest that scholars of institutional change need to better model environmental constraints (including the changing international scene and the constitutional separation of powers), which can induce efficiency and institutional concerns, rather than just zero-sum politics. Viewed in this way, the rise of executive agreements, much like the rise of other institutional tools (i.e., fast-track trade authority or omnibus legislating), is an adaptation by vital democratic political institutions responding to a complicated political and policy reality (Epstein and O'Halloran 1999; Krutz 2001). Continuing to assume that institutional changes bubble up only from political battles will lead scholars to continue to develop woefully incomplete models, and it will inhibit our thinking on the disposition and consequences of institutional change.

Normative Implications

The empirical questions of our study raise several obvious normative questions. Questions of institutional balance within the American political system are driven by normative concerns related to democratic theory. After all, the United States rejected monarchy at the Constitutional Convention, and if the institutional relationship tilts too far to the executive, democracy is compromised. As the system of shared powers demands, the legislature has important effects on the executive as they pursue American diplomacy. The Congress provides significant constraints on presidents in foreign policy. These constraints, however, can frustrate presidents mightily and may compromise, at times, a coherent American foreign policy. To this complaint, we say that it is all part of the larger story of the constitutional design. "Gridlock-ridden" and "inefficient" are common descriptors of the American system of shared powers. Modern institutions struggle to surmount these obstacles, and institutional change occurs as a result.

Democracies must pursue coherent international policies, and they must be able to do so strategically. This reality presented the American political system with an important dilemma that became especially apparent during the interwar years of the last century. Yet the requirement for strategic behavior on the part of the government requires some unity in representing the nation outside of its borders. This is sound reasoning for why, in democracies, legislatures often delegate a number of foreign policy responsibilities to executive actors, while maintaining some degree of oversight and legislative constraint (Martin 2000). The rise in executive agreements, therefore, may promote a more rational foreign policy process. In a domestic political system not designed for the efficiencies required by the complexities of modern international relations, this is certainly a positive implication.

In contrast to the alarms many of the critics sound, the rise in executive agreements also promotes an important democratic outcome. We have found that including the House of Representatives in the treaty process might promote executive accountability on international agreements, as the House, more than the Senate, vigorously pursues its oversight and investigatory functions. Moreover, House involvement promotes majority rule, whereas a Senate-executive monopoly on the treaty power lends too much credence to minority rights, while violating democratic principles of representation and equality. This is the product of equal state representation in the Senate, which violates the "one person, one vote" standard in democratic theory (Dahl 2003). The Senate has been labeled the "most malapportioned legislature in the world," and this undemocratic feature of the constitutional design produces various forms of real inequality among the states (Lee and Oppenheimer 1999: 2, citing Lijphart 1984).

As our results on treaty politics demonstrate, Senate minorities can easily waylay a president's international agreements, and this is especially salient given the supermajority requirement in Article II. A popular treaty, supported by a majority of Americans, policy makers, and the president, can be blocked in the Senate rather easily. Should the treaty ever make it to the floor, it takes just thirty-four votes, or senators representing seventeen states, to kill the treaty. Using 2000 census numbers, these thirty-four senators could conceivably represent a population of 20.5 million Americans, or just 7.3 percent of the nation's population (Dahl 2003: 161). That these floor defeats are extremely rare does not settle this issue, because in many cases, a vote on such a treaty rarely occurs. Treaty proponents anticipate these things and avoid scheduling the vote on a treaty unless they are assured of its passage.

On the flip side, the treaty power, as conceived by the framers of the Constitution, can arguably give too much power to the Senate in promoting binding international action that becomes part of the nation's supreme law, as stated in Article VI of the Constitution. Using the Census figures again, sixty-seven senators (and the president) representing 89.6 million Americans, or just 31.8 percent of the nation's population, could complete a treaty that the representatives of a majority of Americans do not want. Of course, as we have demonstrated, the House could block such action by withholding support for funding and implementing the treaty.

Given the extent to which America's international agreements involve international commerce, monetary policies, promoting the national defense, military interventions, immigration, and so on, all of which are powers of Congress under Article I of the Constitution, the House should be involved. So even if one is not persuaded by the representation and equality argument supported by democratic theory, justification for international agreements other than treaties can be found within the Constitution, as has been argued by numerous legal scholars. We doubt very much that the House would stand idly by and not want its say as the president and Senate completed major trade agreements promoting globalization, for example. Its say, however, might come in the form of refusing to pass implementation or funding legislation, which would make for interesting foreign policy indeed, as domestic law would not correspond with international law. A constitutional crisis might result.

Has the treaty process, as conceived by the framers, outlived its usefulness? Proponents of executive power might argue that it has, given the frustrations that can result when presidents do pursue treaties and the alternative means of completing agreements available to presidents. But we believe that the formal treaty process still serves an important purpose within a system of shared powers. International agreements often impact domestic laws, including the laws of the various states, and minority rights should therefore be given their due when it comes to considering such agreements. We do have a federal system, after all, where the powers of government are shared between the national and state governments. The Brickerites of the 1950s as much as said so in their fight to limit the use of the modern executive agreement, and their complaints were heard. Presidents still utilize the treaty process, despite its problems. This may be a result of domestic pressure but could also occur because treaties signal to other signatories the significance of American commitment to the agreement.

Finally, it is clear to us that the language in Article II is incomplete, as it does not provide clear guidance on how treaties shall be interpreted or how they shall be ended should they no longer benefit the United States, as we discussed in chapter 1. The system of shared powers has not worked this part of the treaty process out as effectively as it has worked out the process that has evolved to handle the numerous international agreements the United States enters. Recent cases have come before the federal courts regarding President George W. Bush's unilateral termination of the ABM Treaty (*Kucinich v. Bush*, 236 F. Supp. 2d 1 [D.D.C. 2002]) and the Defense Department's treatment of suspected terrorists held by the United States at Guantanamo Bay, Cuba (*Hamdan v. Rumsfeld*, 548 U.S. 507 [2006]). As modern presidents have done, President George W. Bush has acted to fill the interpretive void left by unclear language in the Constitution. What Bush has not done, however, is shun treaties for executive agreements, as demonstrated by the fact that there has not been an increased use of executive agreements during Bush's tenure. From 2001 to 2006, 6.2 percent of international agreements have been treaties, a similar percentage as averaged over the previous fifty years. President Bush is well known for behaving unilaterally, especially in regard to guiding foreign policy. This proclivity for unconstrained behavior, however, does not appear to carry over to completing international agreements.

Notes

1. In *Pink*, the Court found that "all international compacts and agreements" are to be treated "with similar dignity" as treaties, but for the purposes of domestic law, important distinctions exist. Executive agreements cannot be inconsistent with existing treaties or federal law or violate the constitutional rights of American citizens (see *United States v. Guy W. Capps, Inc.*, 204 F.2d 655, 660 [4th Cir. 1953]; *Reid v. Covert*, 354 U. S. 1, 16 [1957]). They do, however, trump state laws (as would a treaty), as set forth in *Pink*. Additionally, the Congress retains authority to resist executive action where its powers are clearly delineated, should it decide to act (*Dames and Moore v. Reagan*, 452 U.S. 656 [1981]). The use of executive agreements has sparked controversy among legal scholars surrounding the interchangeability doctrine. We tackle this issue in greater detail in chapter 3.

2. Schlesinger continues, "This reminded Gillette of the time when as a boy on the farm he asked the hired man how to tell the difference between male and female pigeons. The answer was: 'You put corn in front of a pigeon. If he picks it up, it is a he; if she picks it up, it is a she.'"

3. The data on the Bush administration are from the State Department Web site on treaty actions (http://www.state.gov/s/l/treaty/c3428.htm) and from the Library of Congress Web site called THOMAS, which tracks legislation and treaties (http://www.thomas.gov/home/treaties/treaties.html). We counted the number of reported international agreements in documents on the State Department Web site and cross-referenced them with the transmitted treaty documents reported by the Library of Congress.

4. Schlesinger's (1973: 105–8) account of the deal exchanging bases for destroyers indicates that Roosevelt carefully considered how the agreement with Britain would be received in Congress. For a time, Roosevelt argued that he could not legally complete the deal without the assent of Congress. Schlesinger reports that Senator McNary, Republican leader and candidate for vice president in 1940, stated his belief that such an accord

would likely fail in the Senate should Roosevelt submit the agreement under Article II procedures. The president and his advisers agreed with this likelihood. McNary indicated that "he would make no objection if persuasive grounds could be found for going ahead without resort to the Senate."

5. The Supreme Court cases that Howell (2003) references are *U.S. v. Curtiss-Wright* (299 U.S. 304 [1936]), *U.S. v. Belmont* (301 U.S. 324 [1937]), and *U.S. v. Pink* (315 U.S. 203 [1942]). *Pink* and *Belmont* involved the Litvinov Agreement, which gave official recognition to the Soviet Union. *Curtiss-Wright* involved a delegation of power to the president to declare an arms embargo. The majority opinion, however, broadened the findings of the Court significantly (and unnecessarily), to include executive agreements completed unilaterally by the president and other foreign policy powers (Fisher 2000: 29–31).

6. Shull's 2006 book, which devotes an entire chapter to modeling trends in the use of executive agreements, is focused on evaluating his "multiple perspectives" model of presidential prerogative power. His model gains little traction, however, on the usage of executive agreements, particularly when he models his measure of important agreements. His approach more effectively explains other trends, however, including the use of executive orders and presidential uses of force.

7. During many of the presentations we have given of this research, professors who teach Introduction to American Government have chimed in with responses like the following: "Basically, your research is saying that what I have been describing to my students all these years as a neat and clean power grab by the executive branch may be wrong!" We would stop well short of saying it is altogether "wrong." Certain descriptive elements previously described (e.g., the fact that executive agreements can be unilateral) obtain. However, the descriptives are drastically incomplete. Moreover, the inferences drawn from these few descriptive elements have been put together to form a picture that we simply did not see when we wrestled this research project, in all its pieces, to the ground.

8. For instance, in its opinion in *Medellin v. Texas* (552 U.S. __ [2008]), the Supreme Court found that treaties are only executable on the various states if the Congress has passed implementing legislation or if the provisions in the treaty clearly state that it alters the domestic law of signatory nations upon ratification. In *Medellin,* the Court invalidated an order—made by President George W. Bush in response to an International Court of Justice ruling—that the state of Texas reconsider the murder conviction of a Mexican national on death row because the complainant had not received consular advice upon arrest, as is required by the Vienna Convention on the Law of Treaties. The Court ruled, "While a treaty may constitute an international commitment, it is not binding in domestic law unless Congress has enacted statutes implementing it or the treaty itself conveys an intention that it be 'self-executing' and is ratified on that basis."

9. Confidential Senate staff and State Department staff interviews conducted by the authors, August 2004.

10. Confidential State Department staff interviews conducted by the authors, August 2004.

11. Confidential State Department staff and Senate staff interviews conducted by the authors, August 2004.

CHAPTER 1

1. Senator Henry Cabot Lodge (R-MA) sought a number of reservations to the treaty; most important was a clarification that nothing related to the League of Nations would circumvent Congress's "sole power" to authorize the use of military force. President Wilson opposed Lodge's reservations, and his refusal to consider them was important in scuttling the treaty in the Senate (Fisher 2000: 36).

2. See *The Constitution of the United States of America: Analysis and Interpretation*, 104th Cong., 2d sess., 1996, S. Doc. 103-6, as cited in Fisher 1998.

3. The attachment of amendments, reservations, understandings, or declarations (often referred to as RUDs) is a significant policy-making tool given to the Senate under its constitutional role of advice and consent. Such conditions attached to treaties have made the process more difficult for presidents. They often alter the language and meaning of treaty provisions, requiring, in some cases, renegotiation with treaty partners, and they sometimes address a wide-ranging set of policies (see Auerswald and Maltzman 2003; Lindsay 1994: 80–81). The ability of the Senate to attach conditions on treaties already negotiated has also caused consternation among U.S. treaty partners (Crabb, Antizzo, and Sarieddine 2000; Franck and Weisband 1979: 136–37), as some senators view these documents as works in progress once they hit the Senate (Gallagher 1969). The influential Senator Lodge "maintained in an interview that a treaty sent to the Senate is not properly a treaty but merely a project" (Holt 1933: 179).

4. This discussion summarizes the formal process outlined in *Treaties and Other International Agreements: The Role of the United States Senate* (U.S. Senate Committee on Foreign Relations 2001), where the treaty process is broken down into three basic stages: negotiation and conclusion, consideration by the Senate, and presidential action after Senate action (the formal ratification). Each of these stages are broken down into five, four, and three separate stages, respectively; however, this is more complicated than what is required for our purposes here.

5. Presidents are not required to transmit a signed treaty to the Senate for its consent, however. They could, as we discuss later in this chapter, also treat the international agreement as an executive agreement, submitting it to both chambers for approval by joint resolution, as done by President Nixon with the original Strategic Arms Limitation Talks (SALT) treaty. Or the president could refuse to seek congressional (senatorial) consent altogether, for political reasons—as Presidents Clinton and George W. Bush have done regarding the Kyoto Protocol, an amendment to the UN Framework Convention on Climate Change. Moreover, presidents are free to withdraw a treaty from Senate consideration after it has been transmitted, as President Carter did with the second SALT treaty in response to the Soviet Union's invasion of Afghanistan in 1979.

6. Senate Rule XXV grants the Senate Foreign Relations Committee (SFRC) exclusive jurisdiction over "treaties and executive agreements, except reciprocal trade agreements." Other committees may hold hearings, but only the SFRC can report the treaty to the full Senate. Senate Rule XXXVII reduces Senate decisions on the treaty to the "form of resolution, with or without amendments." Such resolutions require a two-thirds vote (Evans and Oleszek 2003: 92).

7. In the legal field, there is much controversy regarding the principle of "self-executing" treaties, yet political practice has largely recognized the existence of the need for

implementation legislation, duly passed by Congress (or the states), in order to carry forth the provisions of certain treaties ratified by the United States (see Paust 1988; Rosenkranz 2005). Despite the ruling in the majority opinion of *Medellin v. Texas* (see this book's introduction, n. 8), much controversy remains over the self-executable nature of treaties.

8. Presidents appear unconstrained by domestic law because the judiciary has largely dodged the issue and because the opponents of presidents unilaterally terminating treaties have been unable to muster legislative majorities. The Courts have chosen to refuse to rule in cases related to the issue, citing the doctrine of the political question (Adler 2004; *Goldwater v. Carter*, 444 U.S. 996 [1979]). However, under international law, presidents remain constrained (diplomatically, at least) by specific treaty provisions dealing with signatory withdrawal from a treaty.

9. Only twice has the issue risen to serious political conflict. In 1978, President Carter unilaterally terminated a mutual defense pact with Taiwan; and in 2001, President George W. Bush unilaterally withdrew the United States from the Anti-Ballistic Missile Treaty.

10. Senate intent, as expressed in ratification documents, is also salient legally when questions of treaty interpretation arise. On several occasions, the Court has relied on accompanying RUDs when interpreting treaties (e.g., *U.S. v. Stuart*, 109 U.S. 1191 [1983]). See Auerswald 2006: 85–86 n. 9. Moreover, the president cannot avoid the requirement of Senate advice and consent on a new treaty by stating that the treaty is an interpretation of an older one (Glennon 1990: 134).

11. In their work on Senate advice and consent on executive branch nominations, McCarty and Razaghian (1999) demonstrate how divided government is particularly problematic for interbranch relations when the parties in the Senate are polarized (see also DeRouen, Peake, and Ward 2005). They demonstrate this using DW-NOMINATE data from Poole and Rosenthal 1997. According to these data, the period between 1880 and 1910 was the most polarized. On a scale of 0–100 (used in DeRouen, Peake, and Ward 2005), with 100 signifying the most polarized Senate, the forty-ninth through sixtieth Senates (1885–1910) ranged from 86 to 100. To compare, the 1990s (through 1996) ranged from 45 to 68. Aldrich, Berger, and Rohde (2002) found a similar pattern in polarization. Political scientists typically focus on the polarized era since 1980 (e.g., Bond and Fleisher 2000) and demonstrate the positive relationship between polarization and legislative gridlock (e.g., Binder 1999; Peake 2002). However, the data suggest that this earlier period was much more polarized than the more studied recent period.

12. The three floor defeats include the Law of the Sea Convention in 1960, the Montreal Protocol No. 4 in 1983, and the Comprehensive Nuclear Test Ban Treaty in 1999 (see O'Brien 2003: 74, table 4.1).

13. The Genocide Convention was eventually ratified in 1989, forty years after it was first transmitted to the Senate by President Truman. We provide a case study of the Genocide Convention in chapter 4.

14. Of important treaties, 9.5 percent failed to ever receive Senate consent. While a success rate of 90 to 93 percent is very high, one must keep in mind that in nearly 10 percent of the cases since 1949, presidents have entered into important international agreements and submitted those agreements for Senate consent, only to have those agreements short-circuited or ignored by the Senate. This is remarkable, given that presidents

have the option of avoiding the Senate consent process altogether, through the use of executive agreements.

15. The odyssey of the Genocide Convention is illustrative, though exceptional. The treaty was transmitted to the Senate first in 1949 by Truman, then again in 1970 by Nixon. Hearings were held in 1950, but the Senate Foreign Relations Committee did not report the resolution of ratification to the full Senate. After Nixon retransmitted the treaty document again, the committee positively reported on the treaty four times, in 1970, 1976, 1984, and 1985. The full Senate did not consent to the treaty until February 1986, nearly forty years after the treaty was first transmitted by President Truman.

16. In *Goldwater*, Justice Powell wrote an important concurring opinion reasoning that the Court should dismiss Goldwater's claims because a constitutional conflict did not exist and therefore was not yet ripe. Congress had not sought legal relief as a whole or on an institutional level. If a majority of Congress had acted to block the president, the question would be justiciable (see Glennon 1990: 146 n. 128).

17. The Supreme Court declared the Military Commissions Act an unconstitutional suspension of the writ of habeas corpus in *Boumediene v. Bush* (553 U.S. __ [2008]).

18. On the significance and use of presidential signing statements, see P. J. Cooper 2005 and Kelley 2003.

19. There is disagreement among scholars regarding when executive agreements first emerged. O'Brien (2003), citing Wallace McClure (1941), argues that the United States completed its first executive agreement in 1817, with the Rush-Bagot Agreement, which President Monroe subsequently submitted to the Senate for consent as a treaty. However, Fisher (1998: 190), Dalton (1999), and a Congressional Research Service study (U.S. Senate Committee on Foreign Relations 2001: 38) all point to a 1792 statute allowing for the executive to negotiate postal agreements. Glennon (1990: 180) points to President John Adams as asserting this executive power in 1799. The difference is due to how different forms of executive agreement are counted—primarily to the difference between sole executive agreements, derived from the president's Article II powers, and statutory (or congressional) executive agreements, derived from some delegation of power from the legislature.

20. Fisher (2000: 27–28) considers these delegations of power as abdications, arguing that Congress willingly, "out of institutional embarrassment and self-doubt," gave up responsibilities over trade, after the unpopularity of its isolationist tariff policies.

21. The judicial nod to congressional delegation did not come so readily in the domestic realm, as the Court struck down several New Deal policies as unconstitutional delegations of power (see, e.g., *Panama Refining Co. v. Ryan*, 293 U.S. 388 [1935]).

22. Commodities agreements are commonly treated as treaties by modern presidents. For instance, the International Natural Rubber Agreements of 1979 (Exec. Doc. D, 96-2), 1987 (Treaty Doc. 100-9), and 1996 (Treaty Doc. 104-27) were all completed as treaties. Similarly, the International Wheat Agreement of 1949 (Exec. Doc. M, 81-1) and several subsequent wheat agreements (e.g., Exec. Docs. I, 84-2; E, 86-1; F, 92-1) were done as treaties.

23. Holding a more expansive view of executive power in this realm, Corwin (1984: 245–47) argues that most of these executive agreements also are derived by congressional delegation, although much of the delegation appears post hoc.

24. For pointed critiques of Sutherland's opinion, see Glennon 1990: 20–23 and Fisher 2000: 29–33.

25. As we noted in the introduction to this book, the Court's finding in *Pink* considered executive agreements to have "similar dignity" with duly ratified treaties, for the purposes of international law. However, in domestic law, executive agreements cannot trump statutes or the constitutional rights of citizens.

26. O'Brien (2003: 81) graphs these data by decade and shows a similar rise in agreements. Our graph masks considerable variation during the modern era. As a percentage of all international agreements, executive agreements range from 86 to 97 percent annually (see Fisher 2001: 39, table II-2). We address and explain this variation in chapter 2 of the present study.

27. There are three types of executive agreements that stem from delegations of congressional authority. First, there are those agreements where Congress provides ex ante authorization to the president to negotiate executive agreements on specific matters. Second are those executive agreements where Congress legislates on a foreign policy matter, instructing the president to verify certain facts before the law can take effect. Reciprocal trade agreements first authorized by statute in 1890 are an example. Finally, there are the congressional-executive agreements that have stirred much legal controversy (see, e.g., Ackerman and Golove 1995; Klarevas 2003; Paul 1998; Spiro 2001; Tribe 1995; Yoo 2001). The third type of congressional-executive agreement involves the president completing an international agreement and then seeking ex post congressional approval through joint resolution. Significant examples include the ascension of the United States to the International Monetary Fund and World Bank in 1945 and the North American Free Trade Agreement of 1992.

28. Shull (2006) refers to a category of congressional-executive agreements, which, for his purposes, include only those agreements that require congressional approval through votes in both the House and the Senate. He does not consider them as executive agreements in his data analysis. However, it is unclear whether or not his aggregate data on executive agreements excludes these agreements.

29. President Truman did not tread as lightly in implementing the UN Charter. He took the nation to war in Korea under UN auspices, without congressional approval, despite his earlier assurances to senators during Senate hearings on the charter that he would first seek congressional approval prior to using American military force to implement its provisions (Fisher 2000: 37–41).

30. Tananbaum (1988) casts doubt on the degree of public support for the amendment, citing the lack of public awareness on the issue in Gallup polls and the relatively limited amount of relevant congressional mail, which, though lopsided, was not especially overwhelming in magnitude. Even so, senators who had publicly opposed the amendment believed they were taking great political risk, as is evidenced in President Eisenhower's memorandum to Secretary of State Dulles and Attorney General Brownell, where he discusses the constituency pressure put on Republican Michigan senator Homer Ferguson (Dwight D. Eisenhower to John Foster Dulles and Herbert Brownell Jr., May 26, 1954, [Galambos and Van Ee [1996: doc. 896], available online in facsimile from the Dwight D. Eisenhower Memorial Commission at http://www.eisen howermemorial.org/presidential-papers/first-term/documents/896.cfm).

31. A two-thirds vote (of those voting) is required to formally propose the amendment and send it to the House of Representatives. The final vote was sixty yeas and

thirty-one nays, with five senators not voting. Senator Harley Kilgore, a liberal Democrat from West Virginia, was the deciding vote. He nearly missed the vote and, according to some accounts, either was intoxicated and had to be fetched from a nearby tavern or was sleeping off a prior drinking binge (see Tananbaum 1988: 180–81). If he had not voted, the amendment would have passed.

32. Dwight D. Eisenhower to Edgar Newton Eisenhower, February 3, 1954 (Galambos and Van Ee 1996: doc. 707), available online in facsimile from the Dwight D. Eisenhower Memorial Commission at http://www.eisenhowermemorial.org/presidential-papers/first-term/documents/707.cfm.

33. The effect of this compromise, when applied to the various forms of executive agreements listed earlier in text, would have eliminated all future executive agreements but congressional-executive agreements where ex post legislative approval is given. This compromise, of course, was offensive to President Eisenhower because it would have significantly hampered the executive's authority to carry out expedient diplomacy.

34. Somewhat related to conservatives' concern for international organizations and American sovereignty was the fear that such treaties might provide a legal argument for the national government imposing its will on the states with regard to civil rights legislation. This concern led many states' rights advocates to support the Bricker Amendment (see Tananbaum 1988).

35. Such resolutions continued to be offered during the 1970s. For example, Senator Clifford Case (R-NJ) introduced Senate Resolution 214 (92nd Cong., 2d sess. [1972])—originally cosponsored with Senators Church (D-ID), Fulbright (D-AR), Javits (R-NY), Ribicoff (D-CT), and Symington (D-MO)—which requested that basing agreements with Portugal and Bahrain be submitted as treaties (Dear Colleague letter from Senator Case to Senator Harris, January 17, 1972, Papers of the Honorable Fred P. Harris, Carl Albert Center Congressional Archives, Norman, OK). The Senate Foreign Relations Committee held extensive hearings on the underlying issues of unpublished executive agreements and military commitments and successfully reported the sense of the Senate resolution, which was passed by the full Senate (Congressional Information Service 1972: S. Rpt. 92-632; Glennon 1990: 180).

36. The Senate's distaste during the 1970s for unfettered use of executive agreements, especially when completing major international agreements, is clear in the legal and political arguments surrounding the Vienna Convention on the Law of Treaties, transmitted to the Senate in 1971 but never given consent. The convention, specifically Article 46, could be interpreted as recognition of the validity, under international law, of executive agreements, even should the president enter into such an agreement when he is not permitted to under domestic law. Opponents of the convention argue that by giving consent without a condition, the Senate would provide constitutional support for unrestrained use of executive agreements; and the executive has been unwilling to accept conditions to the convention (Glennon 1990: 183–88).

CHAPTER 2

1. Martin (2000) offers a third perspective encompassed somewhat by both perspectives tested in this chapter. She argues that presidents cannot evade the Senate when

making foreign policy, and her analysis demonstrates that the use of executive agreements does not vary with the typical variables noted as important by previous literature.

2. An example of one of Roosevelt's important executive agreements leading up to World War II was the 1940 agreement to trade U.S. destroyers to Great Britain in exchange for bases in the Caribbean.

3. Citing a congressional study for the period 1946–72, Loch Johnson (1984) states that 87 percent of the international agreements were congressional-executive agreements, 7 percent were sole executive agreements, and 6 percent were treaties.

4. Martin (2000: 66, 69–70) found that presidents appear to decrease the percentage of executive agreements (versus treaties) when their party has greater numbers in the Senate, but when she simply examined counts of executive agreements and treaties separately, she found that the change is a result of the increased use of treaties when presidents have greater support, rather than the decreased use of executive agreements. She concludes that presidents are not substituting executive agreements for treaties, as claimed under the evasion hypothesis. Instead, executive-legislative conflict, as measured by presidential support scores, accounts for the number of treaties (but not for the executive agreements) presidents conclude. Oddly, however, she finds that presidential support in the House (not the Senate) accounts for the yearly use of treaties.

5. Senate Rule XXV mandates that the SFRC has exclusive jurisdiction over all "treaties and executive agreements, except reciprocal trade agreements" (Evans and Oleszek 2003: 92).

6. In early 1993, Bush, in one of his final actions as president, signed the Chemical Weapons Convention, a treaty that both nations had signed and that superseded the original bilateral agreement. The convention was eventually ratified in April 1997 (Hersman 2000).

7. Refusal is uncommon but not unheard of. For example, the St. Lawrence Seaway agreement was originally submitted to the Senate as a treaty by President Roosevelt and rejected. When President Truman later sent the agreement to Congress for approval as an executive agreement in 1946, it was again defeated.

8. Confidential State Department staff interviews conducted by the authors, August 2004.

9. Confidential State Department staff and Senate staff interviews conducted by the authors, August 2004.

10. In the case of treaties, much like with vetoes, the pivotal senator is the individual located at the two-thirds spot on a one-dimensional ideological scale. Since international agreements are presidential policies, the pivotal member of the Senate is the sixty-seventh most liberal senator when the president is a Republican and the sixty-seventh most conservative senator when the president is a Democrat.

11. Confidential Senate staff interviews conducted by the authors, August 2004.

12. The two primary problems deal with accuracy and the lack of an up-to-date accounting. Margolis's (1986) data end in the 1970s, and Loch Johnson's (1984) data end in 1972.

13. Ragsdale compiled a list of international agreements by form up through 1985. In table 7-2 of *Vital Statistics on the Presidency* (1998), Ragsdale presents the yearly number of international agreements according to successive volumes of the *Current Treaty Index* (*CTI*). The list subdivides the number of agreements into two categories: executive agreements and treaties. However, from 1985 onward, only the total number of in-

ternational agreements is reported. Ragsdale explains, "Beginning in 1985 the *Current Treaty Index* no longer clearly distinguishes between treaties and executive agreements" (319). We made attempts to both replicate Ragsdale's count for certain years and update her data through our time period. We turned to the 1995 revision of the *United States Treaty Index: 1776–1990 Consolidation.* This source revealed many more agreements than we had originally counted in the *CTI* (Ragsdale's source), yet it also contained many more agreements than evidenced in Ragsdale's list. Other sources suggest that Ragsdale's accounting of international agreements seriously undercounts the number of executive agreements and possibly overcounts treaties. Lindsay (1994: 82, table 3) lists by decade the number of treaties and executive agreements compiled using Nelson 1989 and Stanley and Niemi 1994. Lindsay finds 3,040 executive agreements and 173 treaties from 1970 to 1979, whereas Ragsdale finds 2,524 executive agreements and 379 treaties during the same period. In the 1980–90 time period, Lindsay finds 4,021 total international agreements, whereas Ragsdale finds 1,871. These numbers, especially for the most recent period examined, are wildly different.

14. The State Department's Office of the Assistant Legal Adviser for Treaty Affairs is primarily responsible for overseeing and processing treaties and executive agreements on behalf of the administration. Through a process described in Circular 175 (the *Foreign Affairs Manual*), the legal advisor is responsible for providing legal advice regarding the classification of international agreements. A look at the list by year suggests that we are correct to be leery of Ragsdale's (1998) data on international agreements.

15. A better test of the evasion hypothesis would be to break down the agreements other than treaty by form, into congressional-executive agreements versus presidential agreements (see chap. 1). Presidential agreements, for example, are completed with much greater presidential discretion than are congressional-executive agreements. We include all types of agreements in our aggregate analysis. In chapter 3, we analyze agreement data on an agreement-by-agreement basis for a test of presidential decision making, and we are there able to disaggregate the agreements by policy topic. Loch Johnson (1984) does this for the period 1946–72. Furthermore, including congressional-executive agreements (what Johnson calls "statutory agreements") would focus the efficiency tests to only the presidential side of the equation, not the senatorial side, though efficiency may benefit the Senate as well. We disaggregate the following analysis by examining the major international agreements—those agreements where the president is likely, if at all, to take a direct interest. Moreover, some run-of-the-mill international agreements are required by statute to be treated as treaties—presidents cannot complete them as executive agreements. The best example is extradition treaties (*Crimes and Criminal Procedures,* U.S. Code 18 [1996], § 3184). Additionally, some types of agreements, given their effects on state laws, are, by convention, always handled as treaties, including tax treaties and treaties concerning mutual legal assistance. As these agreements are nearly always done as treaties, they are excluded from the set of important international agreements.

16. It is unclear—and much debated in the legal literature (see chap. 3)—whether or not presidents can ignore such a statute. Moreover, as we explain in previous chapters, executive agreements and treaties are not completely interchangeable in a legal sense.

17. See the discussion of the State Department Circular 175 process (Senate Committee on Foreign Relations 2001: 358–59). Detailed procedures are identified to help

practitioners make the determination for agreement classification. In most cases, discretion is not as great as the conventional wisdom suggests. In fact, the preference of the Congress is to be taken into consideration, according to the *Foreign Affairs Manual* (11 *FAM* 710). We explore these issues in greater depth in chapter 3.

18. We supplemented Axelrod's list by examining *CQ Almanac* for each year, looking for treaties and executive agreements that were discussed as being politically salient. In addition, we examined State Department documents on significant international agreements. Based on these reviews, we added several additional agreements to Axelrod's list of major agreements. We exclude from our analysis of significant agreements all extradition and tax treaties, should they appear in Axelrod's accounting. He includes a few of these as examples of an agreement type (we exclude any executive agreements that he included as examples for similar reasons). Axelrod's approach is similar to the method used by Mayhew (1991) to signifying importance when he came up with his much-used list of landmark legislation. Like Mayhew, Axelrod used policy-oriented books and primary sources to compile his list of international agreements. We cross-referenced Axelrod's list by reading over State Department documents on significant international agreements and other available listings and found that Axelrod's list is valid.

19. The time series values range from 86.1 to 96.9, with a mean of 93.9 and a standard deviation of 2.72.

20. The time series values range from 0 to 76.9, with a mean of 17.8 and a standard deviation of 17.8.

21. Divided government (between the president and Senate) and the number of presidential partisans was highly collinear (Kendall's $tau\text{-}b = .76$), so we opted to account for partisan context using a measure of presidential partisans rather than the more traditional approach based on divided government. We ran the model alternatively with both variables. The findings were the same. Alternative measures could have been used to account for the power of the president's party in the Senate. For example, in his models explaining the use of executive orders, Howell (2003) uses scores for divided government and "legislative potential for policy change" (LPPC). The scores measure the size and cohesiveness of the majority party and were developed by Hurley, Brady, and Cooper (1977). Howell and Pevehouse (2007) use "presidential party power scores," which are a variation on LPPC scores, accounting for the president's party in Congress rather than the majority party's strength. We calculated both scores for the Senate and used them in place of our number of presidential partisans variable. The results remain unchanged, and these alternative measures performed similarly to the variable of the number of presidential partisans.

22. We define the treaty pivot in the same manner that Krehbiel (1998) defines the veto pivot, as the sixty-seventh member of the Senate in the direction opposite the ideology of the president. The number represents the thirty-third most conservative member of the Senate during a Democratic presidency and the thirty-third most liberal member of the Senate during a Republican presidency. Our variable measures the absolute distance between the president's and pivot's first-dimension CS-NOMINATE scores. We use the median CS-NOMINATE score of Democrats in the Senate for Truman, as CS-NOMINATE scores for presidents are unavailable prior to Eisenhower. CS-NOMINATE scores are from Poole 2006. NOMINATE scores range from 1 to +1, with the higher score indicating conservatism.

23. While the United States does not have formal relations with every member state

of the United Nations (there are ten members with which the United States does not have relations), the growth in UN membership is a good proxy for new nation-states (emerging in the modern era) with which the U.S. will enter into formal relations. Using nation "background notes" on the State Department Web site (http://www.state.gov/r/pa/ei/bgn/), we cross-referenced a sample of nation-states (nations beginning with the letters *A–C*), assessing when the United States entered into formal relations (through formal recognition, placement of an embassy, etc.), and we found that the year coincided with dates of formal independence and acceptance into the United Nations in most cases, save a few. One exception was Afghanistan, where the U.S. embassy was left unstaffed after violence erupted there in 1978 and lasted until 2002.

24. All Congresses beginning in 1989 (the 101st Congress) are coded 0 for the Cold War variable. All previous Congresses are coded 1.

25. See L. Johnson 1984 and Martin 2005 for examples where agreements are disaggregated.

CHAPTER 3

1. *Congressional Record,* 108th Cong., 1st sess., March 5, 2003: S 3145.

2. According to the Gallup polls, Bush's approval was at 52 percent in March 2005 but was on a downward trend into the 30 percent range by the spring of 2006.

3. See Martin 2005 for an exception.

4. Setear (2002) and Martin (2005) make this simplifying assumption. In doing so, they avoid the complications inherent in the actual decision process outlined by State Department documents (especially Circular 175, the *Foreign Affairs Manual*). Lindsay (1994: 83) mentions the classification process internal to the State Department but concludes that "the criteria are open to interpretation" and that "as a result, only the president decides whether an agreement with other nations will be handled as an executive agreement or as a treaty." His conclusion is problematic, for if the decisions are primarily made at the agency level, as we show, how can the president be the primary decision maker? To be sure, presidents could issue an executive order requiring that a certain type of agreement be handled by either treaties or executive agreements, but no such order has ever been given.

5. Tax agreements and agreements concerning mutual legal assistance are traditionally completed as treaties, due to their effects over state law and due to the ambiguities of the "supremacy" of executive agreements (which does not exist for treaties) under Article VI (confidential Senate staff interviews conducted by the authors, August 2004). Conversely, more recently, science and cultural agreements only take the form of executive agreements (Martin 2005: 456).

6. Law requires that extradition agreements be completed as treaties (*Crimes and Criminal Procedures,* U.S. Code 18 [1996], § 3184). However, exceptions to this rule have been upheld in federal cases (e.g., *Ntakirutimana v. Reno,* 184 F.3d 419 [5th Cir. 1999]; see Klarevas 2003). Moreover, major agreements on arms control require, by law, some form of congressional approval, either through the Senate as an Article II treaty or through their submission to both congressional chambers for majority approval (Arms Control and Disarmament Act of 1961, Public Law 87-297).

7. Caruson and Farrar-Myers (2007) measure presidential elevation of an agree-

ment by examining whether or not the executive agreement is mentioned in *The Public Papers of the Presidents*.

8. Because they require an official transmittal document completed by the president, treaties always involve direct White House action. However, we do not then conclude that all formal treaties are significant, as some areas of agreement making require formal treaties (at least according to State Department rules) because they supersede state law (see the State Department's Circular 175, the *Foreign Affairs Manual*). Examples of such treaties include extradition and tax treaties that have been completed with most foreign nations. Most treaties do not qualify as significant, although the percentage of treaties that are important is greater than the percentage of executive agreements that are important. To illustrate, of the treaties we examine in chapter 5 (from the period 1949–2000), we code only 200 of the 850 treaties (24 percent) as important. Of the over 13,800 executive agreements analyzed in chapter 2 (from the period 1949–98), only 246 (1.8 percent) are coded as important.

9. As discussed in previous chapters, most executive agreements are congressional-executive agreements, pursuant to a previous delegation of power from Congress and, in some cases, subject to a congressional vote of approval.

10. Probably the most notorious executive agreement brokered by Roosevelt at the end of World War II was the Yalta Accord, an agreement between the Allied powers on the postwar divide of power in Europe. Critics believed that Roosevelt essentially gave away Eastern Europe to the Soviets.

11. We are referring to the Bricker Amendment (discussed in depth in chapter 1), which, in its original form, would have eliminated the constitutionality of executive agreements.

12. We address the politics surrounding Case-Zablocki in greater depth in chapter 1.

13. Confidential Senate staff interviews conducted by the authors, August 2004.

14. For contrasting views on this question, see Fisher 1998: 190–91 and Ackerman and Golove 1995: 7. Tribe (1995) and Paul (1998) argue that executive agreements are unconstitutional; however, clearly, the interchangeable theory has dominated legal academic discourse and political practice (Klarevas 2003).

15. Confidential State Department staff interviews conducted by the authors, August 2004.

16. Presidential executive agreements have been recognized as legitimate when there is a clear connection to Article II powers of the president. Controversy arises over the extent of these unilateral powers and their linkage to the president's authority as chief executive or chief diplomat (Ackerman and Golove 1995: 15 n. 49) and over the extent to which the Congress has previously delegated authority to the president.

17. As discussed in chapter 1, in practice, the political branches have recognized areas of policy where the congressional-executive agreement is legally most appropriate and areas where the treaty is most appropriate. As shown by Spiro (2001), when the international agreement deals with a power of Congress (e.g., a trade agreement and the commerce power), both chambers constitutionally play a role, and the congressional-executive agreement is most appropriate. Employing a treaty for such agreements would endanger the prerogatives of the House. However, when an international agreement deals with state law (as reserved by the Tenth Amendment) or powers outside of Article I, a treaty is most appropriate; hence extradition agreements are typically done by treaty,

as most criminal violations are violations of state law. As a result of these practices, Spiro (2001: 993) states that "an ad hoc typology has developed under which some types of international agreements continue to be submitted as treaties, arguably by constitutional mandate, and others might require the form of congressional-executive agreement."

18. Proponents of legal interchangeable theory (e.g., Ackerman and Golove 1995) fail to reconcile with the fact that presidential practice has been to submit politically consequential international agreements in both forms, making the presidents' decisions political. For example, in practice, most arms control agreements and mutual security pacts are submitted as treaties (Spiro 2001: 996); however, presidents still maintain (and have used and considered using) the option of the executive agreement for even those agreements, and they are specifically authorized to do so by the Arms Control and Disarmament Act of 1961 (Public Law 87-297).

19. Furthermore, the Senate has gone on record several times insisting that arms control agreements be done as treaties. In consenting to the 1991 Conventional Armed Forces in Europe Treaty, the Senate attached a declaration stating that its official opinion is that arms control agreements must be completed as treaties (Spiro 2001: 997). That presidents since have considered ignoring this Senate declaration is clear in our discussion on the Moscow Treaty (earlier in the present chapter).

20. In this subsection, we rely heavily on a set of confidential interviews we conducted with senior staff members in the State Department and Senate in August 2004.

21. To catalog the significant international agreements, we relied on Axelrod's list in *American Treaties and Alliances* (2000), supplemented by our own reading of the agreement summaries and State Department documents on significant international agreements. We discussed our use of Axelrod's list in greater depth in chapter 2 (n. 18).

22. We relied on LexisNexis to search for stories in the *New York Times*. We searched the two preceding years of the *Times*, up through the date the agreement was signed. Our intent with the *New York Times* measure is to account for media salience of an agreement at the time of the signing. Only 138 (31 percent) of the 441 international agreements actually garnered attention by the *Times* prior to signing. We collapsed our continuous measure (stories) to a dummy variable (1 for attention in the *Times*), so the measure captures some base level of salience for an agreement. Auerswald (2006) used coverage on the *New York Times* editorial pages as an indicator of a security treaty's importance. Howell (2003) used a similar approach to distinguish important executive orders from run-of-the-mill executive orders.

23. To determine whether or not the president spoke publicly on an international agreement, we turned to *The Public Papers of the Presidents*. We counted the number of lines where the president mentioned the agreements (in spoken word), up to and including the signing date. We collapsed this continuous measure to a dummy variable (1 for public attention by the president), so the measure captures some base level of presidential attention to an agreement. Only 136 (31 percent) of the significant agreements received any public attention by the president. We do not include written statements on the agreements (which would include the actual transmittal documents of the treaties). Of course, we cannot account for nonpublic attention by the president, as these data are not as readily available and do not send signals of significance regarding an international agreement.

24. Martin (2005) found this to be the case in her analysis. Examining the data separately between multilateral and bilateral agreements clearly shows the significance of

multilateralism in structuring presidential choice. Of the 211 multilateral agreements, 165 (78 percent) were completed as treaties, whereas only 29 (13 percent) of the 223 bilateral agreements were completed as treaties.

25. We use the same topical classification used by Auerswald and Maltzman (2003) in their study on treaty reservations. Security and sovereignty agreements constitute "high politics," whereas norms, legal, and economic agreements involve "low politics."

26. Moreover, one could argue that agreements on trade, fisheries, and nuclear materials lack variation due to statutes requiring that presidents submit these types of agreements for congressional approval. However, presidents are still free to choose the treaty route or the congressional-executive agreement route. Our data on treaties show that presidents have used the treaty form to complete several agreements on fishing rights (e.g., the Agreement on East Coast Fishery Resources with Canada, Exec. Doc. V, 96-1) and for multilateral trade agreements (e.g., the International Sugar Agreement of 1954, Exec. Doc. B, 83-2). That presidents most often go the latter route with economic/trade agreements (coded as "low politics" agreements), particularly those that are bilateral, is controlled for in our analysis.

27. We also ran the statistical models using both a measure of divided government and Howell and Pevehouse's (2007) measure of the strength of the president's party. The findings are similar to what we report in the present chapter. Running the models with a measure of ideological distance between the president and pivotal senator (see chap. 2) yields a coefficient near zero and does not change at all the reported results.

28. Each of these variables is explained in chapter 2.

29. Predicted probabilities were calculated in Stata 9.0 using CLARIFY software, available online at http://gking.harvard.edu/stats.shtml (King, Tomz, and Wittenberg 2000).

30. This nonfinding holds no matter how we measure the partisan relationship between the president and Senate. A measure of divided government is insignificant as well.

CHAPTER 4

1. While the House does not have a formal role in the advice and consent process, House members have shown keen interest in treaty politics over the years, as we show in chapter 6.

2. Should the Senate give its consent to a treaty, the treaty then awaits final presidential action (ratification).

3. See, for example, Caldwell 1991a; Hersman 2000; Jorden 1984; Moffett 1985.

4. That domestic politics often guide treaty negotiators is well accepted in the literature on international relations. For example, see Evans, Jacobson, and Putnam 1993; Mo 1995; Schelling 1960; Tarar 2001. The degree to which negotiators are advantaged by domestic ratification requirements is disputed theoretically, however. Yet our understanding of the shape those politics take in the American setting is hampered by the lack of systematic research on the topic.

5. None of the cited works account for committee politics. Moreover, they fail to give full consideration to prefloor processes. Auerswald and Maltzman 2003 and Auerswald 2006 do account for reservations, but their models discount the role played by the

SFRC, even though it is the committee that attaches most of the successful reservations and amendments to treaties that are considered on the floor.

6. For example, Kennedy and Khrushchev completed an important executive agreement in 1963 establishing a direct hotline between the White House and the Kremlin.

7. In searching the archives of several senators available at the Carl Albert Center Congressional Archives in 2005, we found many letters in opposition. A typical example included a letter of August 13, 1965, to Senators Mike Monroney and Fred Harris (of Oklahoma) from Mrs. E. L. Mutzig of Duncan, Oklahoma. She opened, "Are we really so determined to destroy ourselves?" She did not hold anything back later in the letter, where she stated, "I can visualize a Consulate in California where the present riots are going on. The Communists can open the doors of the Consulate to those lawbreakers, murderers, destroyers of property, assaulters, thieves, and any of the other types of criminals, and no officer of the law in the United States can touch the criminal. The boundary of the Consulate is the dead end of law enforcement. It is the same as moving Communist Russia inside the boundaries of the United States" (Papers of the Honorable Fred P. Harris and A. S. Mike Monroney, 1965, Carl Albert Center Congressional Archives, Norman, OK).

8. Prior to Johnson's speech, a State Department official (Douglas MacArthur II, assistant secretary for congressional relations) wrote to all House and Senate members to squelch misunderstandings that had emerged over the treaty (January 27, 1967, Papers of the Honorable Jeffrey Cohelan, 1967, Carl Albert Center Congressional Archives). Basically, the treaty itself did not approve the locating of the consulates, and its core purpose was to protect Americans in Russia.

9. Papers of the Honorable Fred P. Harris, 1965, Carl Albert Center Congressional Archives, Norman, OK. Additional examples include a February 23, 1967, letter to Senate minority leader Everett Dirksen (R-IL) in which Rex Westerfied Sr. of Oklahoma City wrote, "I have gotten accustomed to the Liberals, Socialists, Fabians, Americans for Democratic Action and Communist selling us out . . . I really wouldn't expect a true Republican or Democrat to undermine our government to the point of its falling to the communist" (Papers of the Honorable Everett Dirksen, 1966, Carl Albert Center Congressional Archives, Norman, OK). In a letter to Senator Fred Harris, Mr. Ollie Manow of Grante, Oklahoma, wrote on February 16, "This bill would greatly benefit the Communist party in their constant effort to overthrow the United States government" (Papers of the Honorable Fred P. Harris, 1966, Carl Albert Center Congressional Archives, Norman, OK).

10. Hence there were three treaties (the original in 1903 and two others, in 1936 and 1955, to increase the payment) when the Carter changes were pursued in the 1970s.

11. Despite media reports suggesting that opinion shifted late in the treaty fight to growing support in response to changes in the treaties, scholarly analysis of public opinion polls on the Panama Canal Treaties clearly show that public opposition to the treaties was significant and largely unchanging. Roshco (1978: 562) estimates that throughout the political battle, public opinion stood at the ratio of five opposed to the treaties to three in favor of them. Moffett (1985: 116) concludes, "Despite one of the most extensive public relations efforts ever undertaken on a foreign policy issue . . . public attitudes never budged." The public remained stridently opposed to the ratification of the treaties. See also Smith and Hogan 1987.

12. That President Carter pursued such a change in the framework in response to

the likelihood of failures in the Senate defies the logic of a pro forma treaty consent process. We cannot fathom a better example of the difficulty that presidents may face (and the politics that can emerge) than one where a president was so concerned about these possibilities potentially occurring that he would return to rehash part of the pact.

13. For example, "Memorandum. March 17, 1978. Telephone calls received regarding Senator Bellman's vote on Canal Treaty." Papers of the Honorable Dewey F. Bartlett, 1977, Carl Albert Center Congressional Archives, Norman, OK.

14. If the treaty were later amended in the Senate, Panama would have the choice to approve it or not ratify it. Hence this was an important question to ask, and the answer was a promising one.

15. Memorandum from Senator Paul Laxalt to Senator Dewey Bartlett, March 6, 1978, Papers of the Honorable Dewey F. Bartlett, 1977, Carl Albert Center Congressional Archives, Norman, OK. When legislators would prefer to vote a certain way (often for constituency purposes) but would be available to the leadership should their votes be pivotal for the greater good, they are called "if-you-need-me" votes. There were four such senators in the case of the neutrality treaty to which this letter refers. This meant that the opponents needed to actually gather four more votes than the one-third needed to block the treaty. It also suggests that President Carter had a bit more breathing room on the neutrality treaty than others have previously assumed.

16. Internal office memorandum from a staff member to Senator Dewey Bartlett, February 7, 1978, summarizing an attached February 7 strategy letter from Laxalt, Papers of the Honorable Dewey F. Bartlett, 1977, Carl Albert Center Congressional Archives, Norman, OK.

17. Such a claim has been proved invalid in subsequent analysis. Smith and Hogan (1987: 6) argue that the proponents' argument was a "massive misinterpretation of public opinion," brought on by significant mistakes on the part of news reporters.

18. As shown regularly on CSPAN-2, there typically are only a few persons on the floor of the Senate chamber during sessions. Senators watch from their offices, only coming to the floor as needed to cast a vote and then leaving.

19. The one exception to this tradition pertains to the Budget Reconciliation Act. When the Congress completes a budget resolution at the start of the congressional budget process, they are required, in the authorization stage, to then follow the parameters of the resolution. The process of reconciling authorizations to be in line with the budget resolution is called "reconciliation." The outcome is typically a massive Omnibus Budget Reconciliation Act (OBRA). Senate Rules state that senators cannot filibuster this act.

20. The United States ratified two antislavery conventions during the 1950s: the International Agreement for the Suppression of the White Slave Traffic (Exec. Doc. B, 81-2) and a protocol amending the Slavery Convention of September 25, 1926 (Exec. Doc. F, 83-2). A refugee protocol was also ratified in 1968 (Protocol Relating to the Status of Refugees, Exec. Doc. K, 90-2).

21. The three treaties include the Convention against Torture (Treaty Doc. 100-20), the International Covenant on Civil and Political Rights (Exec. Doc. E, 95-2), and the International Convention on the Elimination of All Forms of Racial Discrimination (Exec. Doc. C, 95-2).

22. Of course, no senator promoted such practices. The implicit argument was that the United States could handle these issues within its own governmental framework.

23. March 16, 1971, letter from Senator Sam J. Ervin (NC) to Senator Fred R. Har-

ris (OK). From the papers of Senator Fred Harris, Carl Albert Center Congressional Archives.

24. The Liberty Lobby, which loomed large in the debate over the U.S.-Soviet Consular Treaty (discussed earlier in this chapter), made three separate appearances opposing the Genocide Convention at ratification hearings—on May 22, 1970; May 26, 1977; and December 3, 1981.

25. Senate Rule XXX, which governs treaty proceedings, requires that at least one day "elapse between the time the Senate completes action (amends) on the treaty itself and the time it begins consideration of the resolution of ratification, although this requirement . . . is frequently waived by unanimous consent." Once the resolution or ratification is under consideration, the treaty can no longer be amended (Rundquist and Bach 2003: 2). If even one senator opposes the waiving of this rule, the treaty is further delayed.

26. Senate rules allow any senator to access the floor once the senator currently speaking yields the floor. Senators may speak for as long as they wish. Speaking for a long period of time and not yielding the floor in an attempt to kill legislation (or a resolution of treaty ratification or a presidential nominee for the courts or executive branch) is called a filibuster. In order to run the Senate floor, therefore, the floor leaders seek unanimous consent to proceed under particular conditions. If no senator rises on the floor to object, unanimous consent is granted, and the floor debate on whatever was considered in the unanimous consent agreement is regulated. If even one senator opposes such an agreement, it fails, and delayed floor consideration becomes a reality.

27. The final treaty passed with two reservations and five understandings. LeBlanc (1991: 241) refers to these agreements as the "Sovereignty Package," meant to "reduce the convention to no more than a symbol of opposition to genocide." The reservations and understandings stipulated that the convention would not become "binding on the United States until implementing legislation was passed" (Lowery 1993: 203).

28. President Kennedy's commencement address at American University, Washington, DC, June 10, 1963.

29. One account indicates that Senator Kyl (R-AZ), an outspoken opponent of the treaty, had been quietly making a head count of Republican votes earlier in the spring and had received pledges to vote against the treaty from forty-two out of fifty-five Republican senators, enough to doom the treaty should it come to a vote (Deibel 2002).

30. The forty-four Annex 2 states include those states that currently possess nuclear power or research reactors and that formally participated in the 1996 session of the Conference on Disarmament (CTBTO 2007; see http://www.ctbto.org/glossary).

31. The CTBTO Preparatory Commission maintains a list of signatories and ratifying states on its web site, http://www.ctbto.org/member-states/status-of-signature-and-ratification/ (accessed September 29, 2008).

32. See UN General Assembly, GA/DIS/356, available at http://www.un.org/News/Press/docs/2007/gadis3356.doc.htm (accessed September 29, 2008).

CHAPTER 5

1. Despite the president's focus on START II, the Senate did not consent to the treaty until January 26, 1996. The politics of START II and the CWC were intertwined

once Republicans took control of the Senate following the 1994 congressional elections, as leaders in the Senate conditioned movement on START II for concessions on the CWC.

2. His ideology scores, using CS-NOMINATE (Poole 2006), rank him as the most conservative senator for the 102nd through the 106th Senates.

3. A review of President Clinton's public statements indicates that he spoke publicly on the CWC more than on any other treaty during his eight years in office, save for the Comprehensive Nuclear Test Ban Treaty, which failed in a Senate vote in 1999.

4. Among the treaties completed within three years, the mean period to ratification is 276 days, with a great deal of variance around the mean (the standard deviation is 240 days).

5. While presidents typically will transmit a treaty within months of signing the agreement, delays of a year or more are not uncommon. An extreme example occurred when President Nixon transmitted the Convention on the Privileges and Immunities of the United Nations (Exec. Doc. J, 91-1) on December 19, 1969. The treaty was originally signed by the Truman administration on February 13, 1946.

6. Confidential State Department staff interviews and Senate staff interviews conducted by the authors, August 2004. Unfortunately for our purposes, the priority lists are unavailable.

7. This is especially the case for significant treaties, including arms control agreements. In several instances, world opinion on American prestige has proven significant in prodding conservative senators to support arms control agreements despite their initial hesitations. The Limited Test Ban Treaty, for example, was given Senate consent rapidly (forty-seven days after transmittal) despite clear misgivings from conservative senators who regarded the Soviets as untrustworthy treaty partners and despite a protracted floor debate that lasted two weeks (Loeb 1991: 176, 202).

8. Additionally, substantial delay in the ratification of a treaty can cause a technical problem when considering international law. In some cases, if signatories fail to ratify a treaty prior to the treaty entering into force, they may be shut out of administration of the treaty. This nearly happened with the CWC, as the Senate gave its consent to the treaty only five days prior to the treaty entering into force (Hersman 2000: 94).

9. Similarly, during the public battles of judicial and executive nominations during the Clinton and George W. Bush administrations, much of the Senate obstruction occurred within committee.

10. Of the 850 treaties under Senate consideration from 1949 to 2000, the median number of days that passed until the SFRC made its report was 192. The median number of days to Senate consent was 216. The median difference between duration to floor consent and duration to the SFRC reporting was only eight days. Thus, in the median case, the SFRC accounts for 89 percent of the duration of the consent process. We use median values here because mean values are not representative due to severe outliers. For instance, the longest a treaty languished in the SFRC prior to being reported was 9,835 days, in the case of the 1949 Inter-American Convention on Granting of Political Rights to Women.

11. Two important exceptions exist. In this chapter, we discuss at length the work of Auerswald and Maltzman (2003) on Senate propensity to attach reservations to treaty documents. DeLaet and Scott (2006), in their study of arms control treaties, found important partisan and ideological effects on Senate floor voting.

12. Lindsay's account includes treaties the president decided not to ratify—even after Senate consent was given—because of alternations to the treaty in the Senate.

13. Pivotal and partisan explanations are clearly related. The ideologies of the pivotal players discussed in this section diverge in the context of polarized political parties.

14. Krepon and Caldwell (1991) cite the importance of the Senate leadership and pivotal senators. In each of their five modern cases, the SFRC chair proved pivotal. Chairs of the Senate Armed Services Committee were also pivotal, but that is primarily due to their case selection, which included only arms control treaties. Since we examine all treaties, focusing on the SFRC chair makes sense theoretically.

15. Exceptions to this general rule occurred while Senator Helms was the SFRC chair during the Clinton administration. During that period, he was the most conservative senator in the Senate (according to CS-NOMINATE ideology scores), and he is renowned for his efforts in opposing liberal foreign policies, including human rights and arms control treaties, during his long career on the foreign relations committee (R. Johnson 2006: 253). As shown earlier, Helms would condition SFRC approval for a treaty on considerations by the administration on conservative priorities.

16. Of course, presidents often spoke on behalf of treaties both prior to transmittal and afterward; hence the sum of these numbers is higher than the 12 percent aggregate figure.

17. Krepon and Caldwell (1991: 462–65) also identify the president's legislative skills and reputation as a "staunch defender" of U.S. security interests as being important indicators of presidential success in traversing the Senate during ratification debates. Such concepts are difficult to measure systematically (see Edwards 1989) and are excluded from our theoretical model.

18. Auerswald (2006) found that security treaties he coded as important were more likely to attract consequential reservations and amendments than were less significant treaties.

19. We end in 2000 to allow sufficient time for treaties transmitted in the more recent periods to be processed.

20. That treaties remain on the Senate calendar until they are rejected (or returned) by the Senate or withdrawn by the president complicates our analysis significantly. Normally, the legislative calendar ends with the swearing in of each new Congress, but this is not the case regarding treaties before the Senate. The methodological problem is obvious: which variables of political context do we examine, variables at the time of transmission or variables at the time of reporting, if in a different Senate? We minimize this problem in a variety of ways in the analysis in terms of how we right-censor our variables in the hazard analyses that follow. Specifically, while we report our full population models, we are able to right-censor our data set to include only those treaties processed in a specific time frame. We compare our results reported here to data censored at the end of the original transmittal Senate, as well as the original and subsequent Senate. We base these formulations on the logic that treaties that take a lengthy period of time to ratify signify failed policy change for presidents, at least in terms of getting the Senate to consent to their treaties. This operationalization also helps minimize the concerns inherent in studying treaties that carry over from one Senate to the next. The results are quite similar.

21. Senate consent within the transmittal Senate is the ideal for presidential success in the treaty process. We include an analysis in the subsequent Senate because some

treaties are not transmitted until the end of a congressional term and are unlikely to be resolved at that late date. We include time variables (the month the treaty is transmitted during a two-year Senate) to control for the timing of treaty transmittal.

22. From examination of the hazard function graphs for our models, as well as Akaike information criteria (AIC), we conclude that the standard Cox proportional hazards model—or, more simply, Cox regression—is inappropriate for our data. Instead, we employ parametric models that best match the hazard function graphs and that, as indicated using AIC, have the best overall fit. We employ a Gompertz hazard distribution for our analysis of time to SFRC report and a log-logistic survival distribution for our analysis of time between SFRC report and full Senate consent. Additionally, we report Hubert-White (robust) standard errors clustered by Senate to account for the pooling of our data by Senate, thus providing very conservative significance tests for our models (see Zorn 2006).

23. We use this measure, instead of the standard dummy variable of divided government, to account for the partisan context, in order to be consistent with our previous analyses in chapters 2 and 3. We also ran the analysis using the dummy variable of divided government, and the results are very similar. We considered including a party polarization measure in the model, to account for partisanship, but that measure correlates too highly with our measures of preference divergence discussed shortly.

24. As we did in chapters 2 and 3, we define the treaty pivot in the same manner that Krehbiel (1998) defines the veto pivot, as the sixty-seventh member of the Senate in the direction opposite the ideology of the president. See chap. 2, n. 22.

25. We employ the same ideology measures as we used in chapters 2 and 3. See chap. 2, n. 22, for a discussion of these measures.

26. Public approval data for 1949–52 come from King and Ragsdale 1988. Data from 1953–2000 are from Edwards and Wayne 2006.

27. While we also counted the number of lines in the *Papers* on behalf of each treaty after transmittal, using such a measure would be endogenous. In other words, presidents are more likely to speak on behalf of a treaty when it runs into trouble in the Senate, so we cannot be sure whether the president's efforts are contributing to delay in the SFRC or are a result of delay. Lines in the transmittal documents are not included, as they are not public utterances by the president.

28. Legal treaties are held out of the model as the comparison category. The categories are mutually exclusive. Security treaties include alliances, basing agreements, peace agreements, arms control treaties, and so on. Sovereignty treaties include border/territorial treaties, international organizations not specific to another topic, treaties dealing with diplomatic procedures (e.g., consular conventions), and so on. Economic treaties include tax conventions, shipping and aviation treaties, fisheries treaties, commodity agreements, communications agreements, and so on. Norms treaties include human rights conventions, labor rights protocols, environmental or conservation treaties, and so on. Legal agreements include extradition treaties, mutual legal assistance treaties, copyright conventions, terrorism conventions, and so on.

29. We supplemented this historical source with contemporary accounts by *CQ Almanac* (various editions). See chap. 2, n. 18, for further discussion. Through this process, using multiple sources, we identified two hundred treaties as important.

30. We do not include a Senate variable, essentially a control for time, as some previous duration analyses of the Senate have done (see McCarty and Razaghian 1999). We

exclude the variable for two reasons. First, it correlates very highly with two of our other variables: president/pivot difference and Cold War. Second, since we cluster our standard errors by Senate (Zorn 2006), including a Senate variable becomes problematic. Finally, including a Senate variable in the analyses (and not clustering by Senate) does not alter the findings, and the variable is insignificant.

31. For more complete discussion of the use of hazard models in duration analysis, see Bennett and Stam 1996 and Box-Steffensmeier and Jones 1997.

32. This can be done in any number of ways. The chair could simply refuse to schedule hearings on a treaty, thus ignoring it. Or he or she could try to alter the treaty through reservations and amendments, which would add to the time before the committee.

33. Senator Helms, the most ideologically conservative SFRC chair in our data set, is just over two standard deviations above the mean chair ideology. Computing Helms's ideology score (.656) gives an estimated increase in duration of a full year for significant treaties—a clearly substantial contribution to gridlock. The most liberal SFRC chair (Senator Green, at −.412) had a marginal effect of decreasing the median duration by 2.5 months for significant treaties.

34. Moreover, the finding is not very robust. When the distance between the president and pivot variable is removed from the model, the number of presidential partisans becomes statistically insignificant, lending support for our conclusion that the ideology, not the party, is significant.

35. As we showed in chapter 4, this logic fell short as Republican leaders brought the Comprehensive Nuclear Test Ban Treaty to the floor knowing full well that it did not have the necessary votes to receive consent.

36. We use a log-logistic survival analysis distribution due to the accelerated time to process completion (in this case, Senate consent) that normally arises. Log-logistic is the appropriate distribution according to the AIC statistics. The model differs from the model reported in table 5. The signs are interpreted so that a positive coefficient indicates added time to survival—meaning that the duration of the process is increased.

37. We measured party polarization using differences between DW-NOMINATE scores for median Republican and median Democratic senators (Poole 2006).

CHAPTER 6

1. In the area of international trade, research on legislative politics and the constraints they present on the executive has been quite extensive. The research generally focuses on the House of Representatives, since the House is typically where recent trade battles have been won and lost. For example, studies have demonstrated the significance of partisanship and ideology in recent House voting on trade (Biglaiser, Jackson and Peake 2004; Conley 1999; Gartzke and Wrighton 1998; Peake, Jackson, and Biglaiser 2007). More broadly, the legislative politics of trade has seriously constrained presidential efforts on behalf of globalization (Lohman and O'Halloran 1994; Shoch 2001).

2. In an earlier paper, we find that a clear majority (72 percent) of final bills passed to implement treaties are House bills and that House committees tend to be the first mover on implementation legislation (Peake, Krutz, and Jatkowski 2007).

3. The recent nuclear energy deal with India negotiated by President George W.

Bush, which we discussed in chapter 3, is an example. Bush negotiated the deal with the understanding that it would be subject to bicameral legislative approval. The example demonstrates the significance of executive agreements, as the deal with India represents the most significant Bush policy related to India.

4. On the controversy regarding the principle of "self-executing" treaties, an imbroglio we seek to avoid, see chap. 1, n. 7.

5. We do not mean to suggest here that all commercial agreements are completed as executive agreements. Certain international agreements involving commodities (e.g., wheat, rubber, and sugar) have historically been transmitted to the Senate as formal Article II treaties. Other international agreements in the economic domain that are routinely done as treaties include tax conventions and investment treaties.

6. The timing clearly parallels other congressional efforts to constrain presidents in their foreign policy, such as the War Powers Resolution of 1973. While the Case-Zablocki Act and its amendments are primarily procedural, that Congress is kept informed of executive agreements is an important first step in congressional oversight of the procedure. The requirements within the law are quite specific and beyond the scope of our analysis here. For an in-depth discussion of the Case-Zablocki Act, its many amendments, and how it has worked in practice, see U.S. Senate Committee on Foreign Relations 2001: 217–33.

7. In addition to the laws we address later in this discussion, which require congressional approval of an agreement prior to entry into force, several laws require presidents to inform relevant congressional committees before an agreement can enter into force. For example, the International Development and Food Assistance Act of 1978 (Public Law 95-424) requires that all executive agreements concerning debt relief be transmitted to each chamber's foreign relations committee and the Senate Appropriations Committee thirty days prior to entry into force. The requirement enables Congress to block the agreement should it decide to enact legislation doing so (U.S. Senate Committee on Foreign Relations 2001: 236–38).

8. For this section, we draw heavily on U.S. Senate Committee on Foreign Relations 2001 (particularly chap. 10).

9. Approval and disapproval procedures typically require action by joint resolution. However, executive agreements regarding social security require a sixty-day waiting period, and if either the House or Senate vote to disapprove the agreement within the waiting period, the agreement does not enter into force (Social Security Amendments of 1977, Public Law 95-216). A single-chamber disapproval procedure constitutes a legislative veto and seemingly runs afoul of *INS v. Chadha* (462 U.S. 919 [1983]; see U.S. Senate Committee on Foreign Relations 2001: 238).

10. For example, in two instances, Republicans in sugar and textile districts voted for CAFTA because of threats or inducements made by the Republican leadership. Robin Hayes, a North Carolina Republican whose district had suffered the loss of thousands of textile jobs, voted for CAFTA because House Speaker Dennis Hastert promised to help restrict imports of Chinese clothing. As the *New York Times* reported, Mark Foley, a Florida representative from a sugar-producing district, supported CAFTA because "Republican leaders had already made it clear that they would punish the sugar industry in the next farm bill if they managed to defeat the trade pact," and many others would have voted against CAFTA if not for Republican leaders "earmarking billions of dollars for pet projects in a $286 billion highway spending bill" (Andrews 2005: A1).

11. The Case-Zablocki Act, which passed in 1972, requires the State Department to

report all concluded international agreements to the foreign policy committees of Congress. Therefore, 1973 is the appropriate start date for analysis of hearings on international agreements.

12. The words and phrases used in the search included *treaties and conventions, executive agreements, trade agreements,* and *treaty.* Each Congress was searched separately, and each entry that came up under hearings or unpublished hearings (typically Senate hearings held in executive session during the earlier Congresses) was read and coded. The data exclude Indian treaties, pacts with American territories, funding for executive offices that negotiate agreements/treaties, tangential mentions of treaties/agreements in force, and nominations hearings. The data set includes published and unpublished hearings.

13. The topic codes are from Auerswald and Maltzman 2003. See chap. 5, n. 28.

14. For example, hearings on NAFTA prior to its submission to the Congress for approval as a congressional-executive agreement are coded as investigative. Hearings related to the bill approving NAFTA are legislative. Hearings that discuss the Commerce Department's implementation of NAFTA fall under oversight. Hearings that investigate the employment impact of NAFTA, considering possible changes in the agreement, would be categorized as investigative.

15. This difference might exist because the House, having larger membership than the Senate, may conduct more hearings on average across time. We ran comparisons using a baseline of all nonappropriation hearings and all hearings on international affairs and foreign aid, foreign trade, and defense policies (those subtopics relating to international commitments), employing data on congressional hearings from the Policy Agendas Project (http://www.policyagendas.org). Using the baselines did not significantly alter the findings (i.e., reported significant differences remain significant), so we report raw hearings totals because their interpretation remains straightforward. The data used here to construct a baseline for comparison purposes were originally collected by Frank R. Baumgartner and Bryan D. Jones, with the support of a National Science Foundation grant (no. SBR 9320922), and were distributed through the Center for American Politics and Public Policy at the University of Washington (Seattle). Neither the National Science Foundation nor the original collectors of the data bear any responsibility for the analysis reported here.

16. The House hearings are clearly of a different kind than the Senate ratification hearings. Generally, when the House held a hearing on a treaty undergoing ratification, it was held so the House Foreign Affairs Committee could indicate its support for Senate consent to a treaty or so the House Armed Services Committee could discuss the military implications of an arms control treaty or alliance that was currently being considered by the Senate.

17. We cannot say this for certain because we do not separate oversight hearings by treaty/agreement. Since treaty implementation hearings deal, by definition, with treaties, we can make comparisons there.

18. For example, during the 103rd Congress (1993–94), the House's Ways and Means Committee and Government Operations Committee each held fifteen hearings on NAFTA. NAFTA also drew several hearings from the committees on agriculture, small business, and energy and commerce.

19. During the 106th Congress (1999–2000), there were only ten hearings in the House on economic agreements. There were also ten hearings on agreements dealing with international norms (i.e., climate change) and legal agreements (i.e., the International Criminal Court).

20. Other House committees that held hearings regularly were: Merchant Marine (averaged 8.3 hearings during its existence), Ways and Means (6.1), Government Operations/Reform (3.1), Energy and Commerce (3.8), Small Business (3.1), and Agriculture (2.4). Several other committees averaged just fewer than two hearings. The House Committee on Foreign Affairs (International Relations) averaged 16.8.

21. Other Senate committees to hold hearings regularly were: Finance (averaged 7 hearings per Congress), commerce (2.9), Judiciary (2.9), Armed Services (2.8), Government Affairs (1.8), and Environment and Public Works (1.6). The SFRC averaged 21.3 hearings, of which about two-thirds were formal hearings on advice and consent.

22. In just a few cases, hearings for discussion of the ratification documents were held by the Senate Armed Services Committee (e.g., in the case of the Anti-Ballistic Missile Treaty) or the Senate Judiciary Committee (e.g., in the case of the Genocide Convention).

23. We coded a sixth nonexclusive category for process-related hearings. These were hearings devoted to the treaty process or processes related to legislative approval of executive agreements (e.g., fast-track authority). Senate process hearings focused on presidential use of executive agreements and typically decried their use for significant agreements. The SFRC went on record several times with the claim that it expected the most significant agreements to suffer the formal treaty process. House process hearings, however, typically involved using congressional-executive agreements in the area of trade and the specific processes that surrounded approval of trade agreements, including fast-track (or trade promotion) authority, which was reauthorized in 2001 for President George W. Bush (after lapsing in 1997) but lapsed in 2007.

CONCLUSION

1. A condensed version of this passage is etched on Panel Four of the Jefferson Memorial in Washington, D.C.

2. The statistics cited here are derived from Fisher (2001: 39, table II-2) and from our count of agreements from 2000 to 2006, using information from the State Department Web site and the Library of Congress (see n. 3 in this book's introduction).

3. Abdication means a willing relinquishment of power. Fisher (2000) argues that Congress has abdicated its war and spending powers to the executive. We argue that his reasoning, which may apply to war and spending, does not apply in terms of the treaty-making power.

4. Confidential State Department staff interviews conducted by the authors, August 2004.

5. As we demonstrate in chapters 2 and 3, when only significant international agreements are considered, the ratio of executive agreements to treaties is reduced considerably. Forty-four percent of these agreements were completed as treaties, compared to 6 percent of all agreements.

6. Senate Foreign Relations Committee staff interviews conducted by the authors, August 2004.

7. Confidential State Department staff interviews conducted by the authors, August 2004.

References

Aberbach, Joel D. 1990. *Keeping a Watchful Eye: The Politics of Congressional Oversight.* Washington, DC: Brookings Institution.

Abramowitz, Michael. 2008. "Personal Approach Marks Bush's First Saudi Visit." *Washington Post,* January 15, A8.

Ackerman, Bruce A. 1991. *We the People.* Cambridge, MA: Harvard University Press.

Ackerman, Bruce A., and David Golove. 1995. *Is NAFTA Constitutional?* Cambridge, MA: Harvard University Press.

Adler, David Gray. 2004. "The Law: Termination of the ABM Treaty and the Political Question Doctrine: Judicial Succor for Presidential Power." *Presidential Studies Quarterly* 34 (March): 154–66.

Aldrich, John H., Mark M. Berger, and David W. Rohde. 2002. "The Historical Variability in Conditional Party Government, 1877–1994." Chapter 2 in *Party, Process, and Political Change: New Perspectives on the History of Congress,* ed. David Brady and Mathew D. McCubbins. Stanford, CA: Stanford University Press.

Aldrich, John H., and David W. Rohde. 2000. "The Consequences of Party Organization in the House: The Role of the Majority and Minority Parties in Conditional Party Government." Chapter 3 in *Polarized Politics,* ed. Jon R. Bond and Richard Fleisher. Washington, DC: CQ Press.

American Law Institute. 1987. *Restatement of the Law Third, Foreign Relations Law of the United States.* New York: American Law Institute.

Andrews, Edmund L. 2005. "Pleas and Promises by G.O.P. as Trade Pact Wins by 2 Votes." *New York Times,* July 29, A1.

Associated Press. 2006. "U.S.-India Deal Faces Fight in Congress." *MSNBC.com,* March 2. http://www.msnbc.msn.com/id/11645988/pring/1/displaymode/1098/.

Auerswald, David P. 2006. "Senate Reservations to Security Treaties." *Foreign Policy Analysis* 2 (1): 83–100.

Auerswald, David, and Forrest Maltzman. 2003. "Policymaking through Advice and Consent: Treaty Consideration by the United States Senate." *Journal of Politics* 65 (November): 1097–1110.

Axelrod, Alan. 2000. *American Treaties and Alliances*. Washington, DC: CQ Press.

Bardwell, Kedron. 2000. "The Puzzling Decline in House Support for Free Trade: Was Fast Track a Referendum on NAFTA?" *Legislative Studies Quarterly* 25 (November): 591–610.

Barrett, Andrew W. 2005. Going Public as a Legislative Weapon: Measuring Appeals regarding Specific Legislation. *Presidential Studies Quarterly* 35 (March): 1–11.

Bartlett, Dewey. 1977a. Personal letter to President Carter, November 11. Senator Dewey Bartlett Papers, Carl Albert Center Congressional Archives, Norman, OK.

Bartlett, Dewey. 1977b. "Special Report on the Panama Canal." Constituent newsletter, September. Senator Dewey Bartlett Papers, Carl Albert Center Congressional Archives, Norman, OK.

Baumgartner, Frank R., and Bryan D. Jones. 1993. *Agendas and Instability in American Politics*. Chicago: University of Chicago Press.

Bennett, A. LeRoy, and James K. Oliver. 2002. *International Organizations: Principles and Issues*. 7th ed. Upper Saddle River, NJ: Prentice Hall.

Bennett, D. Scott, and Allan C. Stam III. 1996. "The Duration of Interstate Wars, 1816–1985." *American Political Science Review* 90 (June): 239–57.

Biglaiser, Glen, David J. Jackson, and Jeffrey S. Peake. 2004. "Back on Track: Support for Presidential Trade Authority in the House of Representatives." *American Politics Research* 32 (November): 679–97.

Binder, Sarah A. 1997. *Minority Rights, Majority Rule: Partisanship and the Development of Congress*. New York: Cambridge University Press.

Binder, Sarah A. 1999. "The Dynamics of Legislative Gridlock, 1947–1996." *American Political Science Review* 93 (September): 519–34.

Binder, Sarah A., and Forrest Maltzman. 2002. "Senatorial Delay in Confirming Federal Judges, 1947–1998." *American Journal of Political Science* 46 (January): 190–99.

Bond, Jon R., and Richard Fleisher. 1990. *The President in the Legislative Arena*. Chicago: University of Chicago Press.

Bond, Jon R., and Richard Fleisher. 2000. *Polarized Politics*. Washington, DC: CQ Press.

Bond, Jon R., Richard Fleisher, and Glen S. Krutz. 2006. "The Presumption of Success on Presidential Appointments Reconsidered: How Delay Has Become the Primary Method of Defeating Nominees." Paper presented at the annual meeting of the Midwest Political Science Association, Chicago.

Box-Steffensmeier, Janet M., and Brandon S. Jones. 1997. "Time Is of the Essence: Event History in Political Science." *American Journal of Political Science* 41 (October): 1414–61.

Brady, David W., and Craig Volden. 1998. *Revolving Gridlock*. Boulder: Westview.

Burns, James MacGregor. 1979. "Jimmy Carter's Strategy for 1980." *Atlantic Monthly* 243 (March): 41–46.

Caldwell, Dan. 1991a. *The Dynamics of Domestic Politics and Arms Control: The SALT II Treaty Ratification Debate*. Columbia: University of South Carolina Press.

Caldwell, Dan. 1991b. "The SALT II Treaty." Chapter 6 in *The Politics of Arms Control Treaty Ratification*, ed. Michael Krepon and Dan Caldwell. New York: St. Martin's.

Canes-Wrone, Brandace, William G. Howell, and David E. Lewis. 2007. "Toward a Broader Understanding of Presidential Power: A Reevaluation of the Two Presidencies Thesis." *Journal of Politics* 69 (January): 1–16.

Carter, Jimmy. 1977. Personal letter to Senator Dewey Bartlett, November 5. Senator

Dewey Bartlett Papers, Carl Albert Center Congressional Archives, Norman, OK.

Caruson, Kiki. 2002. "International Agreement-Making and the Executive-Legislative Relationship." *Presidency Research Group Report* 25 (Fall): 21–28.

Caruson, Kiki, and Victoria A. Farrar-Myers. 2007. "Promoting the President's Foreign Policy Agenda: Presidential Use of Executive Agreements as Policy Vehicles." *Political Research Quarterly* 40 (December): 631–44.

Chiou, Fang-Yi, and Lawrence S. Rothenberg. 2003. "When Pivotal Politics Meets Partisan Politics." *American Journal of Political Science* 47 (July): 503–22.

Cirincione, Joseph. 2006. "The US's Nuclear Cave-in." *Asia Times Online,* March 4. http://www.atimes.com/atimes/South_Asia/HC04Df03.html.

Cloud, David S. 2007. "U.S. Set to Offer Huge Arms Deal to Saudi Arabia." *New York Times,* July 28. http://www.nytimes.com/2007/07/28/washington/28weapons.html.

Coleman, John J. 1999. "Unified Government, Divided Government, and Party Responsiveness." *American Political Science Review* 93 (4): 821–35.

Congressional Information Service, Inc. 1966–2006. *CIS/Annual: Abstracts of Congressional Publications.* Washington, DC: CIS.

Conley, Richard S. 1999. "Derailing Presidential Fast-Track Authority: The Impact of Constituency Pressures and Political Ideology on Trade Policy in Congress." *Political Research Quarterly* 52 (December): 785–99.

Cooper, Joseph. 1977. "Congress in Organizational Perspective." In *Congress Reconsidered,* ed. Lawrence Dodd and Bruce Oppenheimer. New York: Praeger.

Cooper, Joseph, and Cheryl Young. 1989. "Bill Introduction in the Nineteenth Century: A Study of Institutional Change." *Legislative Studies Quarterly* 14 (February): 67–105.

Cooper, Phillip J. 2002. *By Order of the President: The Use and Abuse of Direct Executive Action.* Lawrence: University of Kansas Press.

Cooper, Phillip J. 2005. "George W. Bush, Edgar Allan Poe, and the Use and Abuse of Presidential Signing Statements." *Presidential Studies Quarterly* 35 (September): 515–32.

Corwin, Edward S. 1984. *The President: Office and Powers, 1787–1984.* 5th ed. New York: New York University Press.

Cox, Gary W., and Mathew D. McCubbins. 1993. *Legislative Leviathan: Party Government in the House.* Berkeley: University of California Press.

CQ Almanac. 1949–2000. Washington, DC: Congressional Quarterly.

CQ Weekly. 1990. "Chemical Weapons: Both Chambers to Get Pact." June 11, 1898.

Crabb, Cecil V., Jr., Glenn J. Antizzo, and Leila E. Sarieddine. 2000. *Congress and the Foreign Policy Process.* Baton Rouge: Louisiana State University Press.

Crabb, Cecil V., and Pat M. Holt. 1984. *Invitation to Struggle: Congress, the President, and Foreign Policy.* Washington, DC: CQ Press.

Crenson, Matthew, and Benjamin Ginsberg. 2007. *Presidential Power: Unchecked and Unbalanced.* New York: W. W. Norton.

Current Treaty Index. 2000. Buffalo, NY: William S. Hein, Inc.

Dahl, Robert A. 2003. *How Democratic Is the American Constitution?* 2nd ed. New Haven: Yale University Press.

Dalton, Robert E. 1999. "National Treaty Law and Practice: United States." Chapter 6 in *National Treaty Law and Practice,* ed. Monroe Leigh, Merritt R. Blakeslee, and L. Benjamin Ederington. Washington, DC: American Society of International Law.

Dangerfield, Royden J. 1933. *In Defense of the Senate: A Study in Treaty Making*. Norman: University of Oklahoma Press.

Davidson, Roger H. 1988. "'Invitation to Struggle': An Overview of Legislative-Executive Relations." *Annals of the American Academy of Political and Social Science* 499 (September): 9–21.

Davidson, Roger H., and Walter J. Oleszek. 2004. *Congress and Its Members*. Washington, DC: CQ Press.

Deering, Christopher J. 2003. "Alarms and Patrols: Legislative Oversight in Foreign and Defense Policy." Chapter 6 in *Congress and the Politics of Foreign Policy*, ed. Colten C. Campbell, Nicol C. Rae, and John F. Stack Jr. Upper Saddle River, NJ: Prentice Hall.

Deering, Christopher J., and Forrest Maltzman. 1999. "The Politics of Executive Orders: Legislative Constraints on Presidential Power." *Political Research Quarterly* 52 (December): 767–83.

Deibel, Terry L. 2002. "The Death of a Treaty." *Foreign Affairs* 81 (5): 142–61.

DeLaet, C. James, and James M. Scott. 2006. "Treaty-Making and Partisan Politics: Arms Control and the U.S. Senate, 1960–2001." *Foreign Policy Analysis* 2 (2): 177–200.

DeRouen, Karl, Jr., Jeffrey S. Peake, and Kenneth Ward. 2005. "Presidential Mandates and the Dynamics of Senate Advice and Consent." *American Politics Research* 33 (January): 106–31.

Diermeier, Daniel, and Timothy J. Feddersen. 2000. "Information and Congressional Hearings." *American Journal of Political Science* 44 (January): 51–65.

Divine, Robert A. 1978. *Blowing on the Wind: The Nuclear Test Ban Debate, 1954–1960*. New York: Oxford University Press.

Dobriansky, Lev E. 1967. "Ten Reasons for Opposing the U.S.-U.S.S.R. Consular Treaty." *Human Events*, February, 88–89. Senator Fred Harris Papers, Carl Albert Center Congressional Archives, Norman, OK.

Edwards, George C., III. 1989. *At the Margins*. New Haven: Yale University Press.

Edwards, George C., III, Andrew Barrett, and Jeffrey Peake. 1997. "The Legislative Impact of Divided Government." *American Journal of Political Science* 41 (April): 545–64.

Edwards, George C., III, and Stephen J. Wayne. 2006. *Presidential Leadership*. 7th ed. Belmont, CA: Thomson Wadsworth.

Edwards, George C., III, and B. Dan Wood. 1999. "Who Influences Whom? The President, the Media, and the Public Agenda." *American Political Science Review* 93 (June): 327–44.

Epstein, David, and Sharyn O'Halloran. 1999. *Delegating Powers: A Transaction Cost Politics Approach to Policy Making under Separate Powers*. New York: Cambridge University Press.

Eshbaugh-Soha, Matthew. 2006. *The President's Speeches: Beyond "Going Public."* Boulder: Lynne Rienner.

Evans, C. Lawrence, and Walter J. Oleszek. 2003. "A Tale of Two Treaties: The Practical Politics of Treaty Ratification in the U.S. Senate." Chapter 5 in *Congress and the Politics of Foreign Policy*, ed. Colten C. Campbell, Nicol C. Rae, and John F. Stack Jr. Upper Saddle River, NJ: Prentice Hall.

Evans, Peter B., Harold K. Jacobson, and Robert D. Putnam, eds. 1993. *Double-Edged Diplomacy: International Bargaining and Domestic Politics*. Berkeley: University of California Press.

Felton, John. 1990a. "Approval Seen on Chemical Weapons." *CQ Weekly,* June 9, 1800.

Felton, John. 1990b. "In the Bag: Chemical Weapons Pact." *CQ Weekly,* May 26, 1664.

Fenno, Richard F. 1973. *Congressmen in Committees.* New York: Little, Brown.

Finch, George A. 1949. "The Genocide Convention." *American Journal of International Law* 43 (October): 372–78.

Finney, John W. 1972. "U.S. Agreement with Bahrain to Set Up Navy Base Disclosed." *New York Times,* January 5, A1.

Fisher, Louis. 1985. *Constitutional Conflicts between Congress and the President.* Princeton: Princeton University Press.

Fisher, Louis. 1988. *Constitutional Dialogues: Interpretation as Political Process.* Princeton: Princeton University Press.

Fisher, Louis. 1991. *Constitutional Conflicts between Congress and the President.* 3rd ed. Lawrence: University of Kansas Press.

Fisher, Louis. 1998. *The Politics of Shared Power: Congress and the Executive.* 4th ed. College Station: Texas A&M University Press.

Fisher, Louis. 2000. *Congressional Abdication on War and Spending.* College Station: Texas A&M University Press.

Fisher, Louis. 2001. "Historical Background and Growth in International Agreements." Chapter 2 in U.S. Senate Committee on Foreign Relations, *Treaties and Other International Agreements: The Role of the United States Senate,* 106th Cong., 2d sess. Committee Print.

Fleisher, Richard, Jon R. Bond, Glen S. Krutz, and Stephen Hanna. 2000. "The Demise of the Two Presidencies." *American Politics Quarterly* 28 (January): 3–25.

Fleming, Denna Frank. 1930. *Treaty Veto of the Senate.* New York: G.P. Putnam's Sons.

Flemming, Roy B., B. Dan Wood, and John Bohte. 1999. "Attention to Issues in a System of Separated Powers: The Macrodynamics of American Policy Agendas." *Journal of Politics* 61 (February): 76–108.

Franck, Thomas M., and Edward Weisband. 1979. *Foreign Policy by Congress.* New York: Oxford University Press.

Frye, Alton. 1994. "Searching for Arms Control." In *The President, the Congress, and the Making of Foreign Policy,* ed. Paul E. Peterson. Norman: University of Oklahoma Press.

Furlong, William L., and Margaret E. Scranton. 1984. *The Dynamics of Foreign Policymaking: The President, the Congress, and the Panama Canal Treaties.* Boulder: Westview.

Galambos, Louis, and Daun Van Ee. 1996. *The Papers of Dwight David Eisenhower. The Presidency: The Middle Way.* Baltimore: Johns Hopkins University Press.

Gallagher, Hugh G. 1969. *Advise and Obstruct: The Role of the United States Senate in Foreign Policy Decisions.* New York: Delacort.

Gartzke, Erik, and J. Mark Wrighton. 1998. "Thinking Globally or Acting Locally? Determinants of the GATT Vote in Congress." *Legislative Studies Quarterly* 23 (February): 33–55.

Glennon, Michael J. 1990. *Constitutional Diplomacy.* Princeton: Princeton University Press.

Grimmett, Jeanne. 2001. "International Agreements and U.S. Law." Chapter 4 in U.S. Senate Committee on Foreign Relations, *Treaties and Other International Agreements: The Role of the United States Senate,* 106th Cong., 2d sess. Committee Print.

Grimmett, Richard F. 2001. "Overview of the Treaty Process." Chapter 1 in U.S. Senate Committee on Foreign Relations, *Treaties and Other International Agreements: The Role of the United States Senate,* 106th Cong., 2d sess. Committee Print.

Hall, Richard L. 1996. *Participation in Congress.* New Haven: Yale University Press.

Hastedt, Glenn P. 2000. *American Foreign Policy, Past, Present, Future.* 4th ed. Upper Saddle River, NJ: Prentice Hall.

Hastedt, Glenn P. 2006. *American Foreign Policy, Past, Present, Future.* 6th ed. Upper Saddle River, NJ: Prentice Hall.

Henkin, Louis. 1995. "U.S. Ratification of Human Rights Conventions: The Ghost of Senator Bricker." *American Journal of International Law* 89 (April): 341–50.

Henkin, Louis. 1996. *Foreign Affairs and the United States Constitution.* 2nd ed. Oxford: Clarendon.

Hersman, Rebecca K. C. 2000. *Friends and Foes: How Congress and the President Really Make Foreign Policy.* Washington, DC: Brookings Institution.

Hess, Gary R. 2001. *Presidential Decisions for War.* Baltimore: Johns Hopkins University Press.

Holt, W. Stull. 1933. *Treaties Defeated in the Senate.* Baltimore: Johns Hopkins University Press.

Howell, William G. 2003. *Power without Persuasion: The Politics of Direct Presidential Action.* Princeton: Princeton University Press.

Howell, William G. 2005. "Unilateral Powers: A Brief Overview." *Presidential Studies Quarterly* 35 (September): 417–39.

Howell, William G., and Jon C. Pevehouse. 2007. *While Dangers Gather: Congressional Checks on Presidential War Powers.* Princeton: Princeton University Press.

Hulse, Carl. 2008. "House Votes to Put Off Trade Deal Bush Sought." *New York Times,* April 11, C1.

Hurley, Patricia, David Brady, and Joseph Cooper. 1977. "Measuring Legislative Potential for Policy Change." *Legislative Studies Quarterly* 2 (November): 385–98.

Hutcheson, Ron, and Jonathan S. Landay. 2006. "Nuclear Pact between U.S., India Draws Fire." *San Jose Mercury News,* March 3, A6.

Irwin, Neil. 2007. "A Shift in Bush's Trade Policies." *Washington Post,* October 10, D1.

Jackson, Rosemary P., and K. Larry Storrs. 1978. *Panama Canal Treaties: Consideration by the Congress.* Issue Brief no. 78026. Washington, DC: Congressional Research Service.

Jentleson, Bruce W. 2000. *American Foreign Policy: The Dynamics of Choice in the 21st Century.* New York: W. W. Norton.

Johnson, Loch K. 1984. *The Making of International Agreements: Congress Confronts the Executive.* New York: New York University Press.

Johnson, Robert David. 2006. *Congress and the Cold War.* New York: Cambridge University Press.

Jones, Charles O. 1994. *The Presidency in a Separated System.* Washington: Brookings Institution.

Jorden, William J. 1984. *Panama Odyssey.* Austin: University of Texas Press.

Kaiser, Fred. 1977. "Oversight of Foreign Policy: The U. S. House Committee on International Relations." *Legislative Studies Quarterly* 2 (August): 255–79.

Katz, Jonathan N., and Brian R. Sala. 1996. "Careerism, Committee Assignments, and the Electoral Connection." *American Political Science Review* 90 (March): 21–33.

Kaufman, Natalie Hevener. 1990. *Human Rights Treaties and the Senate: A History of Opposition.* Chapel Hill: University of North Carolina Press.

Kaufman, Natalie Hevener, and David Whiteman. 1988. "Opposition to Human Rights Treaties in the United States Senate: The Legacy of the Bricker Amendment." *Human Rights Quarterly* 10 (August): 309–37.

Kelley, Christopher S. 2003. "The Unitary Executive and the Presidential Signing Statement." PhD diss., Miami University.

Kennedy, Kevin C. 1986. "Treaty Interpretation by the Executive Branch: The ABM Treaty and 'Star Wars' Testing and Development." *American Journal of International Law* 80 (October): 854–77.

King, Gary, and Lyn Ragsdale. 1988. *The Elusive Executive: Discovering Statistical Patterns in the Presidency.* Washington, DC: CQ Press.

King, Gary, Michael Tomz, and Jason Wittenberg. 2000. "Making the Most of Statistical Analysis: Improving Interpretation and Presentation." *American Journal of Political Science* 44 (April): 341–55.

Klarevas, Louis. 2003. "The Law: The Constitutionality of Congressional-Executive Agreements." *Presidential Studies Quarterly* 33 (June): 394–407.

Krehbiel, Keith. 1998. *Pivotal Politics.* Chicago: University of Chicago Press.

Krepon, Michael, and Dan Caldwell, eds. 1991. *The Politics of Arms Control Treaty Ratification.* New York: St. Martin's.

Krutz, Glen S. 2001. *Hitching a Ride: Omnibus Legislating in the U.S. Congress.* Columbus: Ohio State University Press.

Krutz, Glen S., and Jeffrey S. Peake. 2006. "The Changing Nature of Presidential Policymaking on International Agreements," *Presidential Studies Quarterly* 36 (September): 391–409.

Ku, Julian. 2006. "U.S. Senate Approves U.S.-India Civil Nuclear Cooperation Deal." *Opinio Juris,* November 17. http://opiniojuris.org/2006/11/17/us-senate-approves-us-india-civil-nuclear-cooperation-deal/.

Lay, S. Houston, and Richard B. Lillich. 1965. "The United States–Soviet Consular Convention." *American Journal of International Law* 59 (October): 876–98.

LeBlanc, Lawrence J. 1991. *The United States and the Genocide Convention.* Durham, NC: Duke University Press.

Lee, Frances E., and Bruce I. Oppenheimer. 1999. *Sizing Up the Senate: The Unequal Consequences of Equal Representation.* Chicago: University of Chicago Press.

Liberty Lobby. 1965. *Emergency Liberty Letter No. 12.* August 10. Washington, DC: Liberty Lobby. Congressman Page Belcher Papers, Carl Albert Center Congressional Archives, Norman, OK.

Liberty Lobby. 1967. *Liberty Letter No. 71: Consular Treaty to Allow Soviet Agents in Your City.* January. Washington, DC: Liberty Lobby. Senator Fred Harris Papers, Carl Albert Center Congressional Archives, Norman, OK.

Library of Congress. 2005. Thomas database: http://Thomas.loc.gov.

Lijphart, Arend. 1984. *Democracies: Patterns of Majoritarian and Consensus Government in Twenty-one Countries.* New Haven: Yale University Press.

Lindsay, James M. 1994. *Congress and the Politics of U.S. Foreign Policy.* Baltimore: Johns Hopkins University Press.

Livingston, C. Don, and Kenneth A. Wink. 1997. "The Passage of the North American Free Trade Agreement in the U.S. House of Representatives: Presidential Leadership or Presidential Luck?" *Presidential Studies Quarterly* 27 (March): 52–70.

Locke, John. [1689] 1988. *Two Treatises of Government*. New York: Cambridge University Press.

Loeb, Benjamin S. 1991. "The Limited Test Ban Treaty." Chapter 4 in *The Politics of Arms Control Treaty Ratification*, ed. Michael Krepon and Dan Caldwell. New York: St. Martin's.

Lohmann, Susanne, and Sharyn O'Halloran. 1994. "Divided Government and U.S. Trade Policy." *International Organization* 48 (Autumn): 595–632.

Lowery, Daniel. 1993. "Review of Kaufman and LaBlanc." *Human Rights Quarterly* 15 (February): 197–204.

Lowi, Theodore J., Benjamin Ginsberg, and Kenneth A. Shepsle. 2004. *American Government: Power and Purpose*. 8th ed. New York: W. W. Norton.

Mack, Gerstle. 1944. *The Land Divided: A History of the Panama Canal and Other Isthmian Canal Projects*. New York: A. A. Knopf.

Mann, Thomas. 1990. "Making Foreign Policy: The President and Congress." In *A Question of Balance: The President, the Congress, and Foreign Policy*, ed. Thomas Mann. Washington, DC: Brookings Institution.

Margolis, Lawrence. 1986. *Executive Agreements and Presidential Power in Foreign Policy*. New York: Praeger.

Martin, Lisa L. 2000. *Democratic Commitments: Legislatures and International Cooperation*. Princeton: Princeton University Press.

Martin, Lisa L. 2005. "The President and International Commitments: Treaties as Signaling Devices." *Presidential Studies Quarterly* 35 (September): 440–65.

Mayer, Kenneth R. 2001. *With the Stroke of a Pen: Executive Orders and Presidential Power*. Princeton: Princeton University Press.

Mayhew, David R. 1991. *Divided We Govern*. New Haven: Yale University Press.

McCarty, Nolan, and Rose Razaghian. 1999. "Advice and Consent: Senate Responses to Executive Branch Nominations, 1885–1999." *American Journal of Political Science* 43 (October): 1122–43.

McClure, Wallace. 1941. *International Executive Agreements: Democratic Procedure under the Constitution of the United States*. New York: Columbia University Press.

McCormick, James M. 2005. *American Foreign Policy and Process*. 4th ed. Belmont, CA: Thomson Wadsworth.

McCormick, James M., and Michael Black. 1983. "Ideology and Senate Voting on the Panama Canal Treaties." *Legislative Studies Quarterly* 8 (February): 45–63.

McCormick, James M., and Eugene R. Wittkopf. 1990. "Bipartisanship, Partisanship, and Ideology in Congressional-Executive Foreign Policy Relations, 1947–1988." *Journal of Politics* 52 (November): 1077–1100.

McCubbins, Matthew D., and Thomas Schwartz. 1984. "Congressional Oversight Overlooked: Police Patrols versus Fire Alarms." *American Journal of Political Science* 28 (February): 165–79.

Medalia, Jonathan. 2007. *Nuclear Weapons: Comprehensive Test Ban Treaty*. CRS Report for Congress, no. RL33548. Washington, DC: Congressional Research Service.

Melanson, Richard A. 2000. *American Foreign Policy since the Vietnam War: The Search for Consensus from Nixon to Clinton*. Armonk, NY: M. E. Sharpe.

Milkis, Sidney M., and Michael Nelson. 1999. *The American Presidency: Origins and Development, 1776–1998*. Washington, DC: CQ Press.

Milner, Helen V. 1997. *Interests, Institutions, and Information: Domestic Politics and International Relations*. Princeton: Princeton University Press.

Mo, Jongryn. 1995. "Domestic Institutions and International Bargaining: The Role of Agent Veto in Two-Level Games." *American Political Science Review* 89 (December): 914–24.

Moe, Terry M., and William G. Howell. 1999. "The Presidential Power of Unilateral Action." *Journal of Law, Economics, and Organization* 15 (1): 132–79.

Moffett, George D., III. 1985. *The Limits of Victory: The Ratification of the Panama Canal Treaties*. Ithaca: Cornell University Press.

Monaghan, Elaine. 2006a. "Senate Endorses Nuclear Deal for India." *CQ Weekly*, November 20, 3136.

Monaghan, Elaine. 2006b. "2006 Legislative Summary: U.S.-India Nuclear Pact." *CQ Weekly*, December 18, 3350.

Moore, Frank. 1977. Memorandum to Members of Congress, Subject: Panama Canal Treaty, August 17. Washington, DC: White House. Senator Dewey Bartlett Papers, Carl Albert Center Congressional Archives, Norman, OK.

Myers, Steven Lee. 2008. "Next-Door Neighbors Back Bush on Trade." *New York Times*, April 23, A8.

Nathan, James A., and James K. Oliver. 1994. *Foreign Policy Making and the American Political System*. 3rd ed. Baltimore: Johns Hopkins University Press.

Nelson, Michael, ed. 1989. *Congressional Quarterly's Guide to the Presidency*. Washington, DC: Congressional Quarterly.

Neustadt, Richard. 1960. *Presidential Power*. New York: John Wiley.

New York Times. 2004. "Rescuing the Law of the Sea." August 22, A21.

New York Times. 2007. "Twenty-Five Years and Counting." October 31, A23.

Nolan, Janne E. 1991. "The INF Treaty." Chapter 7 in *The Politics of Arms Control Treaty Ratification*, ed. Michael Krepon and Dan Caldwell. New York: St. Martin's.

Nowak, Manfred. 2006. "What Practices Constitute Torture? US and UN Standards." *Human Rights Quarterly* 28 (November): 809–41.

O'Brien, David M. 2003. "Presidential and Congressional Relations in Foreign Affairs: The Treaty-Making Power and the Rise of Executive Agreements." Chapter 4 in *Congress and the Politics of Foreign Policy*, ed. Colton C. Campbell, Nicol C. Rae, and John F. Stack Jr. Upper Saddle River, NJ: Prentice Hall.

O'Halloran, Sharyn. 1993. "Congress and Foreign Trade." Chapter 10 in *Congress Resurgent: Foreign and Defense Policy on Capitol Hill*, ed. Randall B. Ripley and James M. Lindsay. Ann Arbor: University of Michigan Press.

Orentlicher, Diane F. 2007. Testimony in *Genocide and the Rule of Law: Hearing before the U.S. Senate Committee on the Judiciary, Subcommittee on Human Rights and the Law*. 110th Cong., 1st sess., February 5.

Palmer, Elizabeth A. 1994. "The Slow Road to Destruction." *CQ Weekly*, September 17, 2586.

Pant, Harsh V. 2006. "The U.S.-India Nuclear Deal: The End Game Begins." *Power and Interest News Report*, January 27. http://www.pinr.com/report.php?ac=view_report&report_id=428&language_id=1.

Paul, Joel R. 1998. "The Geopolitical Constitution: Executive Expediency and Executive Agreements." *California Law Review* 86 (July): 671–773.

Paust, Jordan J. 1988. "Self-Executing Treaties." *American Journal of International Law* 82 (October): 760–83.

Peake, Jeffrey S. 2001. "Presidential Agenda Setting in Foreign Policy." *Political Research Quarterly* 54 (March): 69–86.

Peake, Jeffrey S. 2002. "Coalition Building and Overcoming Gridlock in Foreign Policy, 1947–1998." *Presidential Studies Quarterly* 32 (March): 67–83.

Peake, Jeffrey S., David J. Jackson, and Glen Biglaiser. 2007. "'Don't Go Changing to Try to Please Me': A Preference Consistency Analysis on Trade Policy in the U.S. House." *Congress and the Presidency* 34 (Spring): 79–99.

Peake, Jeffrey S., Glen S. Krutz, and Walt Jatkowski III. 2007. "The Forgotten House? Treaties, Executive Agreements, and the Role of the U.S. House of Representatives." Paper presented at the annual meeting of the American Political Science Association, Chicago.

Peterson, Mark A. 1990. *Legislating Together: The White House and Capitol Hill from Eisenhower to Reagan.* Cambridge, MA: Harvard University Press.

Peterson, Paul E. 1994. "The President's Dominance in Foreign Policy Making." *Political Science Quarterly* 109 (Summer): 215–34.

Pincus, Walter. 2002. "Bush Backs an Accord on Nuclear Arms Cuts." *Washington Post,* March 14, A19.

Platt, Alan. 1991. "The Anti-Ballistic Missile Treaty." Chapter 5 in *The Politics of Arms Control Treaty Ratification,* ed. Michael Krepon and Dan Caldwell. New York: St. Martin's.

Polsby, Nelson W. 1968. "The Institutionalization of the U.S. House of Representatives." *American Political Science Review* 62 (March): 144–68.

Poole, Keith. 2006. *NOMINATE Data.* http://voteview.com/.

Poole, Keith, and Howard Rosenthal. 1997. *Congress: A Political-Economic History of Roll Call Voting.* New York: Oxford University Press.

Putnam, Robert D. 1988. "Diplomacy and Domestic Politics: The Logic of Two-Level Games." *International Organization* 42 (Summer): 427–60.

Ragsdale, Lyn. 1998. *Vital Statistics on the Presidency: Washington to Clinton.* Washington, DC: Congressional Quarterly.

Ripley, Randall B., and Grace A. Franklin. 1984. *Congress, the Bureaucracy, and Public Policy.* 3rd ed. Homewood, IL: Dorsey.

Rosenkranz, Nicholas Quinn. 2005. "Executing the Treaty Power." *Harvard Law Review* 118 (6): 1867–1938.

Roshco, Bernard. 1978. "The Polls: Polling on Panama—Si; Don't Know; Hell, No!" *Public Opinion Quarterly* 42 (Winter): 551–62.

Rudalevige, Andrew. 2005. *The New Imperial Presidency: Renewing Presidential Power after Watergate.* Ann Arbor: University of Michigan Press.

Rundquist, Paul, and Stanley Bach. 2003. *Senate Consideration of Treaties.* CRS Report to Congress, no. 98-384. Washington, DC: Congressional Research Service.

Savage, Charlie. 2006. "Bush Could Bypass New Torture Ban." *Boston Globe,* January 4, available at http://www.boston.com/news/nation/articles/2006/01/04/bush_could_bypass_new_torture_ban/.

Schattschneider, E. E. 1942. *Party Government.* New York: Holt, Rinehart and Winston.

Schatz, Joseph J. 2006. "A New Sales Pitch for Nuclear Pact with India." *CQ Weekly,* March 20, 746–47.

Schelling, Thomas C. 1960. *The Strategy of Conflict*. Cambridge, MA: Harvard University Press.

Schickler, Eric. 1998. "Institutional Change in the House of Representatives, 1867–1986." Paper presented at the annual meeting of the Midwest Political Science Association, Chicago.

Schlesinger, Arthur M., Jr. 1973. *The Imperial Presidency*. Boston: Houghton Mifflin.

Setear, John K. 2002. "The President's Rational Choice of a Treaty's Preratification Pathway: Article II, Congressional-Executive Agreement, or Executive Agreement?" *Journal of Legal Studies* 31 (January): S5–S39.

Shanker, Thom. 2002. "Senators Insist on Role in Nuclear Arms Deals." *New York Times*, March 17, A16.

Shanker, Thom, and David E. Sanger. 2001. "White House Wants to Bury Pact Banning Tests of Nuclear Arms." *New York Times*, July 7, A1.

Shipan, Charles R., and Megan L. Shannon. 2003. "Delaying Justice(s): A Duration Analysis of Supreme Court Confirmations." *American Journal of Political Science* 47 (October): 654–68.

Shoch, James. 2001. *Trading Blows: Party Competition and U.S. Trade Policy in a Globalizing Era*. Chapel Hill: University of North Carolina Press.

Shull, Steven A. 2006. *Policy by Other Means: Alternative Adoption by Presidents*. College Station: Texas A&M University Press.

Smith, Robert Charles. 1977. "The Commander's Message: We Have Again Studied the Treaty; We Still Say 'No.'" *American Legion Magazine*, December. Press clippings, Senator Dewey Bartlett Papers, Carl Albert Center Congressional Archives, Norman, OK.

Smith, Ted J., III, and J. Michael Hogan. 1987. "Public Opinion and the Panama Canal Treaties of 1977." *Public Opinion Quarterly* 51 (Spring): 5–30.

Sollenberger, Mitchel A. 2006. "The Law: The President "Shall Nominate": Exclusive or Shared Constitutional Power?" *Presidential Studies Quarterly* 36 (December): 714–31.

Spiro, Peter J. 2001. "Treaties, Executive Agreements, and Constitutional Method." *Texas Law Review* 79 (April): 961–1035.

Spitzer, Robert J. 1993. *President and Congress: Executive Hegemony at the Crossroads of American Government*. New York: McGraw-Hill.

Squassoni, Sharon. 2006. *India's Nuclear Separation Plan: Issues and Views*. CRS Report to Congress, no. RL33292. Washington, DC: Congressional Research Service.

Stanley, Harold W., and Richard G. Niemi. 1994. *Vital Statistics on American Politics*. 4th ed. Washington, DC: CQ Press.

Sundquist, James L. 1992. *Constitutional Reform and Effective Government*. Washington, DC: Brookings Institution.

Talbert, Jeffery C., Bryan D. Jones, and Frank R. Baumgartner. 1995. "Nonlegislative Hearings and Policy Change in Congress." *American Journal of Political Science* 39 (May): 383–405.

Talbot, Strobe. 1979. *Endgame: The Inside Story of SALT II*. New York: Harper and Row.

Tananbaum, Duane. 1988. *The Bricker Amendment Controversy*. Ithaca: Cornell University Press.

Tannahill, Neal. 2004. *American Government: Policy and Politics*. 7th ed. New York: Pearson Longman.

Tarar, Ahmer. 2001. "International Bargaining with Two-Sided Domestic Constraints." *Journal of Conflict Resolution* 45 (3): 320–40.

Taylor, Andrew J. 1998. "Domestic Agenda Setting, 1947–1994." *Legislative Studies Quarterly* 23 (August): 373–97.

Time. 1967. "Symbolic Span." March 24. http://www.time.com/time/printout/0,8816,836867,00.html.

Tomz, Michael, Gary King, and Langche Zeng. 1999. ReLogit: Rare Events Logistic Regression, version 1.1. Harvard University. http://gking.harvard.edu/stats.shtml.

Towell, Pat. 1997a. "Cover Story." *CQ Weekly*, March 1, 545–50.

Towell, Pat. 1997b. "Pact Would Ban All Chemical Warfare." *CQ Weekly*, March 1, 550.

Trachtenberg, David J. 2004. "Finding the Forest among the Trees: The Bush Administration's National Security Policy Successes." *Comparative Strategy* 23 (March): 1–8.

Tribe, Laurence H. 1995. "Taking Text and Structure Seriously: Reflections on Free-Form Method in Constitutional Interpretation." *Harvard Law Review* 108 (6): 1221–1303.

United States Treaty Index, 1776–2000 Consolidation. 2000. Buffalo, NY: William S. Hein, Inc.

U.S. Department of State. 2007. *Diplomacy: The U.S. Department of State at Work.* Washington, DC: Bureau of Public Affairs. http://www.state.gov/r/pa/ei/rls/dos/46732.htm.

U.S. Government Printing Office. 1949–2000. *The Public Papers of the Presidents of the United States.* Washington, DC: U.S. Government Printing Office.

U.S. Senate Committee on Foreign Relations. 2001. *Treaties and Other International Agreements: The Role of the United States Senate.* 106th Cong., 2d sess. Committee Print.

Uslaner, Eric M. 1998. "Let the Chits Fall Where They May? Executive and Constituency Influences on Congressional Voting on NAFTA." *Legislative Studies Quarterly* 23 (August): 347–65.

Vagts, Detlev F. 1995. "The Exclusive Treaty Power Revisited." *American Journal of International Law* 89 (January): 40–42.

VandeHei, Jim, and Dafna Linzer. 2006. "U.S., India Reach Deal on Nuclear Cooperation." *Washington Post,* March 3, A1.

Vasquez, Carlos Manuel. 1995. "The Four Doctrines of Self-Executing Treaties." *American Journal of International Law* 89 (October): 695–723.

Warber, Adam L. 2006. *Executive Orders and the Modern Presidency: Legislating from the Oval Office.* Boulder: Lynne Rienner.

Wayne, John. 1977. Personal letter to Senator Dewey F. Bartlett, October 11. Senator Dewey Bartlett Papers, Carl Albert Center Congressional Archives, Norman, OK.

Weaver, William G., and Robert M. Pollitto. 2006. "The Law: 'Extraordinary Rendition' and Presidential Fiat." *Presidential Studies Quarterly* 36 (March): 102–16.

Weisman, Steven R. 2007. "Senate Approves Peru Trade Deal," *New York Times,* December 5, C1.

Whittington, Keith E. 1999. *Constitutional Construction: Divided Powers and Constitutional Meaning.* Cambridge, MA: Harvard University Press.

Wildavsky, Aaron. 1966. "The Two Presidencies." *Trans-Action* 4:7–14.

Wittkopf, Eugene R., and James M. McCormick. 1998. "Congress, the President, and the

End of the Cold War: Has Anything Changed?" *Journal of Conflict Resolution* 42 (3): 440–66.

Woolf, Amy F. 2003. *Nuclear Arms Control: The U.S.-Russian Agenda*. Issue Brief no. 98030. Washington, DC: Congressional Research Service.

Woolf, Amy F. 2007. *Nuclear Arms Control: The Strategic Offensive Reductions Treaty.* CRS Report for Congress, no. RL31448. Washington, DC: Congressional Research Service.

Yoo, John C. 2001. "Laws as Treaties? The Constitutionality of Congressional-Executive Agreements." *Michigan Law Review* 99 (4): 757–852.

Zorn, Christopher. 2006. "Comparing GEE and Robust Standard Errors for Conditionally Dependent Data." *Political Research Quarterly* 59 (September): 329–41.

Index

Note: Numbers in *italics* indicate figures.